Witch Hazels

Royal Horticultural Society Plant Collector Guide

Witch Hazels

Chris Lane

Timber Press
Portland • Cambridge

ROYAL HORTICULTURAL SOCIETY

For my wife, Diane, and daughters, Samantha and Tracey

Published in association with the Royal Horticultural Society in 2005 by

Timber Press, Inc.
The Haseltine Building
133 S.W. Second Avenue, Suite 450
Portland, Oregon 97204-3527, U.S.A.

Timber Press
2 Station Road
Swavesey
Cambridge CB4 5QJ, U.K.

www.timberpress.com

Design by Dick Malt
Printed through Colorcraft Ltd., Hong Kong

Library of Congress Cataloging-in-Publication Data
Lane, Chris, 1948-
Witch hazels / Chris Lane.
p. cm. -- (Royal Horticultural Society plant collector guide)
Includes bibliographical references and index.
ISBN 0-88192-678-7 (hardback)
1. Witch hazels. I. Title. II. Series.
QK495.H3.L36 2005
635.9'76--dc22
2004012689

A catalogue record for this book is also available from the British Library.

Contents

	Foreword	*7*
	Preface	*9*
	Acknowledgements	*15*
Chapter 1	Nomenclature and Taxonomy	19
Chapter 2	Morphology and Distribution	23
Chapter 3	*Hamamelis virginiana* L.: The American Witch Hazel	29
Chapter 4	*Hamamelis vernalis* Sarg.: The Ozark Witch Hazel	45
Chapter 5	*Hamamelis japonica* Sieb. & Zucc.: The Japanese Witch Hazel	61
Chapter 6	*Hamamelis mollis* Oliv.: The Chinese Witch Hazel	77
Chapter 7	*Hamamelis* Hybrids	95
Chapter 8	The Development of Hybrid Witch Hazels	159
Chapter 9	Propagation	171
Chapter 10	Cultivation	181
Chapter 11	Companion Plants	191
Appendix 1	*Gardeners' Selection*	*199*
Appendix 2	*Places to See Witch Hazels*	*201*
Appendix 3	*Where to Buy Witch Hazels*	*204*
Appendix 4	*Metric Conversions*	*207*
	Glossary	*208*
	Bibliography	*212*
	Plant Index	*220*

Colour plates follow page 112

Foreword

No doubt many people have wandered the autumn woods of eastern North America and asked how any sensible plant could be coming into full bloom while the trees overhead were losing their leaves in a riot of colour. The astute gardener can certainly counter that he or she knows of others, equally confused, which bloom during winter with apparent indifference to frost and snow. That all of these hardy plants are members of the genus *Hamamelis* distinguishes witch hazels as perhaps the only flowering shrubs in the Northern Hemisphere whose cheerful blooms frame both sides of our harshest season.

Despite this novelty, witch hazels have never been extensively cultivated, and only a handful of recorded selections had been introduced through the mid-1900s. In 1963 the Arnold Arboretum of Massachusetts released *Hamamelis* ×*intermedia* 'Arnold Promise', one of the first and undoubtedly still the most popular clone in North America today. But, it is the Europeans, especially the de Belder family of Belgium, that we recognize for most of the numerous (more than 100) stunning, floral selections which have been named to date. Many of these are known only to enthusiasts, thereby leaving witch hazels, like a chorus line waiting offstage, poised to take the spotlight and capture our hearts.

Despite what appears to be a manageable inventory, compared to some other important genera, confusion regarding identification and nomenclature of *Hamamelis* has been widespread and is likely to get much worse, as interest in these underused plants increases. This book represents the first attempt to authenticate and describe all of the known selections, varieties, and species in one English text. For more than twenty-five years, Chris Lane has developed his passion for witch hazels into a comprehensive collection of more than 250 unique specimens, using wild-collected stock or propagations from the original introductions whenever possible. Illustrated with outstanding photographs and citing personal research as well as that of collectors, gardeners, nurserymen, and enthusiasts from all over the world, *Witch Hazels* provides practical, comparative information that will assist amateurs and professionals alike. For many readers, *Witch Hazels* will be their first introduction to a group of plants that have no peers in brightening the dullness of winter's retreat. For others, it is the long-awaited authority for which we owe Chris Lane a great debt of gratitude.

Tim Brotzman
Madison, Ohio, USA

Preface

In deciding to write a book on witch hazels, several factors have come together to both stimulate and encourage me. First, a long interest in the genus, collecting and growing them over a period of time, and noting and observing their characteristics have put me in a good position to communicate my findings to the wider gardening public, professional horticulturists, and botanists alike. Second, there is at the moment only one book on *Hamamelis* available, a German publication which is difficult for people to obtain outside of Germany. Third, there is a burgeoning interest in winter gardening, and *Hamamelis* are winter-flowering shrubs par excellence. Their reputation for being difficult is unfounded, and I wish to dispel this myth. "They grow too big for my garden" is a comment one often hears, so I wish to show gardeners how they can limit the size of their plants successfully. Finally, many new cultivars are just starting to become available, and these need to have a wider audience so that discerning gardeners can make wise choices for their gardens.

It is perhaps interesting to recount how I became interested in the genus *Hamamelis*. As a horticultural student at Hadlow College in Kent, I saw my first witch hazels, a small plant of *Hamamelis mollis* 'Pallida' and a much larger plant of *H. mollis* 'Brevipetala', as they were then known. As part of my course, I spent a year at the famous Waterers Nurseries, Bagshot, Surrey, and here I can remember seeing a huge stock plant of *H. mollis*, the scent of which pervaded the air for a considerable distance.

For a few years after college I did not have much contact with *Hamamelis*, but on commencing work at Hadlow College as a technical instructor, I took an interest in them again. The main reason for my rekindled interest in the genus (soon to become an obsession) was the cold winter of 1978–1979. The college nursery had a stock plant of *H.* ×*intermedia* 'Ruby Glow', a red-flowered cultivar which was new to me. I can quite clearly recall this plant in full flower in January 1979. I had not kept close observation of the plant, just noting the flowers on the sunny, though cold, days. Then one night there was a -18°C (0°F) frost. Looking at the very dishevelled flowers the next morning, I remarked to the students with me "That's the end of them." By midday, however, the temperature had risen to around the freezing point, the sun was fully out, and to my amazement the flowers had opened up and the plant looked terrific with the sun shining through the branches.

This was the point at which I decided to collect the genus. I could not think of another winter-flowering shrub whose flowers could tolerate that much frost. I mentioned to the nursery stock lecturer, Bruce Macdonald, that we ought to grow them at the college nursery, so he ordered about ten cultivars from Herman Grootendorst, Boskoop, The Netherlands, and Hillier Nurseries Ltd., Winchester, England, which then formed the nucleus of a collection.

At about this time I met two people who were also very interested in the genus. A nurseryman friend in Kent introduced me to Tim Brotzman, over from Madison, Ohio, who had spent some time at Wisley as a student a few years before. Tim had been exposed to the wonders of witch hazels and was therefore already a convert to the genus. This meeting led to much correspondence and the exchange of propagation material of new acquisitions. Twelve years later I was fortunate enough to visit Tim in Ohio and look at his collection. The other person I met was Chris Sanders from Bridgemere Nurseries, Cheshire, England, and I soon realized his knowledge on the genus *Hamamelis* was far greater than mine. He introduced me to the wonderful *Hamamelis* collections in the English gardens of RHS Wisley, Savill, and Valley Gardens; The Hillier Arboretum; and the Royal Botanic Gardens, Kew. Chris and I also exchanged plant material, with the collection being planted at my nursery.

By the mid-1980s my collection stood at fifty or so cultivars and unnamed clones. In 1990 I was introduced to Robert and Jelena de Belder at Kalmthout Arboretum in Belgium, and in subsequent years I was able to collect numerous cultivars and unnamed hybrids from both Kalmthout and Hemelrijk due to their kind generosity. Also at this time I met Wim van der Werf in Boskoop, The Netherlands, who is the acknowledged expert there, and we also exchanged plant material over the years. More recently I have exchanged material with Helmerich Helmers in Westestede, Germany.

When I started collecting I thought it would not take long to amass all there was to be had in this relatively small genus. Realization soon dawned on me, however, that collecting a particular group of plants will always be a never-ending task as other people raise or introduce new clones or further collections are made from the wild. At present my collection, which was granted National Collection status in 1997, stands at 125 named cultivars and 132 unnamed clones, botanical varietal forms, and synonymous plants.

In this book I provide an introduction to the genus, describe the four species, and look at the origins of the hybrids with a complete descriptive list. The information and descriptions throughout this book (except where original sources have been used) are mine and therefore any errors are also mine. If readers spot any mistakes, I would be grateful to hear from them for future reference.

The descriptions of cultivars have all been made from plants in my collection (unless otherwise stated), all growing under the same conditions. Comparisons have been made with plants well known to the gardening public to give a more realistic idea as to flower colour and performance. It is important to point out that geographical climate, microclimate, aspect, soil type, temperature (including winter chill), rainfall, light levels, rootstock, and age of plant can all have significant effects on growth rates, size and colour of leaves, winter leaf retention, flowering period, and flower size and colour. This is particularly the case with the intensity of colour in the red-flowered hybrids, which can look different from year to year on the same plant.

It should also be noted that young plants can flower earlier and often do not settle down to consistent flowering times until several years old. Drought stress in late summer can also make even well-established plants flower out of season (that is, in early to midautumn). The red-flowered cultivars, if flowering at this time of year, will be a clear yellow. This demonstrates the instability of the anthocyanin pigment, which gives the red colouration, and why the red forms can look better one year than another even when flowering at the normal season. To ensure good colour the plant must not be under stress through lack of water, but light levels and temperature may also have an effect—a bit like autumn colour, with many factors coming into play which are not fully understood as yet.

Rootstock influence has perhaps not received the attention it should. As *Hamamelis* cultivars are grafted onto rootstocks of *H. virginiana*, the variability in those seed-raised plants will influence the cultivars grafted onto them. In a batch of *H. virginiana* plants being raised for grafting, there will often be some of them that retain dead leaves in winter. This trait is, to some extent, passed on to the grafted cultivar. Winter leaf retention can be variable in the same cultivar, and I believe this is a rootstock influence. The rootstock can also influence other aspects, in particular timing of flowering and flower colour, the same cultivar behaving differently because of this rootstock influence. Of course, the gardener with one plant will not see this, but the nurseryman with large numbers of a cultivar will notice these differences. It should be mentioned here that these differences are small and should in no way detract from the gardener enjoying these plants.

Throughout the book the cultivars are described using the following format:

Name of plant: Who named the plant and date of introduction

Comments: Who raised the plant, especially if different than the person who named it, and any facts or points of interest pertinent to the cultivar

Growth habit: Shape, upright, vase shaped, rounded bush, spreading, horizontal spreading, and weeping (see Figure 1)

Vigour: strong, medium, slow, compact, twiggy, branching

Average size of plant: height and width in metres of plants ten to fifteen years of age (this could be plus or minus 15 per cent, depending on growing conditions)

Foliage: Measurements of a leaf in millimetres; an average, taken from a leaf of a healthy plant, midway along a shoot of the current season's growth (this could be plus or minus 20 per cent, depending on growing conditions)

Leaf shape: Broadly elliptic, obovate, orbicular, orbicular-obovate, ovate-orbicular

Leaf colour: Young foliage, mature foliage, and autumn colour

Flowers: Average petal size in millimetres (this can be plus or minus 10 per cent depending on growing conditions), shape of petal (see Figure 2), petal colour, calyx colour, overall colour effect (calyx colour has an effect on overall colour), fragrance, and flowering period (as it occurs in my collection in north Kent).

Flower colour is a very difficult area in which to be precise. I abandoned the idea of using a colour chart, preferring to give an overall impression of flower colour, as it is possible to have half a dozen different conclusions for the same cultivar. The colour can look different on a sunny day and a dull

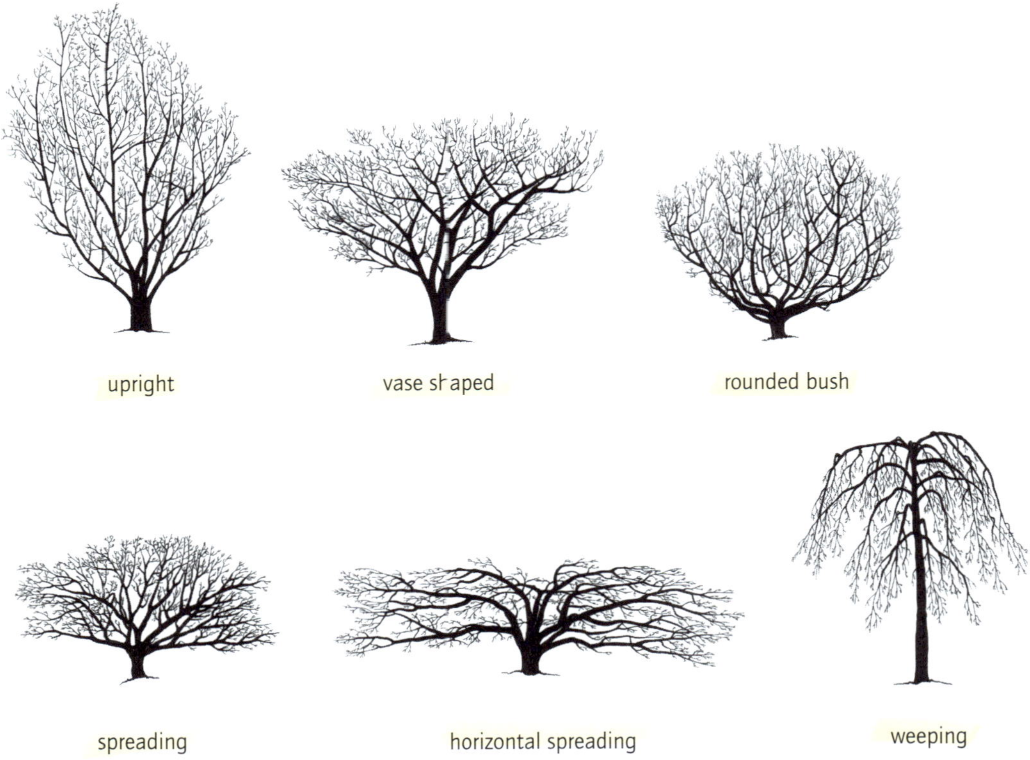

upright
vase shaped
rounded bush
spreading
horizontal spreading
weeping

Figure 1. Witch hazel growth habits

crimped
curled
twisted

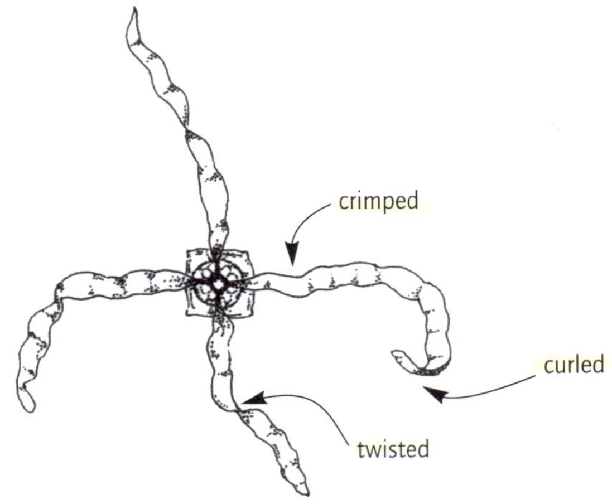

Figure 2. Petal shape characteristics of a *Hamamelis* flower

overcast day, from early in the flowering period until late in the flowering period, when colour changes as it does in virtually all plants. I hope the descriptions, together with the photographs, will enable readers to identify any witch hazel they come across.

An important chapter for the gardener will be basic principles of cultivation, specifically related to witch hazels, thus ensuring success for those wishing to grow these wonderful plants. Another chapter describes a range of companion plants that work well with witch hazels in the garden. Accounts of propagation, pests, and diseases are given, together with lists of places to see witch hazels and sources of supply.

Acknowledgements

On first considering this part of the book, it can be difficult to know where to start—so many people have been instrumental in enabling me to undertake and complete this project. On thinking it through again, the task becomes easier, starting with those individuals to which an enormous debt of gratitude is due and progressing through everyone else, trusting not to forget anyone. If I have done so, I offer my sincere apologies here and now.

First, my wife, Diane, who has typed the drafts for each chapter, from my handwritten script, as each one was ready. This has enabled me to work on each chapter, adding and amending where necessary until I was happy with the outcome. She has done this while holding down a responsible job and running the house. For her support and encouragement, particularly over the last year when trying to meet deadlines, the book is dedicated. To my daughter Tracey, for her support and encouragement also, and many thanks for all her help in sorting computer problems out, when I did not have a clue what to do, and for scanning in various drawings and photographs and generally helping me with more technical aspects of computer work. To my daughter Samantha, for her support and encouragement during the process of compiling my manuscript.

Several people who are witch hazel enthusiasts, some may say fanatics, need a special mention. To Robert and Jelena de Belder, who were enthusiastic, encouraging, and generous in allowing me to visit Kalmthout and Hemelrijk on a regular basis. I shall always be in their debt for the opportunity to observe their plants and collect propagation material for further study and evaluation at home.

To Chris Sanders, who has been a good friend of mine for twenty-four years and a travelling companion on many visits to gardens looking at *Hamamelis* and all manner of other plants. Stimulating me to learn more, to question what does not appear to be right, and to investigate why until the answer is found. For reading through my manuscript and making many helpful suggestions for incorporation or alteration, many thanks.

To Tim Brotzman, who I first met with his wife, Sonia, when they were visiting the United Kingdom about twenty-two years ago. It was a fleeting visit of just a few hours, which however sparked off a lasting friendship, involving annual correspondence on *Hamamelis* matters, exchange of propagating material, and subsequent visits to each other. For reading my manuscript, making useful comments on witch hazels in North America, his tireless efforts in tracking down information for me, and writing the foreword, many thanks.

Thanks to Carole Passey, a colleague who painstakingly drew the outlines of the various shapes of the bushes as I have categorized them and the drawing of a flower. Thanks to Mariko Parslow-Otsu for translating Mikinori Ogisu's article on *Hamamelis japonica* for me. To Chris Brickell, many thanks for steering me in the right direction as far as nomenclature issues were concerned and for other useful comments.

In addition there are a many friends and correspondents who have helped me with valuable information for the book, and to them I am very grateful. In The Netherlands, Wim van der Werf, Ruud van der Werf, Rein Bulk, Mark Bulk, Ronald Houtman, Johan van Heijningen, Andre van Nijnatten, and Harry van der Laar. In Belgium, Harry van Trier, past curator of Kalmthout Arboretum, and Abraham Rammeloo, current conservateur director of Kalmthout Arboretum, for all their help. In Germany, nurseryman Helmerich Helmers, lecturer and advisor at Rostrup Heinrich Beltze, and lecturer at Forschungsanstalt Geisenheim Dr. Volker Behrens. In Japan, botanists Mikinori Ogisu, Professor Masato Yokoi of Chiba University, and Associate Professor Hideki Takahashi of Hokkaido University. In China, Professor Gu Yin of the Nanjing Botanical Garden. In the United States and Canada, Bruce Macdonald, John Wott, Brian Maynard, Charles Tubesing, Chris Strand, Tony Allieo, Paul Capellio, Harald and Alex Neubauer, Anne Southwell, Stephen Spongberg, Alan Jones, Andy Brand, Richard Jaynes, Bob Marquard, Ruth Dix, Carl Hahn, and Phil Normandy. In the United Kingdom, Roy Lancaster, Allen Coombes, Mike Grant, John Hillier, Peter Catt, Peter Chappell, Norman Standbrook, Jim Gardiner, Martin Stanniforth, Mike Buffin, and Brian Humphrey.

I thank the staff at the RHS Lindley Library for tracking down references and organizing photographs for me. I also thank my publishers for their patience over the last eight or so years, six and a half of them gathering information and thinking about the project and eighteen months to write it all up. There must have been times when they thought nothing would materialize. Thanks to Anna Mumford for setting targets, keeping me on track, or nearly so, over the last eighteen months. If any weaknesses or inaccuracies remain in the text, they are entirely mine.

Chapter 1

Nomenclature and Taxonomy

The common name for *Hamamelis*, witch hazel, is an old one and has appeared in English literature in connection with several plants (notably the wych elm, *Ulmus glabra*) and in a variety of spellings. It was applied to the American witch hazel possibly because the foliage, general habit, and the fruits resembled the hazel (*Corylus avellana*) familiar to the early colonists from England.

The word *witch* can be traced back to the Anglo-Saxon words *wice* and *wic*, which apparently come from the Teutonic word *wik*, meaning "to bend." This could refer to the use of the wood to make bows; this certainly happened in England when Henry VIII passed a law stating that craftsmen should, for every bow made from yew (*Taxus baccata*), make several from wych elm. This law was introduced to ensure the supply of yew for the best long bows, the yew being a slow-growing tree.

The other possible derivation of *witch*, and the one I feel most likely, is from the use of forked twigs of wych elm and hazel for water divining, a common practice in western Europe until the end of the nineteenth century. The American colonists coming across the common witch hazel (*Hamamelis virginiana*), with its resemblance to the hazel of the Old World, would have used it for water divining. Or they may have observed the local Indians using the wood to make bows, thus associating it with the wych elm.

With the passage of time, the true derivation cannot be precisely known, and the reader can make his or her own choice. Today the name is in common use and not only applied to the American witch hazel but also the other species and hybrids.

The Latin name for the genus *Hamamelis* was established by Carl Linnaeus in 1742. The name is composed of two Greek words, *hama*, meaning "at the same time or together," and *melon*, meaning "fruit or apple."

Hamamelis was the name used by Hippocrates for the medlar (*Mespilus germanica* L.), which often still had fruits on the plant at flowering time. Linnaeus was impressed that the flowers (the main basis for classification that he used) were borne at the same time as the mature fruits from the previous season, so he selected the ancient Greek name for the genus. In 1753 Linnaeus proposed the presently recognized specific name for the American witch hazel, *virginiana*.

The earliest name that can be linked to the American witch hazel is *Pistachia nigra Coryli folio*, a pre-Linnaean polynomial. This is attributable to John Ray, who applied the name in 1687, to plant material received from Virginia (possibly from Johannes Spragge or John Bannister). He did not publish this name until 1704, in his work *Historia Plantarum*. The earliest published reference is in Leonard Plukenet's *Almagestrum Botanicum* (1696, p. 298), under the name *Pistachia Virginiana nigra Coryli foliis*, a modification of the name given by Ray to indicate the source of the plant by adding *Virginiana*.

The name *Hamamelis vernalis* was given by Charles Sargent (1911) because of its vernal (winter) flowering habit, similar to the Asiatic species but unlike the other North American species, *H. virginiana*, which flowers in the autumn. The name *H. japonica* is attributable to Siebold & Zuccarini, being named after its country of origin, Japan. *Hamamelis mollis* was named by Daniel Oliver (1888) of the Royal Botanic Gardens, Kew. He bestowed the specific epithet *mollis* (meaning "soft") because of the soft hairs on the leaves, particularly the underside of the leaf.

The generic name *Hamamelis* first appeared in John Clayton's *Flora Virginica* (1739, p. 139). Although most of the plants in this flora were collected in Virginia and described by Clayton, the book was largely compiled by Johannes Fredericus Gronovius, with substantial help by Linnaeus, who supplied most of the new names. There is reference in Clayton's work to Linnaeus's *Genera Plantarum*, ed. II (1742), which is why the generic name is cited to Linnaeus. Linnaeus used the name in subsequent works, notably *Species Plantarum*, ed. I (1753), which is the accepted starting point for valid publication under the International Code of Botanical Nomenclature. The generic name *Trilopus* was given by John Mitchell, without the knowledge that Linnaeus had already given the name *Hamamelis* to the genus, which takes nomenclatural priority under the code. Several other specific names have been given to *H. virginiana*, which have all been ranked as synonyms (see chapter 3).

Classification of the genus *Hamamelis* is based on Heywood (1978). The genus belongs to the order *Hamamelidae*, suborder *Hamamelidales*, family *Hamamelidaceae*. Other families which also belong to the suborder *Hamamelidales* are *Cercidiphyllaceae* (katsuras) and *Platanaceae* (plane trees, sycamores).

The *Hamamelidaceae* is a medium-sized family of mainly shrubs but also trees. The distribution of the family is very discontinuous in temperate and subtropical regions of the Northern and Southern Hemispheres. The family contains around 100 species in 23 genera. Two species are of some economic importance. *Hamamelis virginiana* is used in the pharmacy and cosmetics industries, where a concoction of leaves and stems is used for treating cuts and bruises. The fragrant gum (storax) of *Liquidambar styraciflua*, the sweet gum, is extracted for use in perfumery, as an expectorant, as an inhalant, and as a fumigant in the treatment of skin diseases. The sweet gum is a reasonably important timber tree, and the heavy, close-grained heartwood is used for furniture making. *Hamamelis*, *Liquidambar*, and most other members of the family are used in ornamental horticulture.

Members of the *Hamamelidaceae* are trees and shrubs with generally alternate, simple, or palmate leaves with stipules. Stellate hairs are sometimes present. The flowers vary considerably in the different genera and can be bisexual or unisexual, with different sexes on the same plant (monoecious) or on separate plants (dioecious); they are often in a spike or head, sometimes subtended by coloured bracts. The calyx consists of four or five united sepals and the corolla of four or five distinct petals (absent in *Liquidambar*, *Fothergilla*, and *Altingia*). The stamens vary from two to fourteen in number, and the ovary from hypogynous to perigynous and epigynous. The ovary has two locules and two styles; each locule contains one or more ovules. The fruit exocarp is woody and the endocarp somewhat horny. The seeds are straight and with endosperm.

The family is usually divided into five subfamilies: (1) *Disanthoideae*: flowers separate in two-flowered heads, petals long and narrow, and up to six ovules in each locule; includes *Disanthus cercidifolius* (endemic to Japan); (2) *Hamamelidoideae*: bisexual and female flowers clearly separate from each other (male flowers in the male inflorescence sometimes not so) and one or two ovules in each loculus; includes *Hamamelis* (eastern Asia and North America), *Trichocladus* (tropical east and eastern South Africa, the only African genus), *Diocoryphe* (endemic to Madagascar), *Corylopsis* (the largest genus, Himalayas to eastern Asia), and *Parrotia* (Iran and

China); (3) *Rhodoleioideae*: flowers bisexual and borne in a five- to ten-flowered capitulum, surrounded by numerous bracts so as to resemble a single flower; includes *Rhodoleia* (northern Burma, southern China, Malaysia, and Sumatra); (4) *Exbucklandioideae*: plants polygamo-monoecious with unisexual and bisexual flowers in capitula; petals in the bisexual flowers are narrow and two to five in number, with ten to fourteen stamens; the leaves are palmately nerved from the base; the stipules are broad and closely folded face to face, enclosing the young shoot; includes *Exbucklandia* (eastern and south-eastern Asia); and (5) *Liquidambaroideae*: plants dioecious, although female flowers often have staminodia; the male inflorescence is a terminal raceme of globose stamen clusters, with no perianth; the female inflorescence is a globose head, with a perianth of numerous scales; the ovary has two locules, with the stigmas elongate; includes *Altingia* (Assam to South-east Asia, Java, and Sumatra) and *Liquidambar* (eastern Asia, western Asia, and North America).

Some authorities view the *Hamamelidaceae* as being intermediate between the *Rosales* and *Amentiferae* (an assemblage of catkin bearers); others have held the view that they are nearly allied to the *Saxifragraceae* and the small family *Cunoniaceae*. Current data tends to indicate that the ancestral forms of the *Hamamelidaceae* gave rise to the *Casuarinaceae*, *Fagales*, and *Urticales*.

Chapter 2
Morphology and Distribution

The vegetative and floral morphology and the fruit characteristics are remarkably similar in all four species of *Hamamelis*: *H. virginiana*, *H. vernalis*, *H. japonica*, and *H. mollis*. The fact they can all be crossed with each other and will produce fertile offspring substantiates the very close relationship between them. To quote C. S. Sargent, "The different species of *Hamamelis* offer no good morphological characters, the structure of the flowers, fruit and seeds being the same in them all" (1911, p. 137). Distinctions between the species are determined by geography, habit, habitat preference, time of anthesis, and small but distinct morphological differences.

General description of the genus *Hamamelis* (after Rehder 1940)

Deciduous shrubs or small trees with stellate pubescence; buds naked, stalked; leaves short-petioled, oblique at base, sinuate-dentate, with caducous, rather large stipules; flowers perfect, in short-penduncled, axillary few-flowered clusters; calyx four-parted, with spreading ovate obtuse lobes, tomentose outside; petals four linear, crumpled in bend; stamens four with short filaments, alternating with scalelike staminodia; styles distinct, short; capsules two-valved with the calyx-limb about or below the middle; seeds two, lustrous black, oblong. Four species in North America and eastern Asia.

Description

Branches and stems

The following description is adapted from Jenne (1966). The bark is smooth, dark grey to brownish grey with small, dark brown lenticels. As the bark ages it darkens and becomes fissured. The terminal buds are greenish yellow or tan, flattish, crescent-shaped, tomentose, stalked, and naked. The lateral leaf buds are smaller and somewhat cylindrical. Stipules are ephemeral, lanceolate in shape, and pale straw to tan coloured, persisting for a few weeks only.

Foliage

Leaf blades are short petioled, with cuneate to unequally rounded bases and acuminate to rounded tips. The margins are bluntly toothed or wavy especially in the upper half of the leaf, usually thirteen primary veins. Average leaf size 90 mm long and 65 mm wide; however, size is variable between and within species. Underside of leaf tends to be pilose pubescent, the upper side glabrous at maturity.

Inflorescence

The flowers are in clusters of three (rarely two, four, or five) flowers borne on simple axillary peduncles. Each flower in the cluster is subtended by two or three ovate, acute bracts, which are slightly fused at the base to form a cup. The triangular lobes of the deeply four-parted campanulate calyx are usually reflexed and persistent at the base of the mature ovary. These floral characteristics are relatively consistent throughout the genus and are not useful in separating the taxa.

Flowers

Four long, strap-shaped petals, borne separately on the calyx tube, alternate with the calyx lobes. Petals usually 10–20 mm long by 1 mm wide, depending on species; colour is normally pale yellow to sulphur-yellow, rarely orange or reddish. The androecium of the flowers consist of two alternating cohorts of parts, an outer whorl of staminodia and an inner whorl of four stamens. The staminodia are attached separately to the base of the petals. Each staminodium is generally an oblong, fleshy, scalelike organ bending outwards towards the petal. The staminodium is usually laterally winged and secretes fine drops of nectar on the inner face. The fertile stamens are attached separately to the calyx tube, consisting of a short filament, having a single vascular trace, a thickened, nonexerted connective, and two laterally attached, introrse anther sacs. The one-celled, elliptical anther sacs dehisce by means of upcurving or incurving lids hinged on the inner face of the connective.

Gynoecieum

This is formed from two carpels fused basally into a two-locular ovary. The upper portions of the carpels are distinct, forming two horn-shaped styles that have small stigmatic areas at their tips. Two ovules suspended from the terminal placenta develop in each locule, but one ovule of each pair aborts.

Anthesis

Differences in the time of anthesis do appear to have some general taxonomic value. Flowers in *Hamamelis virginiana* extend from early autumn through early winter. The disjunct population in Mexico flowers in from mid to late summer, correlating with the summer rains. *Hamamelis vernalis* flowers from early winter through early spring and *H. japonica* and *H. mollis* early spring through midspring. In cultivation these flower times can vary quite considerably depending on geography and microclimate.

Pollination

The stigmas of *Hamamelis* become receptive (and remain so for quite a time) shortly after the flower opens. The pollen adheres to the valves of the anthers upon dehiscence and is located in the pathway of insects coming to visit the nectiferous staminodia. Pollen is shed during warm periods, when insect activity is likely. Insects visiting a number of flowers in succession are liable to scatter pollen promiscuously, effecting cross-pollination. There is, however, no well-developed mechanism to prevent selfing.

The long, yellow to reddish strap-shaped petals, distinct scents, location of mature pollen, and above all the nectar-secreting staminodia suggest adaptation to insect pollination. I have observed mainly fruit flies, blowflies, wasps, bees, and once a small tortoiseshell (*Aglais urticae*) butterfly at the flowers. Graenicher (1906) collected and identified the insect visitors to *Hamamelis virginiana* in Wisconsin, recording forty-four genera as follows: *Hymenoptera* (wasps), four genera; *Diptera* (flies), thirty-three genera; *Lepidoptera* (moths), five genera; and *Coleoptera* (beetles), two genera.

Fertilization

Although flower times may vary, fertilization occurs around late spring. In the case of *Hamamelis virginiana*, this corresponds to five to seven months after pollination.

Fruit

The fruit matures in the autumn following the blooming season. The partly superior capsule appears to be buried in the torus because in development the calyx tube lengthens disproportionately as compared with the carpels. The pericarp is differentiated into a stony exocarp and fibrous endocarp. The endocarp is the extremely smooth lining which completely surrounds the smooth fusiform seeds. Upon drying the pericarp splits down the midrib and slightly at the upper end of the carpels. The method of dehiscence is loculicidal with slight septicidal tendencies. Pressure is gradually exerted on the pointed lower end of the seeds until this mechanical pinching action forces the sudden ejection of the seeds out of the capsule. Seeds thus ejected may be thrown up to 6–7 m from the parent shrub.

Seeds

The smooth, dark brown to glossy black seeds are fusiform with an apical hilum subtended by a large, light-coloured attachment scar on two sides. Seeds have a spatulate embryo in a fleshy endosperm.

Seedlings

The hypocotyl is glabrous, and the epicotyl is covered with stellate pubescence. The relatively large cotyledons are glabrous. The first true leaf is large for the size of the seedling, stellate pubescent, subcordate-acuminate, and distinctly crenate. The second leaf is much smaller, ovate, and short-pointed at the apex.

Cytogenetics

A chromosome count of $n = 12$ was made by Anderson and Sax (1935) for *Hamamelis vernalis*; Darlington and Wylie (1945) recorded a count, attributed to Whitaker (1933), of $n = 12$ for *H. virginiana*. Although counts of the chromosomes for *H. mollis* and *H. japonica* have yet to be made, I would be surprised if they are different than that recorded for *H. vernalis* and *H. virginiana*, given that all witch hazel species hybridize with each other readily.

Distribution Past and Present

Fossil remains of *Hamamelis* have been found in areas far to the north of present-day distribution; for example, *Hamamelis* leaves of Lower Tertiary age have been found in Spitsbergen, Norway (Schloemer-Jäger 1958), and from the Miocene in Alaska (Chaney and Axelrod 1959). Also in Europe, fossilized leaves have been found in the Pliocene deposits at Auvergne, France (Berry 1923). Pollen grains have been found in the Late Miocene or Early Pliocene lignite seams at Mull in Scotland (Simpson 1953). The Arcto-Tertiary geoflora in Europe was restricted to the south by successive ice ages, and little of the original flora survived to recolonize when the ice receded.

In eastern Asia it was a different story, with not as much continental glaciation. In addition, the climate of southern China has changed little since the Miocene. Most of the plant fossil remains are still represented in today's flora of southern China. Fossil remains of fruit capsules and seeds have been found in Japan

Fossil remains have been found across the entire continent of North America, but changes to climate in western North America in the Pliocene left conditions in which *Hamamelis* could not survive. In eastern North America successive ice ages pushed *Hamamelis* to refugia in the Cumberland Plateau, southern Appalachian Mountains, Ozark Plateau, and the highlands of eastern Mexico. After a considerable amount of time, *Hamamelis* migrated northward onto glacially disturbed territory. This period was sufficiently long to allow slight differences to evolve in *H. virginiana* between the majority of its range and the population in northern Florida and coastal areas of Alabama and Georgia and the disjunct population in Mexico.

Representatives of the genus *Hamamelis* presently grow over extensive areas of eastern Canada and the eastern United States, together with a local population in eastern Mexico. In Asia *Hamamelis* grows over extensive areas of southern China and on the main island of Japan, Honshu, with a presence at the lower end of Hokkaido. This distribution pattern of eastern Asian–eastern North American plants is well known and is repeated in many other plant genera, such as *Magnolia*, *Liquidambar*, *Nyssa*, and *Styrax*, to name a few. This pattern indicates a more widespread distribution in the past which, because of changing climatic factors, has reduced these genera to their present-day distributions.

Chapter 3

Hamamelis virginiana L.: The American Witch Hazel

Synonyms

Hamamelis androgyna Walt., *H. caroliniana* Walt. ex. Steud., *H. communis* Barton, *H. corylifolia* Moench, *H. dentata* Rafin., *H. dioica* Walt., *H. estivalis* Rafin., *H. hyemalis* Rafin., *H. macrophylla* Pursh, *H. monoica* Walt., *H. nigra* Rafin., *H. parvifolia* Rafin., *H. riparia* Rafin., *H. rotundifolia* Rafin., *H. virginica* L., *H. virginiana* L. var. *angustifolia* Nieuwl., *H. virginica* L. var. *macrophylla* (Pursh) Nutt., *H. virginiana* L. var. *orbiculata* Nieuwl., *H. virginiana* L. var. *parvifolia* Fernald, *H. virginica* L. var. *parvifolia* Nutt., *Trilopus dentata* Rafin., *T. estivalis* Rafin., *T. nigra* Rafin., T. *nigra* var. *catesbiana* Rafin., *T. parvifolia* (Nutt.) Rafin., *T. riparia* Rafin., *T. rotundifolia* Rafin., *T. virginica* (L.) Rafin.

Hamamelis virginiana L. was the first species to be discovered and introduced to cultivation by Western botanists and plant collectors. The person responsible was the Rev. John Bannister, who was very active in collecting seeds of plants in North America and making drawings and descriptions of them, which he sent back to England. It was these drawings and descriptions that reached leading European naturalists and botanists such as John Ray and Leonard Plukenet, who were seriously studying the New World fauna and flora.

John Bannister was sent to the British colony of Virginia by the Rev. Bishop Henry Compton in 1678. His reasons were twofold: first, to provide for the spiritual needs of colonists; second, however, Compton was a keen plantsman and he instructed Bannister to obtain as many plants as possible for his garden in England. This Bannister did enthusiastically, and he proposed a natural history of Virginia, which would catalogue the flora and fauna of the region. Unfortunately, before he could begin his life was cut short when he was killed in May 1692. He was accidentally shot while exploring along the Roanoke River, and the wound proved to be fatal.

John Bannister's drawings and descriptions were incorporated into the works of Ray and Plukenet and later Gronovius and Linnaeus. He sent seed to Ray in 1687, which is the first record of introduction of a plant Bannister called *Pistachia nigra coryfolius*, a plant we now know as *Hamamelis virginiana* L., the American witch hazel. Whether these seeds produced plants is not known, and it was not until fifty years later that the American witch hazel was successfully grown in England by the plant collector Peter Collinson, who received seeds in 1736. It was not recorded from whom the seeds were received but is most likely to have been the American plant collector John Bartram.

Distribution

Hamamelis virginiana L. is found on dry woodland slopes, moist woods, bluffs, and high hummocks from sea level to 1500 m. This species grows in the Canadian provinces of Ontario, Quebec, New Brunswick, and Nova Scotia; in the following midwestern and eastern regions of the United States: Minnesota, Wisconsin, Iowa, Illinois, Indiana, Michigan, Ohio, Pennsylvania, New York, New Jersey, Connecticut, Rhode Island, Massachusetts, Vermont, New Hampshire, Maine, Missouri, Kentucky, Tennessee, West Virginia, Virginia, Delaware, Maryland, North Carolina, South Carolina, Georgia, Florida, Alabama, Arkansas, Louisiana, Texas, and Oklahoma; and in the Mexican states of Nuevo León and Tamaulipas (see Maps 1 and 2).

Medicinal Use

The early settlers in eastern North America learnt from the Indian tribes, particularly the Cherokee, Chippewa, Iroquois, Menominee, Mohegan, and Potowatomi, that a distillation of *Hamamelis virginiana* could be used for treating cuts, bruises, scratches, and other injuries and to alleviate colds and kidney complaints. Twigs and small branches were boiled in water to make a decoction for these purposes. It was also used as a lotion for treating sore and damaged eyes. Today's uses have hardly changed from when Peter Kalm reported its use by Native Americans for treating eye diseases in 1751.

The first person to start commercial manufacture of witch hazel extract was Thomas Newton Dickinson, who in 1866 built a distillery in Essex, Connecticut. Originally the stems would have been cut locally and brought in by horse and cart. Today stems are harvested from roadsides and woods by practicing coppicing every five to eight years; the cut bushes readily regenerate so they can be reharvested. The advent of the portable chipper means this process can be done on site, making transport to the distillery more efficient. In the factory, steam is applied to the chopped brushwood for thirty-six hours, the vaporized essence, which is produced from the cambium layer under the bark, is scrubbed in washing chambers, reheated to vapour, condensed, and filtered. Today's preparations are basically manufactured using Dickinson's formula. A bottle of extract is 86 per cent double-distilled witch hazel extract and 14 per cent alcohol.

For a period of time the Optrex Company had a plantation of around 14 ha, near Basingstoke, Hampshire, England, where they cultivated *Hamamelis virginiana* to coppice and harvest for the distillation of witch hazel extract. The original plantation was established in 1947 and after it was well established, harvesting was begun. After coppicing, the plants were allowed to grow for five years before being harvested again. The shoots were harvested from 2.8 ha each year, on a rotational basis. This operation was carried out in the winter months, and from this a yield of 133,000 L of distilled witch hazel was made.

Description

Original description (Hooker 1883, p. 109)

Hamamelis virginiana L.: This, the common witch hazel of the United States, derives its name from its resemblance to the English hazel in leaf, a circumstance, which led to its use as a divining-rod in the early days of the American Colonies. It abounds in moist woods, and especially along the banks of streams east of the Mississippi from Canada to Louisiana, sometimes attaining twenty feet [6 m] in height. Like so many other Eastern American trees and bushes, it puts on gorgeous colour at the fall of the leaf, and contributes not a little to the variegated hues of the forests in autumn. G. B. Emerson, in his account of the trees and shrubs of Massachusetts, says of it, "Amongst the crimson and yellow hues of the falling leaves there is no more remarkable object than the witch hazel, in the moment of its parting with its foliage, putting forth a profusion of gaudy yellow blossoms, and giving to November the counterfeited appearance of spring. The union on the same individual of blossoms, fading leaves, and ripe fruits, not very common in any climate, led Linnaeus to give to an American plant a Greek name, significant of the fact of its producing flowers together with the fruit." In plate 6659 of last year's volume of this work [*Curtis's Botanical Magazine*], the rare *H. japonica* is figured, and the slight diagnostic characters, which separate it from this are alluded to. Of these the chief are the more numerous leaf-nerves, broader revolute brown calyx-lobes, and shorter fruiting calyx of the Japan plant.

Description: A bush or small tree, attaining twenty feet; branchlets puberulous, bifarious, slender. Leaves very irregular in form, from rounded obovate to ovate elliptic or oblong, usually unequally two-lobed at the base, three to six inches long, sometimes nearly as broad, margin waved, coarsely toothed or lobulate; nerves strong, five to seven pairs, stellately pubescent, at length glabrous; petiole rather short; stipules lanceolate. Flowers in small globose peduncled axillary involucrate heads, polygamous. Calyx one-quarter of an inch in diameter, with a brown scalelike bract at its base; tube pubescent, obconic; lobes broadly ovate, obtuse, brown externally, pale within, ciliate. Petals strap-shaped, golden yellow, one half to two-thirds of an inch long. Stamens four, alternating with as many incurved staminodes. Ovary hairy; styles recurved. Capsule ovoid, invested halfway up by the enlarged calyx.

According to some botanists, there are two other species growing in North America apart from *Hamamelis vernalis* that are closely allied to *H. virginiana*, namely *H. macrophylla* Pursh and *H. mexicana* Standl. Having grown plants of three clones of *H. macrophylla* Hort., four of *H. mexicana*, and more than ten of *H. virginiana* for a number of years, I feel the present taxonomic treatment is in need of revision. To further substantiate the need for a revision, Gertrude Jenne (1966) examined more than 5000 herbarium specimens and thousands of examples of live material from across the whole distribution of the American witch hazel. My own observations of my cultivated material led me to concur with the recommendations put forward by Jenne in her thesis. In this book, I therefore follow the taxonomic treatment of *H. virginiana* as proposed by Jenne. Frederick G. Meyer (1997, p. 364) stated, "Infraspecific taxa are not recognized (in this work) for *H. virginiana* because no consistently defined pattern of variation or geographic correlation can be identified with this plant." However, Jenne's work does provide a useful infraspecific framework for use by those interested in variation within the species.

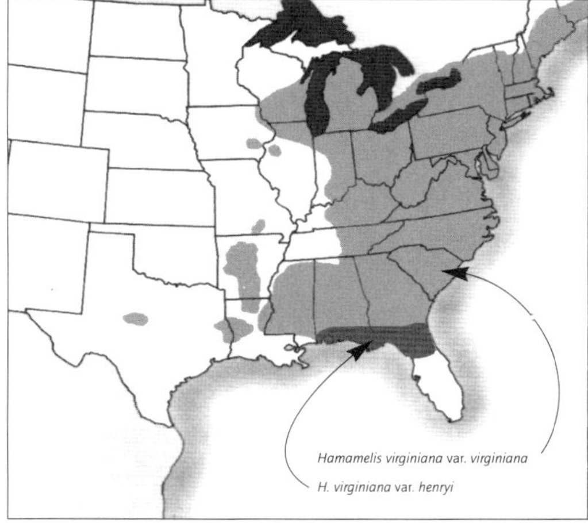

Map 1 Natural distribution of *Hamamelis virginiana* var. *virginiana* and *H. virginiana* var. *henryi* in the United States and Canada

Hamamelis virginiana L. var. *virginiana*

This is the type of the species and is widespread throughout most of the range of distribution. *Hamamelis virginiana* var. *virginiana* is characteristically a plant of dry, shaded woodland slopes. It is common along the edges of woods and along roadsides that pass through wooded or scrubby areas. It also grows in more open woodland situations. Generally preferring well-drained soils, *H. virginiana* var. *virginiana* is sometimes found in the drier parts of swampy or boggy areas, usually forming multiple-stemmed shrubs to 5 m in height or occasionally small trees up to 10 m, rarely suckering to any degree. The following description is from a clone I obtained from Hemelrijk, Belgium.

Comments

This particular clone came from Hemelrijk, where it regularly flowers and fruits well. It also performs well at my nursery in Kent, England.

Growth habit

Upright to rounded bush, 3 m tall by 2.5 m wide.

Foliage

Leaves orbicular-obovate, margins crenate in upper half, shallowly crenate below, apex blunt, base obliquely cordate, 90 mm long by 65 mm wide; petiole 12 mm long; young foliage light green; mature foliage glabrous, dark green, in autumn yellow.

Flowers

Petals 16 mm long by 1 mm wide, slightly twisted, crimped, pale yellow; calyx green with yellowish flush; overall effect pale citron-yellow; sweet scent; flowering mid through late autumn.

Hamamelis macrophylla Pursh

If we look at the original description of *Hamamelis macrophylla* (Pursh 1814), we see that it does not relate to the plants currently given this name, both in the wild and growing in cultivation. The description was based upon a specimen, apparently no longer extant, seen by Pursh in the herbarium of John Lyon. Pursh characterized the plant as having "large, suborbicular, heart-shaped leaves, the margins obtuse-dentate, the blade surface scabrous-punctate below." The plant was said to occur "on the river sides in the western part of Georgia." According to Pursh, "the large leaves punctuated on their lower side, with rough tubercles and other marks give sufficient reason to consider it a distinct species." It seems clear from this description that Pursh intended the name *H. macrophylla* to represent the large-leaved, southern population of *H. virginiana* that occurs in the western part of Georgia.

Sargent (1922, 368–371, fig. 330) included a description and illustration which match that originally described by Pursh. He was obviously unaware that plants originating from the Cumberland Plateau region of northern Florida were being called *Hamamelis macrophylla*. These populations are very distinct from the original description by Pursh, although Jenne (1966) was unable to ascertain how and when the name *Hamamelis macrophylla* was applied to the Cumberland Plateau plants.

It has always puzzled me that the plants available in the horticultural trade and those growing in arboreta both in Europe and North America as *Hamamelis macrophylla* were small-leaved, as the specific epithet indicating a large leaf did not match the material available. The name was accepted by such leading authorities as Sargent and Rehder, although the status of the taxon was questioned by Torrey and Gray (1840), Coker and Totten (1937), Vines (1960), and Jenne (1966). Also this larger-leaved form is found sporadically among populations of *H. virginiana* var. *virginiana* throughout its range. Therefore, in this work the name *H. macrophylla* has been relegated to synonymy under *H. virginiana.*

Hamamelis virginiana L. var. *henryi* Jenne ex. C. Lane

This taxon was named by Gertrude Jenne in 1966 after Mary G. Henry, an avid collector of native plants (Holotype: Herbarium, Academy of Natural Sciences, Philadelphia; *Mary G. Henry 1853*, collected 11 November 1939, 3 miles south of Marianna, Jackson County, Florida). Two or three clones of this plant have been propagated and distributed and are still being called *Hamamelis macrophylla* Pursh. The natural distribution of this variety of American witch hazel is basically in the highland areas of Florida and the adjacent coastal plain of Georgia and Alabama, growing on well-drained soils. How this variety of *H. virginiana* came to be called *H. macrophylla* is unknown.

Original description (Jenne 1966)

Frutex pleurumque 1–3 (8–10) m. Altus, raro innovans ex radice; folium minima longitudine 36 mm. Maxima longitudine 120 mm, minima media latitudine 18 mm, maxima media latitudine 62 mm, circiter 64 mm. Longitudine ad 41 mm. Media latitudine; apex acuminatus vel teres, basis obliquus; superus superficies submentosus vel calvescens, inferus superficies pleurumque tomentosus, pili stellares cum 7–11 radii per pilum; florales partes reapse sic ut *H. virginiana* var. *virginiana.*

Description

Upright shrub, usually 5–7 m tall, occasionally up to 10 m, rarely suckering from the base. Leaf blades with oblique bases and acuminate to rounded apices, averaging 60 mm long by 40 mm wide, the upper leaf surfaces subtomentose to glabrous, the lower tomentose, at least in the case of young leaves, often glabrate to glabrous with age; floral structures as in *Hamamelis virginiana* var. *virginiana,* flower size is smaller, ranging from 7–15 mm long by 0.5–0.8 mm wide. Colour is usually paler than typical *H. virginiana* var. *virginiana,* pale lemon yellow to almost cream.

I have three clones in my collection. One was collected by Mary G. Henry,

3 miles south of Marianna, Jackson County, Florida. The second is from the RHS Garden Wisley that originated from seed sent by the Arnold Arboretum. Wisley's records do not indicate the year, but it is a large plant and must be more than fifty years old. The third clone, obtained from J. C. Raulston at the North Carolina State University Arboretum, has the palest flowers that I have seen on any witch hazel to date.

The characteristics which differentiate this variety from *Hamamelis virginiana* var. *virginiana* are the more upright growth, smaller leaves, smaller flower size, paler flower colour, and later flowering (November through December at my nursery in Kent, England). The following is a description of a clone obtained from the J. C. Raulston Arboretum.

Comments

Selected by Woodlanders Nursery, Inc., of Aiken, South Carolina. Bob McCartney from Woodlanders informs me that they have a large *Hamamelis macrophylla* in the garden, which originated from Dorchester County, South Carolina, and is most probably the clone sent to J. C. Raulston at the North Carolina State Arboretum (now known as the J. C. Raulston Arboretum).

Growth habit

Upright bush, vigorous growth, yet well branched, 3.5 m tall by 2.5 m wide.

Foliage

Leaves ovate-orbicular, margins crenate in upper half, shallowly crenate below, apex acute, base obliquely cordate, 70 mm long by 45 mm wide; petiole 8 mm long; young foliage light green; mature foliage grey-green, in autumn yellow.

Flowers

Petals 8 mm long by 1 mm wide, straight, crimped, very pale yellow; calyx pale green; overall effect of creamy-yellow; scented; flowering mid through late autumn.

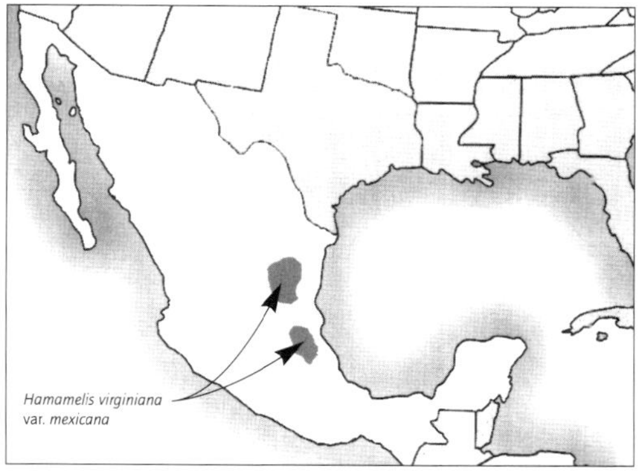

Map 2 Natural distribution of *Hamamelis virginiana* var. *mexicana* in Mexico

Hamamelis virginiana L. var. *mexicana* (Standl.) C. Lane stat. nov.

Synonym

Hamamelis mexicana Standl.

Original description (Standley 1937)

Hamamelis mexicana Standl., sp. nov. Frutex usque 3.5 m. Altus, ramulis vetustioribus teretibus Brunnescenti-ochraceis glabratis obscure rimosis lenticellis paucis elevatis conspersis, annotinis brevibus crassis 1.5–2.5 cm longis conspicue nodosis dense adpresse tomento ochraceo indutis, nodis 4–7, novellis similiter tomento brunnescente indutis; folia ad anthesin persistentia crasse membranacea, petioles solemniter inaequalibus, foliorum inferiorum 8–10 mm tantum longis, foliorum apicalium 2–2.5 cm longis, densissime minute stellato-tomentellis; lamina ambitu rotundato-obovata 5.5–7.5 cm longa 4–6 cm lata, apice obtusa vel rotundata, basin versus interdum subcuneatim angustata, basi ipsa valde inaequali, latere interiore 3–4 mm. Breviore, margine insigniter sinuato-undulato, lamina supra in sicco fusca subdense minute stellato-pilosula, pilis non intertextis, nervis subimpressis, subtus densissime pilis paullo majoribus stellatis ochraceis mollibus pilosa, costa gracili elevata, nervis lateralibus utroque latere 5–6 angulo recto vel angustiore adscendentibus rectis marginem attingentibus, venulis manifestis prominulis laxe reticulatis; flores aestvales; pedunculi e nodis annotinis nascentes crassi 3–4 mm. Longi dense stellato-tomentosi plerumque triflori; calyx ca. 4 mm. Longus extus densissime stellato-tomentosus, intus glaber, lobis ovalibus apice rotundatis; petala pallide lutea liguliformia 10–13 mm. Longa paullo ultra 1 mm. Lata glabra, apice anguste rotundata vel subtruncata.

Description

Upright shrub to 4 m, growth quite twiggy. Leaf blades with oblique bases and acuminate to rounded tips, coarsely toothed or wavy above the middle, averaging 85 mm long by 55 mm wide, pilose stellate pubescent on the upper and lower surfaces. Petals four, strap-shaped, pale yellow, 10–15 mm long by 0.5–0.7 mm wide.

The existence of this taxon in Mexico, disjunct from populations from the United States and Canada, was discovered in 1935 by Cornelius H. Mueller, who made an extensive general botanical collection of plants in Nuevo León for his study of the climate and vegetation of the state (Holotype: Herbarium, Chicago Natural History Museum; *C. H. Mueller 2116*, collected 5 July 1935, Potrero Redondo to [sic] west to Puerto la Laguna Sanchez and beyond, Municipio de Villa Santiago, Nuevo León, Mexico). The collection was originally sent to the Arnold Arboretum and subsequently forwarded to the Chicago Natural History Museum for determination by Paul C. Standley. He described the witch hazel material as representative of a new species, which he named *Hamamelis mexicana*. According to notes accompanying the original description, Standley experienced some difficulty in deciding upon an appropriate taxonomic level, whether specific or varietal.

The known distribution of *Hamamelis virginiana* var. *mexicana* is on the eastern arroyo slopes of the Sierra Madre Orientale ranging in elevation between 1500 and 2800 m (Jenne 1966). It was noted by C. H. Mueller in 1935 along the trail from Potrero Redondo to Laguna Sanchez, in the area of the Municipio de Villa Santiago in the state of Nuevo León. This area has a climate which is, in general, very similar to that of the temperate regions of the United States and Canada. In its natural habitat a very definite winter period exists during which protracted freezes occur, and a period of relatively high temperatures occurs in the summer. The growing season is comparatively short, which is partly due to the late spring frosts, which occur until late spring. Flowering is in mid to late summer, which coincides with summer rainfall. A deep layer of soil, derived from limestone and shale, is present on the slopes and the soil is covered by leaf mould, which varies from 8 to 30 cm or more in depth. Sharp et al. (1950) found *H. virginiana* var. *mexicana* near Rancho del Cielo above Gomez Farias, in southwestern Tamaulipas, in rich temperate woodlands of cloud forests approximately 400 km south of the type locality.

In cultivation in Kent, England, plants of this taxon have proved hardy to

-7°C (20°F). The flowering time is midautumn to early winter, as for *Hamamelis virginiana* var. *virginiana*. The characteristics which distinguish this taxon from *H. virginiana* var. *virginiana* are its twiggy, branching growth habit, leaves more pubescent in spring, not becoming fully glabrous, thicker leaf lamina, and flowers pale, as in *H. virginiana* var. *henryi*.

The disjunct distribution in Mexico is perhaps enough to give this taxon subspecific status; however, until we know more of its distribution and see more plants in cultivation, it is best to regard this as a variety of *Hamamelis virginiana*. The following is a description of a clone I obtained from the U.S. National Arboretum, Washington, D C.

Comments

This is perhaps the strongest growing of the four different clones growing in my collection, and the leaves are slightly larger than the others as well. This year (2003) two of the clones have produced fruit; time will tell if they come true or have hybridized with other clones of *Hamamelis virginiana* in cultivation here. All the clones flower from midautumn to early winter.

Growth habit

Upright to rounded bush, vigorous, well branched, 3 m tall by 3 m wide.

Foliage

Leaves ovate-orbicular, margins shallowly crenate, apex blunt, base oblique, 70 mm long by 50 mm wide; petiole 6 mm long; young foliage light grey-green; mature foliage intensely grey-green, in autumn yellow.

Flowers

Petals 10 mm long by 1.5 mm wide, slightly curled, slightly crimped; calyx light green with faint brownish flush; overall a creamy-yellow; faint scent; flowering mid to late autumn.

Hamamelis virginiana L. var. *virginiana* f. *rubescens*

The following description is based on Rehder (1922). This form, differing in the light red flowers from the type, was first noticed in the autumn of 1921 by C. Vandervoet on an old plant probably brought in from the woods in eastern Massachusetts and now growing in the Arnold Arboretum. When in full bloom this red-flowered form contrasts conspicuously with the typical form with its pale yellow flowers. The form is, however, not entirely new, for a shrub with light red flowers had been observed near Malden, Massachusetts, by Edward L. Rand (Sargent 1893). In the colour of its flowers, *Hamamelis virginiana* var. *virginiana* f. *rubescens* resembles the Japanese *H. incarnata* Makino, a species flowering in winter and early spring, closely related to *H. japonica* Sieb & Zucc., but in that species the sepals are deep red on the inner surface, while in this form they are yellowish green to brownish green. Specimens with reddish corolla colour have been reported to occur in the northern range of *H. virginiana* at widely separated locations.

Cultivars of *Hamamelis virginiana*

Hamamelis virginiana 'Champlin's Red' (Maynard, 2002)

Comments

According to Brian Maynard, the parent plant is located on a roadside in Clayville, Rhode Island, and is about 3 m tall; he has propagated this plant by grafting it onto the species for several years. The original plant was pointed out to him by Richard Champlin of Jamestown, Rhode Island, who is a well-known local plantsman, hence the name 'Champlin's Red'. The leaves and stems are typical of the species. It blooms in midautumn for about two weeks, and the flowers are a dull yellow with a salmon pink centre. The autumn colour is yellow.

Growth habit

Rounded bush, 3 m tall by 2.5 m wide.

Foliage

Leaves orbicular-obovate, margin crenate in upper half, shallowly crenate below, apex blunt, base obliquely cordate, 80 mm long by 60 mm wide; petiole 10 mm long; young foliage light green; mature foliage glabrous, dark green, in autumn yellow.

Flowers

Petals 14 mm long by 1 mm wide, slightly twisted, crimped, yellow at the tip grading to light red at the base; calyx green flushed red; overall light red effect; scented; flowering mid to late autumn.

Hamamelis virginiana 'Green Thumb' (Neubauer, 2002)

Comments

A variegated form, introduced by Alex Neubauer of The Hidden Hollow Nursery, Belvidere, Tennessee, who in 2000 found a sport on a plant in a batch of plants growing in the nursery. The sporting shoot was propagated, assessed for stability, then named and bulked up for release. At my nursery the variegation has remained stable with no sign of reversion, so it is a useful addition to the range of *Hamamelis*. Neubauer also states that the variegated foliage has stood up well to summer heat, with no sign of scorching; the plant is vigorous, flowers well, and does not retain leaves in winter.

Growth habit

Rounded bush, 2.5 m tall by 2.5 m wide.

Foliage

Leaves orbicular-obovate, margin crenate in upper half, shallowly crenate below, apex acute, base oblique, 70 mm long by 40 mm wide; petiole 2 mm long; young foliage yellowish green; mature foliage glabrous with a central splash of green and a wide yellow margin, in autumn yellow.

Flowers

Petals 10 mm long by 1 mm wide, slightly curled and crimped, pale yellow; calyx light green flushed yellow; overall effect of a pale sulphur-yellow; faint scent; flowering mid through late autumn.

Hamamelis virginiana 'Harvest Moon' (Jaynes, 2003)

Comments

This plant derives from the understock of a failed witch hazel cultivar growing on private property in Hamden, Connecticut. It was discovered by Richard Jaynes of Broken Arrow Nursery, Hamden, who plans to introduce this cultivar in 2005.

Growth habit
Vase-shaped, 6 m tall after fifteen years.

Foliage
Size and shape is characteristic of the species; new growth is reddish bronze; rich green during the summer; the autumn colour is not spectacular, shades of yellow and brown at best.

Flowers
Produced profusely and arranged in numerous clusters along the branches, providing a much showier display than most forms of the species. Individual strap-shaped petals are 8–10 mm long and 1–1.5 mm wide and lemon-yellow.

Hamamelis virginiana 'Little Suzie' (Neubauer, 2001)

Comments
Selected and introduced by Harald Neubauer of The Hidden Hollow Nursery from a batch of plants growing in his nursery in 1992. This particular cultivar has a much more compact habit and shorter internodes; it flowers freely as a young plant. This should prove to be a good garden plant—it is floriferous and because of its more compact habit and more dense flowering, it is more likely to stand out in the landscape. There is minimal leaf retention in winter.

Growth habit
Rounded bush, 1.5 m high by 1.5 m wide.

Foliage
Leaves orbicular-obovate, margin crenate in upper half, shallowly crenate below, apex acute, base oblique, 65 mm long by 45 mm wide; petiole 10 mm long; young foliage light green; mature foliage glabrous, dark green, in autumn yellow.

Flowers
Petals 12 mm long by 1 mm wide, slightly curled and crimped, pale yellow; calyx green with brown flush; overall pale sulphur-yellow; scented; flowering mid to late autumn.

Hamamelis virginiana 'Mohonk Red' (Huth, 1998)

Comments

A selection made by Paul Huth, a ranger at the Mohonk Nature Preserve, New Paltz, New York, for its floriferousness and good red flowers. Introduced to the U.S. trade by the Arnold Arboretum and by me in the United Kingdom. 'Mohonk Red' is a larger plant than *Hamamelis virginiana* 'Champlin's Red' and overall a deeper colour.

Growth habit

Rounded bush, 3 m tall by 2.5 m wide.

Foliage

Leaves orbicular-obovate, margin crenate in upper half, shallowly crenate below, apex blunt, base obliquely cordate, 90 mm long by 65 mm wide; petiole 20 mm long; young foliage light green; mature foliage glabrous, dark green, in autumn yellow.

Flowers

Petals 18 mm long by 1 mm wide, slightly curled and crimped, red fading to straw colour at very tip of petal; calyx light red; overall colour light brick-red; scented; flowering mid to late autumn.

Hamamelis virginiana 'Pendula' (de Belder, 1955)

Comments

A selection made at the Kalmthout Arboretum by Robert and Jelena de Belder. It is not truly weeping, although the branch tips are somewhat pendulous; the original plant at Kalmthout is broader than high and mushroom-shaped in habit.

Growth habit

Spreading shrub, tips of branches somewhat pendulous, 2 m tall by 4 m wide.

Foliage

Leaves obovate, margin crenate in upper half, shallowly crenate below, apex acute, base oblique, 90 mm long by 60 mm wide; petiole 15 mm long; young foliage yellowish green; mature foliage glabrous, dark green, in autumn yellow.

Flowers

Petals 15 mm long by 0.8 mm wide, slightly curled and crimped, pale yellow; calyx green with slight brown flush; scented; flowering mid to late autumn.

Hamamelis virginiana 'Tennessee Beauty' (Shadow, 2001)

Comments

A very dense flowering selection made by Don Shadow of Shadow Nursery, Winchester, Tennessee, from a batch of seed-raised plants. As yet it has not been introduced, so information about this cultivar is scant (but see *Proceedings of the International Plant Propagators' Society*, Vol. 51, 2001). I have not seen a plant as yet, but it should be a good addition as Shadow's selections in other genera have nearly always been worthwhile.

Growth habit

Rounded bush to spreading habit.

Foliage

Typical of the species, in autumn yellow.

Flowers

Very dense and yellow.

Chapter 4

Hamamelis vernalis Sarg.: The Ozark Witch Hazel

Map 3 Natural distribution of *Hamamelis vernalis* in the American Midwest

Synonym

Hamamelis ×*vernalis* Jenne

The original description of the Ozark witch hazel, *Hamamelis vernalis*, was made by Charles Sprague Sargent (1911. p. 137) from material sent to him by B. F. Bush, an amateur botanist, who collected material from Swan, Taney County, Missouri. Sargent proposed this as a new species. *Hamamelis vernalis* was known and cultivated long before the formal description of the plant by Sargent, however. The St. Louis botanist George Engelmann had found it growing along the upper reaches of the Meramec River as early as 1845. Today *H. vernalis* is used quite extensively for amenity landscaping purposes in the United States.

Distribution

This species is found on the Ozark Plateau of southern Missouri, Oklahoma, Arkansas, and Louisiana (see Map 3). It grows in the gravely beds and margins of streams, where it forms dense thickets due to its habit of spreading by underground suckers.

Description

The following description of *Hamamelis vernalis* is from Sargent (1911, p. 137). Leaves oblong-obovate, acute or rounded at the apex, cuneate and entire below and sinuate-dentate above the middle; when they unfold, glabrous above and coated on the midribs and veins below with stellate hairs mixed with fascicles of long matted straight hairs, or stellate pubescent on the two surfaces; at maturity thin, dark yellow green above, pale and often glaucous, especially early in the season, on the lower surface, and more or less rusty-pubescent or nearly glabrous on the under side of the midribs and veins, 80–100 mm long and 50–70 mm wide; petioles stout, coated with matted pale or rusty hairs; stipules lanceolate, acuminate, scarious, hoary pubescent, 5–6 mm long, caduceus. Flowers in axillary clusters on stout rusty-tomentose peduncles; calyx lobes rounded, ciliate on the margins, tomentose on the outer surface, dark red on the inner surface; petals light yellow. Fruit about 15 mm long; seeds acute, dark chestnut-brown or nearly black. Growth habit shrub, rarely more than 2 m tall, spreading by stolons into broad thickets, with small pale grey-brown stems and slender branchlets densely stellate-pubescent and covered with long pale deciduous hairs when they first appear, becoming glabrous in their third year. Flowers from the midwinter until spring. Fruit ripens in early summer. Natural habitat gravely banks of streams, often inundated.

Excepting *Hamamelis japonica*, where a high degree of variation is found, *H. vernalis* is the most variable of the four witch hazel species. The range in flower colour from pale yellow to deep red or reddish purple is extraordinary. The petal size is disappointingly small, although some specimens have petals up to 15 mm long. *Hamamelis vernalis* is so variable that Gertrude Jenne, in her thesis on the North American witch hazels (1966), proposed that *H. vernalis* is a hybrid swarm between *H. virginiana* and a relict *Hamamelis* species. She believed this hybrid swarm maintains itself in the region of the Ozark Plateau by introgressive breeding and that the relict species has been so modified by the introduction of genes of *H. virginiana* that it no longer exists in the pure state. She proposed the name *H.* ×*vernalis* (Sarg.) Jenne. While there is much evidence to support this proposal, I feel more work needs to be done to confirm it. Therefore, in this book I will continue to retain the current taxonomic status for the species.

In general *Hamamelis vernalis* and its cultivars are not in the foremost rank of witch hazels for gardeners. They do, however, exhibit good autumn colour and the flowers have a wide colour range, which is starting to have an influence in some recent hybrids (see chapter 8). Two botanical forms have been described, and in recent years many selections have been made and named from seed-raised batches growing in nurseries.

Hamamelis vernalis Sarg. f. *tomentella* Rehder

The original description was based on material collected by Ernest Palmer from Poteau, Le Flore County, Oklahoma, and Moutier, Shannon County, Missouri. The leaves were described as "densely tomentose to subtomentose along the veins with close clustered, shaggy hairs 0.5–1 mm long." Whether this form deserves botanical ranking is doubtful because forms can be found with densely velvety hairy on the lower surface through all intermediates to completely glabrous. Moreover, the complete range of variation from densely hairy to glabrous can be found throughout the distribution of the species.

Hamamelis vernalis Sarg. f. *carnea* Rehder

This was described by Rehder to cover forms of *Hamamelis vernalis* with reddish flowers. I have several clones in my collection that are attributable to forma *carnea*, all varying in morphological characteristics of foliage, size of flowers, and degree of red pigmentation in the petals. Therefore, I do not agree with the validity of this designation.

CHAPTER 4

Cultivars of *Hamamelis vernalis*

Hamamelis vernalis 'Autumn Embers' (Klehm, ca. 1995)

Comments

Introduced by Beaver Creek Nurseries, Poplar Grove, Illinois. This cultivar was raised and selected by Roy Klehm from a large batch of seed-raised plants because of the excellent autumn foliage colour. Roy first noticed this plant because it stood out from all the others in the block, being rich red with overtones of purple, yellow, and orange. He says the breathtaking effect is that of a glowing campfire on a crisp autumn evening. The plant has performed very well for me with respect to consistent autumn colour. I now have several *Hamamelis vernalis* clones and hybrids which regularly outperform *H. vernalis* 'Sandra', the best-known witch hazel in the United Kingdom for autumn colour.

Growth habit

Upright, later a more rounded bush, 3 m tall by 2.5 m wide.

Foliage

Leaves ovate-orbicular, margin crenate in upper half, shallowly crenate below, apex acute, base oblique, 70 mm long by 55 mm wide; petiole 8 mm long; young foliage light green; mature foliage sage-green, in autumn yellow-orange finally turning crimson.

Flowers

Petals 8 mm long by 1 mm wide, twisted and crimped, red at base fading to coppery orange at tip; calyx dull red; overall colour coppery red; spicy scent; flowering throughout midwinter.

Hamamelis vernalis 'Blue Moon' (Kohout, ca.1993)

Comments

The only information I have about this cultivar is that it was discovered as a seedling by Jorg Kohout of Prietitz, Germany. It has violet-blue flowers in early spring and retains no leaves in the winter. The foliage in my opinion, admittedly from just one summer's observation, does not look like *Hamamelis vernalis* but that of a hybrid; time will tell.

Growth habit

My plants are too young to judge fully, but it looks to be spreading, moderately vigorous.

Foliage

Leaves ovate-orbicular, margin shallowly crenate, apex acute, base oblique, 105 mm long by 75 mm wide; petiole 18 mm long; young foliage blue-green; mature foliage grey-green, in autumn yellow.

Flowers

Not observed yet.

Hamamelis vernalis 'Christmas Cheer' (McDaniel, 1971)

Comments

Selected and named by J. C. McDaniel of Urbana, Illinois, because it is one of the first clones of *Hamamelis vernalis* to come into flower. The original plant was brought from the Missouri Ozarks by Dr. James W. Gerdemann, professor of plant pathology at the University of Illinois College of Agriculture. This plant will flower around Christmas and is very fragrant with reddish petals. First grown and introduced by Hoogendorn Nurseries, Newport, Rhode Island, about 1978.

Growth habit

Spreading, 2 m tall by 3.5 m wide.

Foliage

Leaves obovate, margin crenate in upper half, smooth to scarcely crenate below, apex acute, base oblique, 110 mm long by 75 mm wide; petiole 12 mm long; young foliage light yellowish green; mature foliage apple-green, glaucous underneath, in autumn yellow.

Flowers

Petals 8 mm long by 1 mm wide, fairly straight, curled at tip, slightly crimped, red at base fading to golden yellow at tip; calyx carmine-red; overall an orange-red; strong scent; flowering early through midwinter.

Hamamelis vernalis 'Girard Purple' (Girard, ca. 1978)

Synonym

Hamamelis ×*intermedia* 'Girard's Purple'

Comments

This selection by Peter Girard of Geneva, Ohio, is much closer than his *Hamamelis* 'Girard Orange' to being a pure *H. vernalis* clone; there is, however, some evidence that it is a hybrid. Although the flowers are small, they are particularly dark in flower and autumn colour is good. The plant has been propagated and distributed in the United States to some extent by Lake County Nursery, Perry, Ohio.

Growth habit

Upright, 3 m tall by 2.5 m wide.

Foliage

Leaves orbicular-obovate, margin crenate in upper half, shallowly crenate below, apex acute, base oblique, 85 mm long by 65 mm wide; petiole 10 mm long; young foliage medium green, faint bronze flush; mature foliage dark green, in autumn orange to crimson.

Flowers

Petals 10 mm long by 1 mm wide, curled and crimped, dark purplish red; calyx dark purplish maroon; overall a dark reddish purple; spicy scent; flowering mid to late winter.

Hamamelis vernalis 'Holden' (Lane, 2003)

Comments

A selection made by Bob Marquard, who toured the fields of various nurseries in Lake County, Ohio, looking for any *Hamamelis virginiana* in flower showing reddish colouration. This was the only example he found. It was first thought to be a reddish-petalled form of *H. virginiana* but on closer inspection has proved to be *H. vernalis* or possibly even a hybrid of *H. vernalis* and *H. virginiana*. It flowers in early and midautumn, the young twigs resemble *H. vernalis*, foliage midway between the two. It was named and introduced by me, mainly because of its exceptionally early flowering for

H. vernalis; in fact, it finishes flowering before any other *H. vernalis* clone I have begins flowering.

Growth habit

Upright, bushy with many side shoots, 3 m tall by 2.5 m wide.

Foliage

Leaves obovate, margin crenate in upper half, shallowly crenate below, apex acute, base oblique, 90 mm long by 55 mm wide; petiole 10 mm long; young foliage light yellowish green; mature foliage apple-green, in autumn pale yellow.

Flowers

Petal 8 mm long by 0.8 mm wide, curled and crimped, golden yellow, suffused with red from the tip downwards, the colour deepening to the bases; calyx light red; overall colour effect of light orange; spicy scent; flowering mid to late autumn.

Hamamelis vernalis 'January Pride' (Meyer, 1979)

Comments

This plant was selected by F. G. Meyer, of Takoma Park, Maryland, because it regularly started to flower in the first week of January, earlier than most *Hamamelis vernalis* plants he had observed. The original plant was in the Missouri Botanical Garden. He propagated from that plant and took a plant with him when he moved from Missouri to live in Maryland in 1958. His new plant continued to flower consistently in early January, hence the name *H. vernalis* 'January Pride', bestowed after nearly twenty years of close observation. Although the yellow flowers are not that spectacular, it has a pungent spicy scent.

Growth habit

Rounded bush, 2.5 m tall by 2.5 m wide.

Foliage

Leaves broadly elliptic, margin crenate in upper half, shallowly crenate below, apex acute, base oblique, 95 mm long by 55 mm wide; petiole 10 mm long; young foliage medium green; mature foliage apple-green, leaf margins curled upwards, in autumn yellow.

Flowers

Petals 6 mm long by 1 mm wide, straight, slightly crimped, dull yellow; calyx greenish yellow; overall a mustard-yellow; spicy scent; flowering early through midwinter.

Hamamelis vernalis 'Kohankie Red' (Lane, 2003)

Synonyms

Hamamelis carnea Hort., *H. vernalis* 'Boesger', *H. vernalis* 'Carnea', *H. vernalis* 'Carney'

Comments

Raised by the Henry Kohankie Nursery, Perry, Ohio, prior to 1960. It has been propagated and sold by various nurseries under names such as *Hamamelis vernalis* (red form), *H. vernalis* 'Carnea' (as grown in the past by the Herman Losely & Son Nursery), *H. vernalis* 'Carney', and *H. vernalis* 'Boesger' (as grown by Hal Boesger). Before he died Boesger told Tim Brotzman that his source was from Losely's garden. In the Kohankie Nursery catalogue for 1952–1953, it is listed as "*Hamamelis carnea*, the red petal vernal Witch Hazel," although I understand this cultivar was listed as early as the 1930s.

The name *Hamamelis vernalis* f. *carnea* covers any plant with red or reddish flowers. As this clone is a very distinct plant and several names have been given to it, to avoid confusion, it should have a recognized cultivar name. In this book I propose to call it *H. vernalis* 'Kohankie Red', after the nursery where the plant was originally raised. It has been propagated and distributed in the past, mainly by the Losely Nursery in Perry, Ohio, who brought the plant out of the abandoned Kohankie Nursery, as perhaps did others, hence the confusion in naming.

Growth habit

Upright when young, later spreading, 2.5 m tall by 3 m wide.

Foliage

Leaves orbicular-obovate, margin crenate in upper half, smooth to scarcely crenate below, apex blunt, base oblique, 95 mm long by 70 mm wide; petiole 12 mm long; young foliage yellowish green lightly flushed bronze; mature foliage dark green, glaucous underneath, in autumn yellow-orange finally turning crimson.

Flowers

Petals 10 mm long by 1 mm wide, straight, slightly crimped, reddish purple; calyx dull purple; overall effect a dark purplish red; scented but not strong; flowering mid to late winter.

Hamamelis vernalis 'Lombarts Weeping' (Lombarts, 1954)

Synonym

Hamamelis vernalis 'Pendula'

Comments

This plant was selected in Pierre Lombarts Nursery, Zundert, The Netherlands, because of its very spreading, almost weeping habit. The original plant was found in a batch of seed-raised plants imported from a French nursery. In Lombarts's catalogue for 1947–1948, this plant is listed as "*H. vernalis* var. *carnea*, description, up to 2 m tall, flowers from January onward with yellowish brown, strong smelling little flowers, which develop gracefully on weeping branches; very rare plant." In the 1954–1955 catalogue it received its current name, being described as "*H. vernalis* 'Lombarts Weeping', growing up to 2 m tall, own selection, with tiny reddish, nice-smelling flowers in January through March, a beautiful weeping plant."

Growth habit

Horizontally spreading, 1.5 m tall by 3.5 m wide.

Foliage

Leaves broadly elliptic, margin shallowly crenate in upper half, smooth to scarcely crenate below, apex acute, base oblique, 110 mm long by 65 mm wide; petiole 10 mm long; young foliage light yellowish green; mature foliage dark green, glaucous underneath, in autumn yellow.

Flowers

Petals 6 mm long by 1 mm wide, fairly straight, slightly crimped, orange-red; calyx maroon; overall effect orange-red; spicy scent; flowering late winter through early spring.

Hamamelis vernalis 'New Year Gold' (McDaniel, 1971)

Synonym

Hamamelis vernalis 'New Year's Gold'

Comments

Like 'Christmas Cheer', this cultivar was selected from the same batch brought from Missouri by Dr. James W. Gerdemann and named by J. C. McDaniel. It is later flowering than *Hamamelis vernalis* 'Christmas Cheer', not as fragrant, and has yellow flowers. First grown and introduced by Hoogendoorn Nurseries, Newport, Rhode Island, around 1978.

Growth habit

Horizontally spreading, 1.5 m tall by 2.5 m wide.

Foliage

Leaves obovate, margin crenate in upper half, smooth to scarcely crenate below, apex acute, base, oblique, 110 mm long by 70 mm wide; petiole 8 mm long; young foliage yellowish green; mature foliage dark apple-green, glaucous underneath, in autumn yellow.

Flowers

Petals 6 mm long by 1 mm wide, straight and crimped, dull orange; calyx reddish; overall colour yellowish orange; strong spicy scent; flowering mid to late winter.

Hamamelis vernalis 'Orange Glow'

Comments

So far I have not been able to track down the originator of this cultivar; the furthest I can trace it is from information kindly supplied by Jack Alexander of the Arnold Arboretum. According to their accession records, they received two plants from the Tingle Nursery Co., Pittsville, Maryland, on 22 April 1963. This nursery went out of business in the early 1970s, so tracing its origin from there has led to a dead end. Could this possibly be another selection by Henry Hohman of the Kingsville Nursery, who was very active with new plant introductions at this time and in the right vicinity?

Growth habit

Upright when young, later a rounded bush, 2.5 m tall by 2.5 m wide.

Foliage

Leaves obovate, margin crenate in upper half, smooth to scarcely crenate below, apex acute, base oblique, 90 mm long by 55 mm wide; petiole 12 mm long; young foliage light yellowish green; mature foliage apple-green, glaucous beneath, in autumn yellow.

Flowers

Petals 8 mm long by 1 mm wide, fairly straight and crimped, dull ochre-orange; calyx dull light red; overall colour a dull orange, darker than 'New Year Gold'; scent strong and spicy; flowering mid to late winter.

Hamamelis vernalis 'Orange Spangles' (Edwards, 1997)

Comments

This plant arose when the understock of an ailing witch hazel in Pat Edwards's garden in Albrighton, England, started to outgrow the top, began to flower, and proved to be *Hamamelis vernalis*, which is sometimes used for grafting when *H. virginiana* is unavailable. After a period of observation, suckers were transplanted and grown on; because of the abundant flower and good scent, it was eventually named.

Growth habit

Upright, 2.5 m tall by 2 m wide.

Foliage

Leaves obovate, margin crenate in upper half, smooth to scarcely crenate below, apex blunt, base oblique, 90 mm long by 50 mm wide; petiole 12 mm long; young foliage light yellowish green; mature foliage, dark sage-green, glaucous beneath, in autumn yellow.

Flowers

Petals 8 mm long by 1.5 mm wide, straight, red at base fading to orange-yellow at tip; calyx bright maroon-red; overall a coppery orange; strong spicy scent; flowering early to midwinter.

Hamamelis vernalis 'Quasimodo' (Zwijnenburg, 1980)

Comments

A selection made from a batch of seed-raised plants growing in the nursery of Pieter Zwijnenburg, Boskoop, The Netherlands, where he noticed a plant with tighter, more congested growth. This was selected, grown on, and eventually named by him, as it was distinct from other *Hamamelis vernalis* he was familiar with.

Growth habit

Rounded bush, compact, twiggy growth, 1 m tall by 1 m wide.

Foliage

Leaves obovate, margin crenate in upper half, smooth to scarcely crenate below, apex blunt, base oblique, 55 mm long by 35 mm wide; petiole 6 mm long; young foliage light yellowish green; mature foliage sage-green, glaucous beneath, in autumn yellow.

Flowers

Petals 4 mm long by 1 mm wide, straight, slightly crimped, brownish orange; calyx a brownish maroon; overall a dull orange; spicy scent; flowering late winter through early spring.

Hamamelis vernalis 'Red Imp' (Dummer, 1966)

Comments

A selection made at Hillier Nurseries Ltd. by Peter Dummer and Roy Lancaster in February 1966, from a large batch of seed-raised plants growing in the nursery.

Growth habit

Upright, 2.5 m tall by 2 m wide.

Foliage

Leaves obovate, margin crenate in upper half, smooth to scarcely crenate below, apex blunt, base, oblique, 95 mm long by 65 mm wide; petiole 12 mm long; young foliage light yellowish green; mature foliage, medium green, in autumn yellow.

Flowers

Petals 8 mm long by 1 mm wide, twisted and crimped, clear red; calyx purple-red; overall reddish; faint scent; flowering mid through late winter.

Hamamelis vernalis 'Sandra' (Dummer, 1962)

Comments

A selection made by Peter Dummer for spring foliage colour and named after his daughter. According to Roy Lancaster, in the spring of 1962 while examining a large batch of seed-raised plants in the nursery, among a sea of green foliage a patch of purple caught Peter's eye. There was one plant with the young foliage flushed purple. This was duly planted out in some stock beds in a woodland situation, where the plant continued to perform each spring, with the added bonus of brilliant autumn colour of orange and flame, eventually turning scarlet.

Growth habit

Vase-shaped, 2.5 m tall by 2.5 m wide.

Foliage

Leaves obovate, margins shallowly crenate in upper half, smooth to scarcely crenate below, apex acute, base oblique, 90 mm long by 60 mm wide; petiole 20 mm long; young foliage medium green heavily flushed plum-purple; mature foliage dark green, in autumn yellow-orange finally displaying excellent red-crimson colour. Good autumn colour, however, is not a consistent trait and does not always happen on all soil types and localities in the United Kingdom

Flowers

Petals 10 mm long by 1.5 mm wide, very slightly curled, crimped, straw coloured with red tint at very base; calyx light maroon-red; overall a golden yellow; spicy scent; flowering late winter through early spring.

Hamamelis vernalis 'Sashet' (Klein, ca. 1975)

Synonym

Hamamelis vernalis 'Sashay'

Comments

Selected from a batch of open-pollinated *Hamamelis vernalis* plants growing in the nursery of Theodore Klein's garden, Yewdell, in Crestwood, Kentucky. According to Paul Cappiello, it roots readily from cuttings, grows into a large suckering plant, with wide arching branches. It does retain some of its leaves in the winter, most dropping during the flowering period. Flowers are borne as heavily as Paul has seen on any witch hazel, crowded along the branches and best described as a coppery orange. The fragrance is strong and sweet. The staff at the Bernheim Arboretum rated it in the top three of sixty cultivars growing there. It flowers late winter through early spring and is not susceptible to mildew.

Growth habit

Upright, twiggy, 3 m tall by 4 m wide.

Foliage

Leaves obovate, margin crenate in upper half, shallowly crenate below, apex acute, base oblique, 95 mm long by 65 mm wide; petiole 18 mm long; young foliage yellowish green; mature foliage apple-green, glaucous beneath, in autumn butter-yellow, lightly flushed orange.

Flowers

Petals 8 mm long by 1.5 mm wide, dull orange tinted red at base; calyx light red; overall a coppery orange; strong sweet yet spicy scent; flowering early to midwinter.

Hamamelis vernalis 'Spring Magic' (Willoway Nurseries, 1980)

Comments

A selection made from a batch of seed-raised plants growing in Willoway Nurseries, Avon, Ohio, with very apparent differences in morphology from the normal run of *Hamamelis vernalis* plants. An interesting plant for its small leaf size and tight, congested growth habit. The flowers are very small and do not contribute very much to the winter scene in the garden.

Growth habit

Rounded bush, dwarf in growth with many tight congested branches, 1 m tall by 1 m wide.

Foliage

Leaves broadly elliptic, margin crenate in upper half, shallowly crenate below, apex acute, base oblique, 65 mm long by 35 mm wide; petiole 6 mm long; young foliage light yellowish green; mature foliage, dull sage-green, in autumn yellow.

Flowers

Petals 4 mm long by 1 mm wide, straight, slightly crimped, coppery orange; calyx brownish maroon; overall a rusty-orange colour; spicy scent; flowering late winter through early spring.

Hamamelis vernalis 'Squib' (Dummer, 1966)

Comments

Another selection made at Hillier Nurseries Ltd. by Peter Dummer and Roy Lancaster from the same seed batch as *Hamamelis vernalis* 'Red Imp'.

Growth habit

Upright, later rounded bush, 2.5 m tall by 2.5 m wide.

Foliage

Leaves broadly elliptic, margin crenate in upper half, smooth to scarcely crenate below, apex blunt, base oblique, 90 mm long by 45 mm wide; petiole 6 mm long; young foliage medium green; mature foliage sage-green, glaucous underneath, in autumn yellow.

Flowers

Petals 6 mm long by 1 mm wide, straight, slightly crimped, light yellow; calyx greenish yellow; overall a pale yellow; light scent; flowering mid through late winter.

Hamamelis vernalis 'Washington Park' (Lane, 2003)

Synonyms

Hamamelis purpurea Hort., *H. vernalis* 'Purpurea'

Comments

From a plant growing in the Washington Park Arboretum, Seattle, Washington, which originally came from the Henry Kohankie Nursery, Perry, Ohio. It was listed in the nursery's 1952–1953 catalogue, as "*Hamamelis purpurea*, the purple-flowered vernal Witch Hazel," and later as *H. vernalis* 'Purpurea'. Similar in many respects to *H. vernalis* 'Kohankie Red' but if anything the flowers are nearer to a purple colour. I have seen the plant in the Washington Park Arboretum, and it is a sizeable specimen, possibly 3 m tall by 7 m wide. There are two other easily recognizable differences between this cultivar and *H. vernalis* 'Kohankie Red': the leaf margin is more irregular and autumn colouring begins seven to ten days later.

Growth habit

Upright, later a rounded bush, 2.5 m tall by 2.5 m wide.

Foliage

Leaves orbicular-obovate, margin crenate in upper half, shallowly crenate below, apex blunt, base oblique, 90 mm long by 70 mm wide; petiole 10 mm long; young foliage medium yellowish green; mature foliage dark green, glaucous beneath, in autumn yellow-orange finally turning scarlet-red.

Flowers

Petals 12 mm long by 1.5 mm wide, straight and slightly crimped, reddish purple; calyx dark purple; overall a deep reddish purple; faint scent; flowering mid through late winter.

Chapter 5

Hamamelis japonica Sieb. & Zucc.: The Japanese Witch Hazel

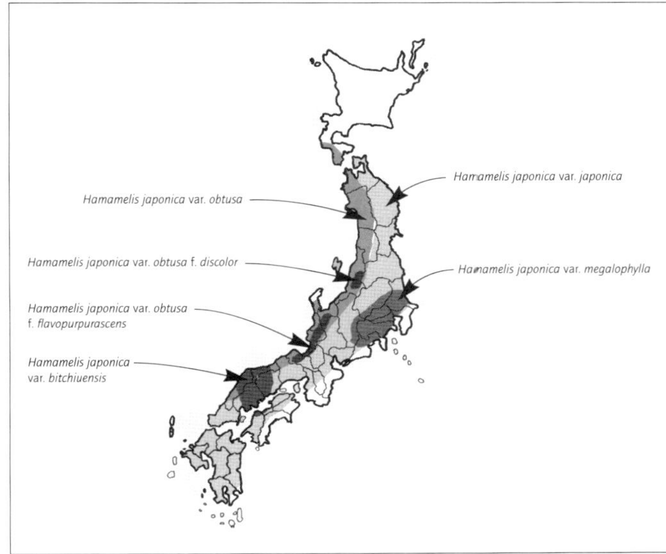

Map 4 Natural distribution of *Hamamelis japonica* varieties in Japan

Synonyms

Hamamelis arborea Ottol. ex. Masters, *H. zuccariniana* Ottol., Japanese name *Mansaku*

The Japanese witch hazel, *Hamamelis japonica*, was introduced to Europe by Philipp Franz von Siebold, a German doctor and naturalist. His career in the Far East began when he joined the Dutch East India Company as a physician naturalist. His first trip to Japan was in 1822, the Dutch being the only foreigners with access to Japan because of the sole trade agreement they had with them. The Japanese distrust of all foreigners was evident in the fact that the Dutch were confined to a small man-made island in Nagasaki Harbour called Deshima.

The Dutch East India Company were hoping that Siebold's appointment and his skill as a physician would improve and strengthen the trading relationship the Dutch had with the Japanese. The fact that Siebold could perform cataract surgery and was able to restore the sight of some important Japanese people enabled him to travel freely around Nagasaki collecting plants.

On a trip to Edo (now Tokyo) in 1826 with the Dutch ambassador, he acquired many plants together with a map of Japan, which he hoped would help him in the future. Unfortunately, on their return to Deshima the ship encountered a storm and foundered on the shores of Deshima. The map, which was a military secret, was discovered and as a punishment Siebold was interred on Deshima. After one year he was given a pardon and told to leave the country, which he had come to love. He also had a Japanese wife and daughter whom he had to leave behind. Siebold departed Deshima with 485 different kinds of plants and arrived in Antwerp in July 1830.

All his surviving plants, 260 in number, were sent to the botanic garden in Ghent. On the outbreak of civil war between The Netherlands and what was to become Belgium, Siebold decided to leave the country. His plants in the botanic garden were confiscated and distributed among the professional and amateur horticulturists of the area. On his return after the war, he discovered his plants were all missing and through much effort was able to locate only 80 plants.

This experience of losing the plants gave Siebold a more business-like approach to plant introduction, and he tried to set up a monopoly on imported Japanese plants. This was made much easier for him when in 1842 he received a royal decree from the Dutch government that gave his business, the Jardin d'Acclimation, reduced shipping rates with the Dutch East India Company and first choice of plant material from Japan. In 1859 Siebold returned to Japan as a guest of the Shogun. Despite being popular with the Japanese, the Dutch government considered him an embarrassment. He was therefore offered a post in the Dutch government, which he could not refuse, and was thus enticed out of Japan. Siebold left in 1861, never to return to the country he loved.

Though Siebold had named and described *Hamamelis japonica* in his 1843 publication *Florae Japonicae*, it was not until his last trip that he collected living plants of *H. japonica*. He offered it for sale in his 1863 catalogue, which listed two types, *H. japonica* and *H. arborea* (known today as *H. japonica* 'Arborea'). The Japanese witch hazel was first offered for sale in a nursery trade catalogue issued by Messrs. Ottolander, of Boskoop, The

Netherlands, as *H. arborea*, under which name it was described by Masters. Since Siebold's time, several different forms of *H. japonica* have arrived in Europe, mainly through nurserymen importing plants rather than European plant collectors searching for them.

The Japanese name for *Hamamelis* is *Mansaku*; it is said to derive from "rich crop," although there are various opinions depending on the translator. Folklore has it that when *H. japonica* produces inflorescences in great number, the year's harvest is promised to be good. Another theory says the name indicates the Japanese words for "earliest flowering." In Okayama, Hiroshima, and Shimane Prefectures it is also called "early in the valley," and in parts of the prefectures Gifu and Nagano it is called "not knowing the timing."

Hamamelis japonica is not of much interest to the Japanese horticultural industry, and little selection and propagation is done in Japan. The people of Japan do make use of them, however, particularly in rural areas. Branches are nicely flexible and are used to make various objects such as rafts, baskets, and shelves and as traditional building and binding materials. Witch hazels are used to a limited extent as garden plants, but prized as cut flowers, particularly at the scene of traditional tea ceremonies.

I have imported two forms in recent years, thanks to the help of Mikinori Ogisu. The variety and gene pool in *Hamamelis japonica* is wide, and I feel there is great potential in searching for and introducing new forms.

Distribution

This species is distributed in mountainous regions of the temperate to warm temperate zone, between the south-western part of Hokkaido and Kyushu in the south (the southern-most limit lies near Mount Takakuma in the Osumi region), at elevations of 200–1700 m (see Map 4). *Hamamelis japonica* favours comparatively sunny sites with reasonably moist soils on mountain slopes and occasionally grows on ridges.

Hamamelis japonica Sieb. & Zucc. var. *japonica* grows on the mainland, along the east coast, and on Shikoku and Kyushu. *Hamamelis japonica* var. *megalophylla* (Koidz) Kitamura grows in mainland areas, in Tohoku (north-east), Kanto (mid-east), and Chuba (mid-west). *Hamamelis japonica* var. *bitchiuensis* (Makino) Ohwi grows in the mainland area, Chuba, and in the Ahime Prefecture of Shikoku Island. *Hamamelis japonica* var. *obtusata*

Matsumura grows in Chuba, in mountainous regions along the west coast. *Hamamelis japonica* var. *obtusata* f. *flavopurpurascens* (Makino) and *H. japonica* var. *obtusata* f. *incarnata* (Makino) Ohwi are rare, growing in the mountains in Toyama and Fukui Prefectures and along the upper Yura River. *Hamamelis japonica* var. *obtusata* f. *discolor* (Nakai) Ohwi is found only on the higher mountains in Nigata Prefecture, such as Mount Komagatake and Mount Sumondake.

Description

Original description (Hooker 1882, p. 108)

Hamamelis japonica Sieb. & Zucc.: A very interesting plant, so closely allied to the North American Witch Hazel, *H. virginica*, that it might easily be mistaken for that plant, the principal differences being the rather larger flowers with red revolute calyx lobes, and the short fruiting calyx of this; in foliage they are almost indistinguishable; the leaves of *H. virginica* are however usually narrower and often more lobulate. Franchet and Savart, who discuss the differences between the two species, overlook the calyx, and attach most importance to the statement that the leaves of *H. japonica* are six- to nine-nerved, and of *H. virginica* five- to six-nerved, a distinction that does not at all hold good; they further observe that the calyx in fruit of *H. japonica* is sometimes half as long as the capsule, whilst in all the specimens which I have examined it is confined to the base. A plate has been prepared of *H. virginica* from plants growing in the Royal Botanic Gardens, Kew, to show the differences. The genus *Hamamelis*, consisting only of these two species, is one of the best proofs of that close connexion between the Floras of Japan and Eastern North America, to the exclusion of the Western side of the continent, which has been so ably discussed by Dr. Gray, and which he has shown to throw so much light on the origin and distribution of the North American Flora.

Hamamelis japonica was introduced into cultivation by Messrs. Veitch; it flowers, like its American kinsman, as the leaves fall in autumn [obviously a mistake by Hooker, as this species flowers in mid to late winter] and fruits the next summer. The petals in our specimen are narrower and less crumpled than in that figured in the *Gardeners' Chronicle*, and in some dried specimens from Japan. There is a plant of it in the Kew Arboretum presented by Messrs. Veitch, to whom I am indebted for the specimens here figured, of which the leaves were drawn in September, and the flowers the following February.

Description

A shrub or small tree; branches rather stout, covered with brown bark; young branchlets, buds, petioles, and often leaf-nerves beneath bracts and calyx externally clothed with a fine close pubescence. Leaves ovate-oblong or rounded, 50–88 mm long and broad, obtuse or acute, sinuate-toothed or crenate, firm in texture, dark green; base acute obtuse cordate or rounded; nerves deeply sunk above, very prominent beneath; petiole very short, stout. Flowers in sessile or subsessile globose heads 13–19 mm in diameter, crowded; bracts small, rounded, appressed to the calyx. Calyx 8 mm across the lobes, tube campanulate; lobes broadly ovate, revolute, dull red, margins villous. Petals 17 mm long, strap-shaped, waved, tip acute obtuse or notched, golden yellow, involute in aestivation. Stamens very short, filaments stout; anthers opening by valves in front. Carpels two, silky, styles filiform. Capsule subglobose, 13 mm long, densely brown-tomentose, girt at the base by the calyx tube.

As *Hamamelis japonica* is variable in the wild and the information from Japanese botanists has not been published in the West, apart from Ohwi, I give descriptions here after Ogisu (1980) and consulted the work of Kitagawa (under the name Ohwi 1983) as well as Kitamura and Murata (1979). I will also describe them myself, where I have plants representative of the various types. In the text that follows, Mikinori Ogisu's descriptions are comparative in the main from one botanical form to another, while mine follow the format used elsewhere in the book.

Hamamelis japonica Sieb. & Zucc. var. *bitchiuensis* (Makino) Ohwi

Synonym

Hamamelis bitchiuensis Makino, Japanese name *Atetsu-Mansaku*

Description

Light brown stellate hairs on both surfaces of the leaf remain well after the leaf matures, petals are shorter than the type *japonica* and pale gold. Not known to have been introduced to cultivation in the West.

Hamamelis japonica Sieb. & Zucc. var. *japonica*

Synonyms

Hamamelis arborea Ottol. ex. Masters, *H. zuccariniana* Ottol., Japanese name *Mansaku*

Description

Multiple-stemmed deciduous shrub 5–10 m tall, bark grey or light brown with lenticels, which split horizontally. Apical branches are grey, with numerous roundish lenticels and when young densely covered with stellate hairs. Leaves alternate, ovate or obovate, asymmetrical, and somewhat cordate at the base, 50–100 mm long by 30–70 mm wide, apex mildly acute, though never sharply, margins deeply serrate, thin and leathery, dark green and glossy on upper surface, light green with stellate hairs when young but later almost glabrous on lower surface, leaving only some hairs at the vein axils. Petiole 5–12 mm long, grooved above. Flowers open in late winter through early spring prior to foliage growth, flower stalk usually bent, 5–10 mm long, sepals ovate, 3 mm long, reflexed, and cruciform, smooth and usually with a dark red-purple tinge on upper surface, with dense short brown hairs on lower surface. Petals linear, 12–20 mm long, colour varying from yellow to reddish yellow.

Comments

I have a plant of the typical form which I obtained from Royal Botanic Gardens, Kew, under the collector's number WAHO.975. This is proving to be a moderately vigorous plant, twiggy growth habit; flowering reasonably profusely with the typical yellow, curled petals.

Growth habit

Rounded to spreading bush, 3 m tall by 3.5 m wide, moderately vigorous and well branched.

Foliage

Leaves orbicular-obovate, margins crenate, apex blunt, base oblique, 80 mm long by 80 mm wide; petiole 10 mm long; young foliage medium green; mature foliage glabrous, dark green, in autumn yellow.

Flowers

Petals 15 mm long by 1.5 mm wide, quite curled and crimped, lemon yellow; calyx green, heavily flushed maroon-red, giving an overall effect of a pale sulphur-yellow, scent faint; flowering in late winter.

Hamamelis japonica var. *japonica* Sieb. & Zucc. f. *flavopurpurascens* (Makino) Rehd.

Synonym

Hamamelis flavopurpurascens Makino, Japanese name *Mansaku*

Description

Petals yellow suffused red.

Comments

I have a plant of this form, which I obtained from the Royal Botanic Gardens, Kew, in 1994; the original plant was very old and died a few years later. All other plants that I have come across in the trade or in gardens are the clone *Hamamelis japonica* 'Rubra'. It was introduced to the United States by E. H. Wilson in 1919 and probably to England about the same time.

Growth habit

Spreading, medium vigour, 2 m tall by 3 m wide.

Foliage

Leaves orbicular-obovate, margins crenate, apex blunt, base oblique, 75 mm long by 65 mm wide; petiole 10 mm long; young foliage medium to dark green, heavily flushed bronze; mature foliage glabrous, dark green, in autumn yellow flushed orange red.

Flowers

Petals 13 mm long by 1.5 mm wide, curled and crimped, straw yellow flushed red, particularly at base of petal; calyx deep purplish red; overall a red-yellow bicolour effect; faint scent; flowering late winter through early spring.

Hamamelis japonica Sieb. & Zucc. var. *megalophylla* (Koidz.) Kitamura

Synonyms

Hamamelis japonica Sieb. & Zucc. subsp. *megalophylla* (Koidz.) G. Murata, *H. megalophylla* Koidz., Japanese name *Ohba-Mansaku*

Description

Leaf larger than the type *japonica*, 50–150 mm long by 40–100 mm wide, petals are larger, up to 15–18 mm long.

Comments

I have a plant from scion material given to me by Mikinori Ogisu. This is an interesting botanical variety in that it has very pale flowers and the summer foliage is dark green and somewhat glossy.

Growth habit

Rounded bush, medium vigour, 2.5 m tall by 2.5 m wide.

Foliage

Leaves orbicular-obovate, margins crenate in upper half, smooth to scarcely crenate below, tip acute, base oblique, 75 mm long by 70 mm wide; petiole 10 mm long; young foliage medium to dark green, heavily flushed bronze; mature foliage glabrous, dark green, in autumn orange red, finally scarlet.

Flowers

Petals 15 mm long by 1.5 mm wide, slightly curled and crimped, pale creamy yellow; calyx green with slight maroon flush; overall colour a very pale creamy yellow; no scent; flowering late winter through early spring.

Hamamelis japonica Sieb. & Zucc. var. *obtusata* Matsumura

Synonyms

Hamamelis japonica Sieb. & Zucc. f. *obtusata* (Matsum.) H. Ohba, *H. obtusata* (Matsum) Makino, Japanese name *Maruba-Mansaku*

Description

Leaf obovate or obovate-orbicular, apex obtuse; stellate hairs above, retained only when young and disappearing when the leaf matures, becoming glabrous above, but a few hairs remaining at axil of veins on the lower surface. Small yellow flowers.

Comments

I have plants raised from three wild-collected sources; the following description is from a plant I obtained from the Hillier Arboretum.

Growth habit

Rounded to spreading bush, densely twiggy, 2 m tall by 2.5 m wide.

Foliage

Leaves obovate, margins crenate in upper half, smooth to scarcely crenate below, apex blunt, base oblique, 65 mm long by 60 mm wide; petiole 8 mm long; young foliage medium green; mature foliage glabrous, dark green, in autumn yellow.

Flowers

Petals 2 mm long by 2 mm wide, curled and crimped, pale yellow; calyx green; overall effect of pale yellow; does not stand out well; little scent; flowering late winter.

Hamamelis japonica Sieb. & Zucc. var. *obtusata* (Matsum) H. Ohba f. *discolor* (Nakai) Ohwi

Synonyms

Hamamelis japonica f. *discolor* (Nakai) Ohwi ex. H. Ohba, *H. obtusata* var. *discolor* Nakai, Japanese name *Urajiro-Maruba-Mansaku*

Description

A form with powdery white lower leaf surfaces.

Hamamelis japonica Sieb. & Zucc. var. *obtusata* (Matsum) H. Ohba f. *flavopurpurascens* Makino

Synonym

Hamamelis obtusata (Matsum) H. Ohba var. *flavopurpurascens* Makino, Japanese name *Nishiki-Maruba-Mansaku*

Description

A form with petals flushed red at the base.

Comments

Another plant in my collection where scion material was received from Mikinori Ogisu.

Growth habit

Upright, vigorous, 3 m tall by 2.5 m wide.

Foliage

Leaves obovate, margins crenate in upper half, smooth to scarcely crenate below, apex blunt, base oblique, 65 mm long by 60 mm wide; petiole 8 mm long; young foliage medium green; mature foliage glabrous, dark green, in autumn orange red and finally scarlet.

Flowers

Petals 13 mm long by 1.5 mm wide, slightly curled and crimped, red at base, pale yellow in upper half; calyx deep maroon-red; overall a red-yellow bicolour effect, scent faint; flowering late winter through early spring.

Hamamelis japonica Sieb. & Zucc. var. *obtusata* (Matsum) H. Ohba f. *incarnata* (Makino) Ohwi

Synonym

Hamamelis incarnata Makino, Japanese name *Akabana-Maruba-Mansaku*

Description

A form with red colouring over the entire petals.

Cultivars of Hamamelis japonica

Hamamelis japonica 'Arborea' (Ottolander, 1862)

Synonyms

Hamamelis arborea Ottol. ex. Masters, *H. japonica* Sieb. & Zucc. var. *arborea* (Masters) Gumbleton

Comments

First imported into Europe by von Siebold in 1862 and distributed by the nursery K. J. W Ottolander, Boskoop, The Netherlands, first as *Hamamelis arborea* and afterwards as *H. japonica* var. *arborea*. All plants in cultivation are the same clone, hence it has been given cultivar status. *Hamamelis japonica* 'Arborea' is a useful shrub for large gardens and parks, because of its distinctive growth habit, not treelike as the name suggests, but a large wide spreading plant; this trait is readily visible in young plants and continues into maturity. It received a First Class Certificate when shown before the Royal Horticultural Society by James Veitch in 1881.

Growth habit

Spreading, strong growth, 3 m tall by 4.5 m wide.

Foliage

Leaves orbicular-obovate, margins crenate in upper half, shallowly so below, apex blunt, base oblique, 80 mm long by 70 mm wide; petiole 8 mm long; young foliage medium green with faint bronze flush; mature foliage glabrous, dark green, in autumn yellow.

Flowers

Petals 13 mm long by 1 mm wide, twisted and crimped, yellow-orange; calyx reddish purple; overall very deep golden yellow; faint scent; flowering throughout midwinter.

Hamamelis japonica 'Brentry' (Lane, 1999)

Comments

Named by me from a plant growing in the Brentry area in the Hillier Arboretum. Origin unknown. This is a particularly fine flowering clone and worthy of cultivar status.

Growth habit

Vase-shaped when young, later spreading, twiggy growth, 3 m tall by 3.5 m wide.

Foliage

Leaves orbicular-obovate, margins crenate in upper half, shallowly crenate below, apex blunt, base oblique, 80 mm long by 65 mm wide; petiole 10 mm long; young foliage medium to dark green; mature foliage glabrous, dark green, in autumn butter-yellow.

Flowers

Petals 15 mm long by 1.5 mm wide, twisted and crimped, pale sulphur-yellow; calyx dull maroon; overall pale yellow; no scent; flowering mid through late winter.

Hamamelis japonica 'Canary Yellow' (de Belder, 2001)

Comments

A Hemelrijk cultivar under the number H.10566, selected by Jelena de Belder because of the late flowering period in early spring. I have not been to Hemelrijk late enough to see it in flower there. At my nursery in Kent, England, it is a late-flowering yellow, but I need to observe it more closely against other yellow *Hamamelis japonica* cultivars before making judgement.

Growth habit

Vase-shaped, to spreading, twiggy vigorous growth, 2.5 m tall by 3 m wide.

Foliage

Leaves obovate, margins crenate in upper half, shallowly crenate below, apex blunt, base oblique, 75 mm long by 55 mm wide; petiole 15 mm long; young foliage light green; mature foliage glabrous, dark green, in autumn yellow.

Flowers

Petals 16 mm long by 1.5 mm wide, twisted and crimped, pale sulphur-yellow; calyx light maroon-red; overall a bright canary yellow; no scent; flowering late winter through early spring.

Hamamelis japonica 'Paleface' (Bond, 1985)

Comments
Named by John Bond from a plant in the Savill Garden, Windsor Great Park, England, that arose as sucker growth on a plant of *Hamamelis mollis* imported from Boskoop in the early 1970s

Growth habit
Upright, strong growing, 3 m tall by 2 m wide.

Foliage
Leaves orbicular-obovate, margins crenate in upper half, smooth to scarcely crenate below, apex acute, base oblique, 70 mm long by 55 mm wide; petiole 10 mm long; young foliage medium green with bronze flush; mature foliage glabrous, shiny dark green, glaucous beneath, in autumn deep butter-yellow.

Flowers
Petals 12 mm long by 1 mm wide, twisted and crimped, pale sulphur-yellow; calyx deep maroon-red; overall a pale yellow, no scent; flowering throughout midwinter.

Hamamelis japonica 'Pendula'

Comments
Of unknown origin, first seen in the Japanese exhibition at the Floriade of 1990 in The Netherlands. *Hamamelis japonica* 'Pendula' is the only truly weeping witch hazel so far.

Growth habit
Weeping, unless trained up a cane makes a mound 1 m tall by 3 m wide.

Foliage
Leaves obovate, margin shallowly crenate in upper half, smooth to scarcely crenate below, apex blunt, base oblique, 65 mm long by 50 mm wide; petiole 10 mm long; young foliage light yellowish green; mature foliage glabrous, dark green, somewhat shiny, in autumn butter-yellow.

Flowers

Petals 12 mm long by 1 mm wide, slightly twisted and crimped, pale sulphur-yellow; calyx bright maroon-red; overall sulphur-yellow; faint scent; flowering late winter through early spring.

Hamamelis japonica 'Rubra' (Chenault, ca. 1915)

Synonyms

Hamamelis japonica Sieb. & Zucc. var. *flavopurpurascens* Makino, *H. zuccariniana rubra* Hort.

Comments

Originally considered to be synonymous with *Hamamelis japonica* var. *flavopurpurascens*. As this is a botanical variety, it can be variable; virtually all plants found in cultivation are referable to the clone 'Rubra', raised at the Chenault Nursery, Orleans, France, prior to 1915. Introduced as *H. zuccariniana rubra*, the first witch hazel with reddish flowers, now surpassed by many red-flowered hybrids. It cannot be stressed too much, however, that 'Rubra' has mainly been responsible for producing the wonderful red-flowered hybrids which we grow today.

Growth habit

Vase-shaped when young, later more spreading, twiggy growth, 3 m tall by 3 m wide.

Foliage

Leaves orbicular-obovate, margin crenate in upper half, smooth to scarcely crenate below, apex acute, base oblique, 80 mm long by 65 mm wide; petiole 15 mm long; young foliage medium green; mature foliage glabrous, dark green, in autumn yellow, flushed orange and red.

Flowers

Petals 15 mm long by 1.5 mm wide, twisted and crimped, yellow grading to red at the base; calyx purple-red; overall a muddy yellow-red bicolour; faint scent; flowering throughout midwinter.

Hamamelis japonica 'Sulphurea' (Russell, 1958)

Comments

A fairly large-flowered selection raised in the nursery of J. R. Russell, Sunningdale, Surrey, England. It received an Award of Merit when shown at the Royal Horticultural Society in 1958 by the Crown Estate Commissioners (Windsor Great Park).

Growth habit

Spreading, medium vigour, twiggy, 2 m tall by 3 m wide.

Foliage

Leaves orbicular-obovate, margin shallowly crenate in upper half, smooth to scarcely crenate below, apex acute, base oblique, 90 mm long by 70 mm wide; petiole 15 mm long; young foliage medium green; mature foliage glabrous, dark green, in autumn yellow.

Flowers

Petals 18 mm long by 1 mm wide, twisted and crimped, yellow; calyx red; overall a strong sulphur-yellow; strong scent; flowering throughout mid-winter.

Hamamelis japonica 'Superba' (Kort. ca. 1939)

Comments

Most probably, an original introduction by von Siebold; there are records of this plant at Kalmthout in Antoine Kort's time, but it has not been widely distributed. There is, however, an old plant at Wisley, which almost certainly originated from Kalmthout. There is no longer a plant at Kalmthout, thus making the one at Wisley the oldest one around, possibly the only plant of that age. I have propagated from this plant, and it is now in my collection. Both Wisley and the Hillier Arboretum now have young specimens of 'Superba'.

Growth habit

Vase-shaped when young, later more spreading, medium vigour, 2.5 m tall by 3 m wide.

Foliage

Leaves orbicular-obovate, margin crenate in upper half, smooth to scarcely crenate below, apex acute, base oblique, 70 mm long by 50 mm wide; petiole 15 mm long; young foliage medium to dark green; mature foliage glabrous, dark green, in autumn yellow.

Flowers

Petals 16 mm long by 1 mm wide, twisted and crimped, yellow; calyx red-purple; overall an acid-yellow; faint scent; flowering throughout midwinter.

Hamamelis japonica 'Zuccariniana' (Ottolander, 1868)

Synonym

Hamamelis zuccariniana Ottol.

Comments

An original introduction, possibly by von Siebold (1868), referable to *Hamamelis japonica* var. *obtusata*. This is a very distinct plant, easily recognized, by growth habit, foliage, and late flowering. Received a First Class Certificate at the Royal Horticultural Society as long ago as 1891, when shown by James Veitch. First distributed by the Ottolander Nursery, Boskoop, The Netherlands, in 1874.

Growth habit

Upright to vase-shaped, medium vigour, very twiggy, 2.5 m tall by 2 m wide.

Foliage

Leaves obovate, margin crenate in upper third, smooth to scarcely crenate below, apex blunt, base oblique, 75 mm long by 45 mm wide; petiole 12 mm long; young foliage medium to dark green with a heavy bronze flush; mature foliage glabrous, leaf edges curl upwards somewhat, dark green, glaucous underneath, in autumn yellow.

Flowers

Petals 10 mm long by 1.5 mm wide, curled at the tip and crimped, yellow; calyx yellow-green; overall a lime-yellow; no scent; flowering late winter through early spring.

Chapter 6

Hamamelis mollis Oliv.: The Chinese Witch Hazel

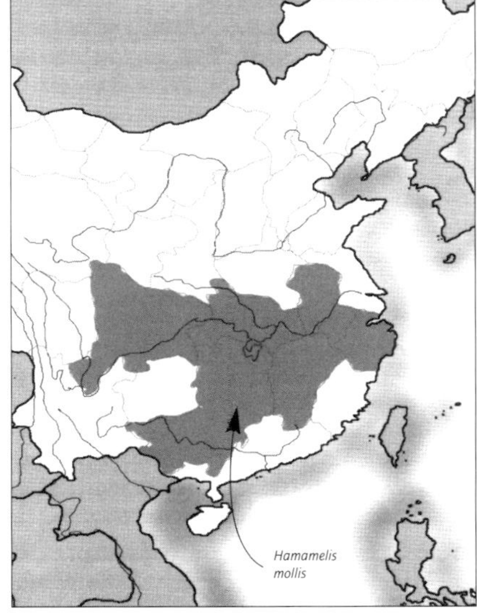

Map 5 Natural distribution of *Hamamelis mollis* in China

Synonym

Hamamelis mollis Oliv. var. *oblongifolia* M. B. Deng & G. Yao

Charles Maries, a British plant explorer who was employed by James Veitch & Sons, Chelsea, London, introduced *Hamamelis mollis* to cultivation in 1879. He had studied botany under the tutorship of Professor G. Henslow and then for seven years worked for his brother, R. Maries, at his nursery in Lytham, Lancashire. This background meant he was familiar with both Japanese and Chinese plants when he joined the firm of Veitch & Sons, in 1877. Because of this knowledge of Asian plants, Maries was sent to collect interesting plants on behalf of the firm.

He left England in February 1877 for Shanghai, and from there he explored the mountains near Ning po, where Robert Fortune collected.

Maries then left for Japan, where he collected many rare plants before returning to China in 1878. In the spring of that year he went to Chin-kiang and Kiu-kiang, where he found *Hamamelis mollis* in the Lushan Mountains. Maries did not record the precise locality where he collected seed; however, the Veitch Nursery indicated it came from Kiang-su. Maries certainly saw many plants here in flower in the spring, but when returning in the autumn he found most of the vegetation had been cut down, presumably for firewood. He did collect some seed, as in 1879 seed was received by the Veitch Nursery. This was immediately sown but only one plant survived to maturity, in the Coombe Wood Nursery.

This plant was not recognized as *Hamamelis mollis* for twenty years, when George Nicholson, curator of the Royal Botanic Gardens, Kew, visited the nursery and recognized it as something different from *H. japonica*, of which the nursery had thought it to be a form. Nicholson realized it was something different because of an herbarium specimen that Augustine Henry had sent to the botanist Daniel Oliver at Kew, who had named it as a new species, *H. mollis*, publishing a description in the 1888 issue of Hooker's *Icones Plantarum*. Nicholson brought the plant to the attention of George Harrow, foreman at the Coombe Wood Nursery, who then grafted as many plants as he could from the original plant. This clone is now known as *H. mollis* 'Coombe Wood' and was awarded a First Class Certificate by the Royal Horticultural Society in 1918 and an Award of Garden Merit in 1922.

Later both Augustine Henry and E. H. Wilson found *Hamamelis mollis* in the woods and thickets of Hupeh (now Hubei), thereby extending its known range into west-central China. In 1902 Henry sent seed to Kew, who distributed some to other botanic gardens in Europe. Wilson in *Plantae Wilsonianae* (Sargent 1913) described it as one of the commonest shrubs in western Hupeh, occurring between 1300 and 2500 m elevation. He found it equally abundant on the Lushan Mountains near Kiukiang, where Maries first found it, noting that it flowered in late March and early April.

Hamamelis mollis introductions to the Arnold Arboretum by E. H. Wilson are reasonably well recorded. The first (under accession number 14691) was seed collected in Hsingshan Hsien in Hupeh Province received at the arboretum on 28 February 1908. The second (accession number 14692) was also of seed but from an unspecified location; this accession was also received at the arboretum in 1908, but the exact date is not given. Between 1914 and 1946, seed, plants, and graft wood was distributed from the Arnold Arboretum to just over 200 individuals and nurseries.

Distribution

Today, according to *Flora Republica Popularis Sinicae* (Chang and Yan 1979), the distribution covers a large area in the provinces of Sichuan, Hubei, Anhui, Zhejiang, Jiangxi, Hunan, and Guangxi (see Map 5). *Hamamelis mollis* is often found in secondary forests or thickets at elevations of 800–1400 m. For such a large distribution, it must be fairly local within its range, as few Western botanists and plant collectors have come across it in the wild in recent times. In a letter I received from Professor Gu Yin of the Nanjing Botanical Garden, she stated that the distribution of *Hamamelis mollis* is scattered in seven provinces in south-eastern and south-western China. She also stated that significant variations have not yet been found in the wild. This is not borne out, however, by the number of distinct named selections from the early collections and from Japan.

Recent collections and introductions have been made by Mikinori Ogisu, who collected some seedlings under his collection number Ogisu 98037 on 4 June 1998 from Wufeng, south-west Hubei, at an elevation of about 1320 m; several plants are now established in cultivation. The plants were growing as understory shubs on wooded slopes in association with *Acer davidii*, *Corylopsis willmottiae*, *Cornus japonica* var. *chinensis*, *Weigela japonica* var. *sinica*, and a *Carpinus* species. On 25 April 1999 he observed *Hamamelis mollis* in flower at Wugang, southern Hunan, at an elevation of about 1350 m; on this occasion they were growing in company with *Quercus serrata*, *Corylopsis sinensis*, *Castanea seguinii*, *W. japonica* var. *sinica*, *Rhododendron simsii*, *Hosta ventricosa*, and a *Lindera* species. He reported that all that were flowering were yellow, not showing much variation in depth of colour. There was, however, a fair amount of variation in flower size, some being quite small, and some individuals were less floriferous than others.

This bears out my initial observations on my own plants, raised from seed obtained from Lushan Botanic Garden, Jiangxi Province, and collected locally. These are showing minor variations in foliage characteristics, but as yet there have not been sufficient flowers for detailed assessment to be made. With the degree of variation in the named cultivars described in this chapter, I am sure that a species with such a wide but local distribution must have interesting forms waiting to be discovered.

In an autumn 1991 letter, Dr. Guo Cheng-ze of the Nanyue Arboretum, Hengyang, Hunan, informed me that they had collected seed from a *Hamamelis mollis* plant, at least fifty years old and growing as a solitary specimen at an elevation of 900 m in Hengshan. He went on to say that it is a rare plant in the locality. From 4 September to 11 October 1994, an American expedition with representatives from the Morris Arboretum, U.S. National Arboretum, Arnold Arboretum, and Longwood Gardens, together with botanists from Nanjing Botanical Garden, botanized and collected in the Wundang Shan region of north-western Hubei. They discovered *H. mollis* (many plants) growing on a dry shady hillside; most were without seed, but a few had fruited, and seed was collected.

Description

Original description (Oliver 1888, p. 18)

Hamamelis mollis Oliv. (sp. nov.); foliis late obovato-ellipticis cuspidatus basi oblique cordatis sinuato-denticulatis supra minute subscabride stellulato-pubescentibus subtus dense stellato-tomentosis, breviter petiolatis, stipilis caducis dense tomentosis.

Description of a herbarium specimen at Kew (*Patung, Province Hupeh, China, Dr. Augustine Henry No. 3791, 3793A*; Hooker 1903, p. 129)

Of *Hamamelis* only three species are as yet known. *Hamamelis virginiana* Linn. t.6684, of the Eastern United States. *Hamamelis japonica* Sieb. & Zucc. t.6659 (*H. zuccariniana* Ottol. in *Gard. Chron.* 1874, vol. i, p. 187), and *H. mollis*, which extends the distribution of the genus into Western China. Though so widely apart geographically, the three species hardly differ in any essential characters of habit, inflorescence, or floral structure, but the Japanese and Chinese are more akin than either is to the American, which is nearly glabrous, and has smaller flowers, with the calyx lobes green within. *Hamamelis mollis* differs from its two congeners in the stellate tomentum of the leaves beneath, which are rather deeply cordate at the base, and in the broader petals. Its calyx-lobes are, as in *H. japonica*, purplish red. All three flower in winter, and leaf and fruit in summer or autumn, the foliage colouring before it falls.

Hamamelis mollis was first described and figured in *Icones Plantarum*, from specimens collected by Henry in the Patung district of the Province of Hupeh. It has since been found in Kiangsu, in the district of Kiukiang by Maries, who sent seeds to Veitch, by whom plants were raised and presented to the Royal Gardens, Kew, in 1902. It is, no doubt, a mountain plant in China, being hardy in England.

A large bush or small tree, sometimes thirty feet [9 m] high, with straggling branches and nearly black bark. Leaves four to five inches [100–125 mm] long, shortly petioled, orbicular-obovate or oblong, cuspidate, toothed, scaberulous above, stellate-tomentose beneath, base obliquely cordate, basal lobes more or less unequal, sinus acute, nerves eight or ten pair; stipules three-fourths of an inch [19 mm] long, linear-lanceolate, externally tomentose; glabrous within, caduceus. Flower heads sessile or very shortly peduncled. Calyx tomentose; lobes broadly ovate, glabrous, purplish red within, about a tenth of an inch [2.5 mm] long. Petals a third of an inch [8.3 mm] long by less than a tenth of an inch [2.5 mm] broad, golden yellow. Filaments short, stout. Ovary hirsute.

Cultivars of *Hamamelis mollis*

Hamamelis mollis 'Bonny Brook' (Bonny Brook Nursery, ca. 1990)

Comments

A selection of *Hamamelis mollis* that has possibly been confused with another plant called 'Bonny Brook', which arose as a seedling in the Bonny Brook Nursery, Bothell, Washington. The latter was acquired by Brian Mulligan, director of the Washington Park Arboretum, which he planted in his garden. As Mulligan's garden has not survived and it was in 1978 that he described the plant, there is little chance of finding it now—but you never know.

The plant I have is not the one mentioned by Mulligan; he related that it is an *Hamamelis* ×*intermedia* type, with bright lemon-yellow flowers and good red autumn colour, which is unusual for a yellow-flowered witch hazel. I obtained material with the help of John Wott of the Washington Park Arboretum, from a plant they received from the Bonny Brook Nursery. This plant is definitely an *H. mollis* clone that the nursery has applied its name to and unfortunately is not distinct. *Hamamelis mollis* 'Bonny Brook' is for all intents and purposes identical to *H. mollis* 'Jermyns Gold'.

Growth habit

Upright plant, at least while young, later a more rounded bush, vigorous growth, 3 m tall by 3 m wide.

Foliage
Leaves ovate-orbicular, margin crenate in upper half, shallowly crenate below, apex acute, base obliquely cordate, 95 mm long by 80 mm wide; petiole 8 mm long; young foliage olive-green; mature foliage pubescent, dull green, in autumn yellow.

Flowers
Petals 17 mm long by 1.5 mm wide, slightly curled and crimped, golden yellow with slight red tint at base; calyx brownish red; overall a good clear golden yellow; pleasant fragrance; flowering early through midwinter.

Hamamelis mollis 'Boskoop' (van de Laar, 1988)

Comments
Named by Harry van de Laar, of Boskoop, The Netherlands, as the best clone in the nursery trade in Holland and the clone that is most universally grown by nurserymen in Holland. According to van de Laar, *Hamamelis mollis* 'Boskoop' is most likely to have come from seed sent back to Europe by Augustine Henry and is a clone selected from one of the seedlings. This is the most widely distributed clone in existence, usually sold as just *H. mollis*. First offered for sale in Holland in 1910 by Firma K. Wezelenburg & Zoon, Hazerswoude, and in 1911 by Keesen & Zn, Aalsmeer.

Growth habit
Upright, at least as a young plant, later a more rounded shape, 3 m tall by 3 m wide.

Foliage
Leaves orbicular, margin shallowly crenate, apex blunt, base obliquely cordate, 95 mm long by 80 mm wide; petiole 6 mm long; young foliage light green; mature foliage pubescent, dull green, in autumn yellow.

Flowers
Petals 17 mm long by 1.5 mm wide, slightly curled and crimped, golden yellow with slight red tint at base; calyx brownish red; overall a good clear golden yellow; pleasant fragrance; flowering early through midwinter.

Hamamelis mollis 'Coombe Wood' (Veitch, 1909)

Comments

This cultivar originated from the only plant that survived in the Veitch, Coombe Wood Nursery, Surrey, England, from seed collected and sent by Maries to Veitch in 1879. It was not realized to be *Hamamelis mollis* until some twenty years later and not offered for sale by Veitch until the early part of the twentieth century.

Growth habit

Spreading, vigorous growth, 2 m tall by 3.5 m wide.

Foliage

Leaves ovate-orbicular, margin shallowly crenate, apex acute, base obliquely cordate, 120 mm long by 90 mm wide; petiole 10 mm long; young foliage light green; mature foliage pubescent, dull sage-green, slightly bullate upper surface, in autumn yellow.

Flowers

Petals 20 mm long 1.5 mm wide, slightly curled and crimped, golden yellow, tinted red at the base; overall a dark golden yellow, appears darker than *Hamamelis mollis* 'Jermyns Gold' due to the more extensive red tinting; calyx brownish red, fragrant, not so free flowering as 'Boskoop', later flowering from mid through late winter.

Hamamelis mollis 'Early Bright' (Scott Arboretum, 1988)

Comments

A selection released at the Scott Arboretum, Swarthmore, Pennsylvania, out of a batch of seed-raised plants received from the Koster Nursery, Bridgeton, New Jersey, in 1951. It was registered by Andrew Bunting, named because the plant flowered three to four weeks earlier than other *Hamamelis mollis* plants growing in the arboretum and it had brighter yellow flowers. The original plant was thirty-seven years old at the time of being registered. It hardly differs from *Hamamelis mollis* 'Boskoop' and *H. mollis* 'Jermyns Gold', flowers possibly a bit larger.

Foliage

Leaves ovate-orbicular, margin shallowly crenate, apex blunt, base obliquely cordate, 100 mm long by 90 mm wide; petiole 6 mm long; blade feels somewhat smoother than *Hamamelis mollis* 'Wisley Supreme'; young foliage light green; mature foliage pubescent, grey-green, in autumn yellow.

Flowers

Petals 17 mm long by 1.5 mm wide, slightly curled and crimped, golden yellow with slight red tint at base; overall a good clear golden yellow; calyx brownish red; pleasant fragrance; flowering early through midwinter.

Hamamelis mollis 'Emily' (Sanders, 1985)

Comments

A selection made by Chris Sanders, of Eccleshall, Staffordshire, England, and named after his mother. The original plant was from a batch of *Hamamelis mollis* imported from Japan by T. Hilling and Co. Ltd., Chobham, Surrey, in 1963. Chris was working for them at the time and he noticed that they were grafted onto *Distylium racemosum*.

Growth habit

Spreading shrub, somewhat slow-growing, well branched, smaller than *Hamamelis mollis* 'Coombe Wood', 2 m high by 3 m wide.

Foliage

Leaves orbicular, margin shallowly crenate, apex acute, base obliquely cordate, 105 mm long by 95 mm wide; petiole 20 mm long; young foliage light green; mature foliage pubescent, dull green, slightly bullate upper surface, in autumn yellow.

Flowers

Petals 18 mm long by 1.5 mm wide, slightly curled and crimped, golden yellow with slight red tinting at base; calyx maroon-red; overall a golden yellow; strong scent; flowering throughout midwinter.

Hamamelis mollis 'Fred Chittenden' (RHS Garden Wisley, 2003)

Synonym

Hamamelis mollis var. *pallida* Hort.

Comments

This clone was named by Mike Grant, botanist at Wisley, to avoid any confusion with the widely grown and well-known *Hamamelis ×intermedia* 'Pallida' (see chapter 7 for a detailed description). It received an Award of Merit in 1932 as *H. mollis* var. *pallida*; as this plant is not the same as *H. ×intermedia* 'Pallida', Mike named it after the long-serving director of the RHS Garden Wisley (from 1919 to 1931), who retired twelve days before it received its Award of Merit.

The original plant still grows in Seven Acres at Wisley; it was probably a ten-year-old plant at the time it received the award, so today is probably eighty years old. The only other plant I have discovered that corresponds with the Wisley plant was one that grew in the Valley Garden, Windsor. I was able to propagate both, grow them alongside each other, and prove to my satisfaction that they were one and the same. The Windsor plant has since died, but was most likely propagated from the Wisley plant, whose origin is unknown. I have distributed a few plants to various gardens and collections, but this cultivar is not readily available.

Growth habit

Upright form of *Hamamelis mollis* with more twiggy growth than most other clones, moderately vigorous, 3 m tall by 2 m wide.

Foliage

Leaves ovate-orbicular, margin shallowly crenate, apex acute, base obliquely cordate, 90 mm long by 70 mm wide; petiole 10 mm long; young foliage light yellowish green; mature foliage pubescent, sage-green, lighter beneath, in autumn yellow.

Flowers

Petals 18 mm long by 1.5 mm wide, straight, crimped, clear sulphur-yellow, very base tinted red; calyx bright maroon-red; overall sulphur-yellow; sweet scent; flowering early through midwinter.

Hamamelis mollis 'Goldcrest' (Aberconway, 1961)

Comments

A selection made at Bodnant Gardens in Wales, England, from seed sent by the Arnold Arboretum from a collection made by E. H. Wilson in 1907–1908. The original plant still grows at Bodnant along with others propagated from it. An excellent clone for flower but unfortunately prone to late spring frost damage when young. Received an Award of Merit when exhibited by Lord Aberconway in 1961.

Growth habit

Spreading shrub, not quite as flat as *Hamamelis mollis* 'Coombe Wood', 3 m tall by 4 m wide.

Foliage

Leaves ovate-orbicular, margin shallowly crenate, apex acute, base obliquely cordate, 105 mm long by 85 mm wide; petiole 15 mm long; young foliage light yellowish green; mature foliage pubescent, dull green, in autumn yellow.

Flowers

Petals 21 mm long by 2 mm wide, slightly wavy, curled at tips before fully open, slightly crimped, golden yellow tinted red at the base; calyx brownish red; overall a dark golden yellow; fragrant; flowering late winter through early spring.

Hamamelis mollis 'Gold Edge' (Nutt, ca. 1985)

Comments

A variegated selection which arose as a branch sport on a plant of the typical *Hamamelis mollis*, selected by Richard Nutt, of Bradenham, High Wycombe, Bucks, England, who was an alpine and bulbous plant enthusiast.

Growth habit

Rounded bush, slow to moderate growth, making a shrub 2.5 m tall by 2.5 m wide.

Foliage

Leaves ovate-orbicular, margin crenate in upper half, shallowly crenate below, apex acute, base obliquely cordate, 90 mm long by 65 mm wide; petiole 10 mm long; young foliage light yellowish green; mature foliage pubescent, somewhat distorted, sage green; in autumn yellow; the variegation is a thin creamy margin to the edge of the leaf, extending part way along the veins, possibly caused by a virus.

Flowers

Petals 12 mm long by 1.5 mm wide, slightly curled and crimped, golden yellow; calyx purplish red; overall a deep golden yellow; fragrant; flowering in midwinter.

Hamamelis mollis 'Imperialis' (Wada, ca. 1960)

Comments

Imported into England by Peter Chappell in about 1980. A selection made by Kochiro Wada, Hakoneya Nursery, Japan, a very distinct clone of *Hamamelis mollis* which needs a wider audience. The flowers are much larger than any other clone I have come across.

Growth habit

Upright, vigorous, 3.5 m tall by 3 m wide.

Foliage

Leaves orbicular, margin shallowly crenate, apex blunt, base obliquely cordate, 95 mm long by 95 mm wide; petiole 10 mm long; young foliage light sage-green; mature foliage pubescent, darkish green, slightly bullate, in autumn yellow, the last *Hamamelis mollis* clone to turn.

Flowers

Petals 24 mm long by 2 mm wide, pale yellow, tinted red at base; overall a sulphur-yellow; strong, sweet scent; flowering early through midwinter, not very profusely as a young plant.

Hamamelis mollis 'Iwado' (Wada, ca. 1970)

Comments

Another selection by Kochiro Wada, imported into United States by the U.S. National Arboretum, Washington, D.C. in about 1980. This is another very distinct clone of *Hamamelis mollis*; the petals are fairly straight and a deep golden yellow.

Growth habit

Upright, vigorous, 3.5 m tall by 3 m wide.

Foliage

Leaves ovate-orbicular, margin shallowly crenate, apex acute, base obliquely cordate, 95 mm long by 80 mm wide; petiole 12 mm long; young foliage light yellowish green; mature foliage pubescent, dull sage-green, in autumn yellow.

Flowers

Petals 18 mm long by 1.5 mm wide, petals straight, golden yellow; calyx purplish red; overall a good clear, strong golden yellow; fragrant; flowering early through midwinter.

Hamamelis mollis 'James Wells' (Hess, ca. 1965)

Synonym

Hamamelis mollis 'Wells Form' Hort.

Comments

There is a lot of confusion regarding this cultivar, and it is now questionable as to whether it is lost to cultivation. It is worthwhile to relate here Jim Wells's story as to the origin of this cultivar.

Soon after he arrived in the United States in 1946, Wells was introduced to John Wister and subsequently went to see him at the Swarthmore Arboretum, Swarthmore, Pennsylvania. They became firm friends, and Wister helped Wells with propagation material of various plants when he was just getting started at the Koster Nursery, Bridgeton, New Jersey. Witch hazels were a favourite plant of Wells, and Wister gave him a bag of seed from a plant of *Hamamelis mollis* growing in the arboretum. From this he was able to return a number of plants to Wister, and the remainder he grew on in the nursery.

Wells took the plants with him when he went to Bobbinks Nursery in East Rutherford, New Jersey, where he planted them as a hedge. When Wells started his own nursery at Redbank, George White, owner of Bobbinks Nursery, allowed Wells to take the plants with him. These were also planted out as a hedge, and after a while Wells selected one plant which stood out for being a stronger grower than the others, with many more flowers; in fact, the bunches of flower buds were so dense they resembled corn-on-the-cob.

Hans Hess of Hess Nurseries, Cedarville, New Jersey, saw the plant and obtained propagation material. Wells then moved the plant to his garden, where it grew in leaps and bounds up to 6 m tall by 3.5 m wide. The branches were strong enough that he could climb into the plant to pick seed. Hess had propagation material for several years, and it was he who named it after Wells.

When Wells moved to New Hampshire, the plant was too large to move and he left it at his old garden. He did, however, obtain a young plant from Princeton Nursery to plant in his new garden. Plants received by Tim Brotzman from Hess turned out to be muddled; he is fairly sure there were some true plants mixed in with *Hamamelis* 'Brevipetala'. Because they were mixed, Brotzman sold them all as a mixed batch.

Wells also sent material to Brian Humphrey, then at Hillier Nurseries Ltd., as *Hamamelis mollis* (Wells Form), which turned out to be *H.* 'Brevipetala'. When Brotzman questioned Wells on this matter, he said he knew the plant *H.* 'Brevipetala' (or *H. mollis* 'Brevipetala' as it was then known), and that *H. mollis* 'James Wells' was altogether a much stronger growing plant and very floriferous. What I think must of happened is that the plant received by Wells from Princeton Nursery was in fact *H.* 'Brevipetala' and not *H. mollis* 'James Wells', and Humphrey had material from this and not the true 'James Wells'. Somewhere in New Jersey there must be the true *H. mollis* 'James Wells', as Hans Hess propagated this plant for several years, even though he may have muddled it with *H.* 'Brevipetala'.

Growth habit
Upright, vigorous strong growth, making a bush 5 m tall by 3.5 m wide.

Foliage
No description available.

Flowers
Golden-yellow, very floriferous.

Hamamelis mollis 'Jermyns Gold' (Hillier, 1990)

Comments

A selection from a plant growing at the Hillier Arboretum that most likely originates from seed collected by E. H. Wilson and distributed from the Arnold Arboretum. From a practical point of view, this clone is virtually identical to *Hamamelis mollis* 'Boskoop', 'Early Bright', and 'Bonny Brook'.

Growth habit

Upright when young, later making a more rounded bush, moderately vigorous, 3 m tall by 3 m wide.

Foliage

Leaves orbicular, margin shallowly crenate, apex blunt, base obliquely cordate, 100 mm long by 90 mm wide; petiole 6 mm long; young foliage light green; mature foliage pubescent, sage-green, in autumn yellow.

Flowers

Petals 17 mm long by 1.5 mm wide, slightly curled and crimped, golden yellow with slight red tint at base; calyx brownish red; overall a good clear golden yellow; pleasant fragrance; flowering early through midwinter.

Hamamelis mollis 'Kort's Yellow' (Lane, 1995)

Synonyms

Hamamelis ×*intermedia* 'Kort's Select', *H.* ×*intermedia* 'Selection Kort', *H. mollis* 'Kort's Select'

Comments

A selection that I first obtained from Brookside Gardens, Maryland, as *Hamamelis* ×*intermedia* 'Kort's Select'. Phil Normandy of Brookside informed me that they received it from the Kingsville Nursery in 1975 as 'Selection Kort'. After I grew the plant for a while, it became obvious that it was a clone of *H. mollis*. The plant probably came from Kalmthout Arboretum, which was started by Antoine Kort. It would also be nice to think that intrepid plantsman Henry Hohman was responsible for introducing it to the United States. As it is a distinct clone of *H. mollis* which needed to be recognized, I renamed it 'Kort's Yellow'.

Foliage

Leaves broadly elliptic, margin crenate in upper half, shallowly crenate below, apex acute, base obliquely cordate, 100 mm long by 60 mm wide; petiole 10 mm long, more bullate on the upper leaf surface than other clones of *Hamamelis mollis* in cultivation; young foliage light yellowish green; mature foliage pubescent, dull green, greyish green underneath, in autumn yellow.

Flowers

Petals 20 mm long by 1.5 mm wide, straight, slightly crimped, pale yellow; calyx bright red; overall a clear sulphur-yellow; fragrant; flowering early through midwinter.

Hamamelis mollis 'Princeton Gold' (Princeton Nursery, 1990)

Synonym

Hamamelis mollis 'Select'

Comments

I am grateful to Paul Meyer for the following narrative regarding this selection and Tony Aiello for sending it to me. A selection made by Bill Flemer of Princeton Nurseries, New Jersey, from a plant growing on the campus of Princeton University in the 1960s or early 1970s. In 1975 the Morris Arboretum received a plant from Princeton Nursery propagated from the original. It grew there unnoticed for several years. Then Meyer quite independently noticed its robust growth and bright, heavy flowers around 1980 and checked the origin in their records. It stood out among others in the collection, and when Meyer contacted Bill Flemer, he was delighted the arboretum still had it. Flemer's plants were lost and the original plant had been removed. The Morris Arboretum then began propagating it and sent a plant back to Princeton Nursery. For many years, it was casually called "select form" or simply "select." This name was never meant to be applied formally, though some grew it under the name 'Select'. Princeton Nursery later named it *Hamamelis mollis* 'Princeton Gold'.

It is a precocious bloomer, has prolific bright yellow flowers and good quality foliage, and the colour shows up well on gloomy winter days. My view is that this particular cultivar is not as precocious and free-flowering as some other *Hamamelis mollis* cultivars. Tim Brotzman mentions that it is always easy to recognize this cultivar from a distance when in leaf, as leaves hang in a limp fashion.

Growth habit

Spreading plant, of twiggy growth as in *Hamamelis mollis* 'Fred Chittenden', moderately vigorous, 2 m tall by 3 m wide.

Foliage

Leaves ovate-orbicular, narrower than other clones of *Hamamelis mollis*, margin shallowly crenate, apex acute, base obliquely cordate, 105 mm long by 80 mm wide; petiole 15 mm long; young foliage light yellowish green; mature foliage pubescent, dull green, grey-green below, in autumn yellow.

Flowers

Petals 20 mm long by 1.5 mm wide, tips of petals stay curled for a long time before fully unfurling, slightly crimped, pale yellow; calyx red; overall a good clear sulphur-yellow; not as profuse as some *Hamamelis mollis* clones; scented; flowering mid through late winter.

Hamamelis mollis 'Wisley Supreme' (RHS Garden Wisley, 1995)

Comments

This superb clone remained unnoticed at Wisley until 1993, when Chris Sanders and I spotted it in flower in early January. The plant, which is fairly old, was partly smashed by a falling tree in a storm in January 1990. Perhaps what drew it to our attention was the good size of the flowers on the young regrowth from the smashed stem. It may have originated from Exbury Gardens, which had a number of plants from E. H. Wilson's seed introductions to the Arnold Arboretum. Francis Hanger introduced many plants from Exbury to Battleston Hill at Wisley, some of which are recorded, some not; it is possible this witch hazel was one of them.

Growth habit

Upright, more spreading with age, vigorous, 3.5 m tall by 3 m wide.

Foliage

Leaves ovate-orbicular, almost as large as *Hamamelis mollis* 'Imperialis', slightly bullate, margin shallowly crenate, apex acute, base obliquely cordate,

115 mm long by 80 mm wide; petiole 12 mm long; young foliage light yellowish green; mature foliage, pubescent dark green, in autumn yellow.

Flowers

Petals 22 mm long by 2 mm wide, fairly straight, slightly crimped, pale yellow; calyx red; overall a clear light yellow; sweetly scented; flowering early through midwinter.

Chapter 7
Hamamelis Hybrids

In this chapter I describe all the named *Hamamelis* ×*intermedia* clones and other hybrids of different parentage. *Hamamelis* ×*intermedia* was first described by Alfred Rehder (1945, pp. 69–70):

Hamamelis intermedia (*H. japonica* Sieb. & Zucc. × *H. mollis* Oliv.), hybr. nov.
Synonym *Hamamelis* ×*japollis* Lange
A *Hamamelide japonica* differt ramulis pubescentibus; foliis supra initio sparse stellato-pubescentibus maturis fere glabris, subtus initio satis dense stellato-pubescentibus, demum glabrescentibus; petiolis pubicentibus; petalorum parte inferiore plerumque rubris vel rubecentibus; capsula subglobosa vel late ovoidea ad 1.2 cm diam., paulo longiora quam lata apice vix attenuata calyce plus quam tertiam partem fructus aequante.
A *H. molli* differt ramulis demum glabrescentibus vel glabris; foliis plerisque obovatis, basin versus plus minusve angustatis, ima basi inaequilateraliter truncatis vel late cuneatis, raro uno latere subcordatis, supra initio pubescentibus demum glabris vel fere glabris, subtus initio stellato-pubescentibus, demum plerumque glabrescentibus, petiolis gracilioribus glabris vel leviter pubescentibus; capsula apice minus distincte quadrangulari.

Reference is also made to awards given by the Royal Horticultural Society of the United Kingdom and the Royal Boskoop Horticultural Society of The Netherlands. The RHS award, the Award of Garden Merit, is given after trial at Wisley or elsewhere, visits to specialist collections, and/or round-table discussion drawing on the committee members' collective expertise, with the opportunity to draw on further specialists when necessary. To win an Award of Garden Merit, a plant must be excellent for garden use, of good constitution, available in the horticultural trade, or available for propagation; it must not be unduly susceptible to pests and disease, not require highly specialized care, and not be unduly subject to reversion of vegetative or floral characteristics. The Royal Boskoop Horticultural Society grades their awards as follows: three stars, excellent; two stars, very good; one star, good; s, for special purposes (for example, weeping); o, can be eliminated because the plant is of no garden value. This grading system allows the nursery trade to produce the best plants for the public.

Cultivars of *Hamamelis* ×*intermedia*

Hamamelis ×*intermedia* 'Adieu' (de Belder, 1992)

Comments

A selection raised at Kalmthout Arboretum, Belgium, by de Belder, under the number K.962, this plant was named because of its late flowering. It resembles *Hamamelis japonica* in habit and appearance, the flowers in particular having that twisted petal shape characteristic of that species. Introduced by me a few years later. This cultivar is not of the first order and unlikely to become popular outside of large collections.

Growth habit

Upright, 3.5 m tall by 2.5 m wide, moderately vigorous and fairly twiggy.

Foliage

Leaves ovate-orbicular, margin crenate in upper half, shallowly crenate below, apex acute, base oblique, 90 mm long by 65 mm wide; petiole 10 mm long, slightly bullate; young foliage a medium yellowish green; mature foliage glabrous, dark green, in autumn yellow.

Flowers

Petals 20 mm long by 2 mm wide, quite curled and crimped, yellow, very faintly tinted red at base; calyx a pale maroon with light green flush; overall effect of a good sulphur-yellow; no scent; flowering in late winter.

Hamamelis ×*intermedia* 'Advent' (Hillier, 1979)

Comments

Raised at the Hillier Nurseries Ltd., Winchester, England. An interesting cultivar, because of its early flowering habit, sometimes in early winter. There are much better yellow-flowered cultivars available, so it is not likely to become popular, except that it can in most years reliably be out for Christmas. Received two stars in the Royal Boskoop Horticultural Society trials in 2002.

Growth habit

Upright when young, becoming more spreading with age, 3 m tall by 3 m wide, moderate vigour.

Foliage

Leaves ovate-orbicular, margin crenate in upper half, shallowly crenate below, apex acute, base oblique, 100 mm long by 75 mm wide; petiole 15 mm long; young foliage light yellowish green; mature foliage glabrous, sage-green, in autumn yellow.

Flowers

Petals 22 mm long by 1.5 mm wide, do not open fully straight, slightly curled with crimped edges, bright clear yellow, faintly tinted red at the base; calyx maroon-red; overall effect of pale sulphur-yellow; scent faint; flowering early through midwinter.

Hamamelis ×*intermedia* 'Agnes' (de Belder, 1996)

Comments

A selection raised at Hemelrijk by de Belder, under the number H.10627. Named after a cousin of Robert de Belder because this was one of her favourite plants at Hemelrijk. She unfortunately died of cancer, and her children asked if this plant could be named in her memory. Introduced by me soon after naming, this plant is very much like *Hamamelis japonica* 'Arborea' in growth habit and makes an imposing specimen plant. The original plant at Hemelrijk is nearly 4 m tall by 9 m wide; growing in a perfect setting with other witch hazels and rhododendrons, it is especially striking.

Growth habit

Spreading, strong growth, yet quite twiggy like *Hamamelis japonica*, 3 m tall by 5 m wide.

Foliage

Leaves orbicular-obovate, margin crenate in upper half, shallowly crenate below, apex acute, base oblique, 80 mm long by 50 mm wide; petiole 15 mm long; young foliage a medium green lightly flushed maroon; mature foliage glabrous, dark grey-green, in autumn orange-red.

Flowers

Petals 17 mm long by 1.5 mm wide, slightly curled and crimped, maroon-red paler towards tip; calyx purple-red; overall effect of dark red; no scent; flowering mid through late winter.

Hamamelis ×intermedia 'Alexander' (van Heijningen, 1995)

Comments

A very interesting cultivar, raised by J. H. M. van Heijningen, Breda, The Netherlands, with exceptional orange flowers which stand out well from a distance. Appears to suffer from a fungal disease on the foliage during the latter part of the summer. This cultivar is slow growing and flowers so profusely one year that it tends to become biennial in flowering.

Growth habit

Upright, compact twiggy growth, 2.5 m tall by 2 m wide.

Foliage

Leaves orbicular-obovate, margin shallowly crenate in upper half, smooth to scarcely crenate below, apex blunt, base oblique, 65 mm long by 60 mm wide; petiole 12 mm long; young foliage a light yellowish green; mature foliage glabrous, dark green, in autumn turning butter-yellow, goes brown quite quickly, however.

Flowers

Petals 18 mm long by 2 mm wide, slightly twisted and crimped, orange-red; calyx greyish red; overall effect of burnt orange; scent faint; flowering mid through late winter.

Hamamelis ×*intermedia* 'Allgold' (Hillier, 1973)

Comments

This plant was received by Hillier Nurseries Ltd. from an unknown source and later named and introduced by them. An attractive, delicate, thin-petalled cultivar that has now been superseded by later introductions, *Hamamelis* ×*intermedia* 'Allgold' is still worth a place in large gardens, however. In fact, many people find the light, airy nature of the petals very attractive. Tim Brotzman comments that in Madison, Ohio, this is a very early flowering selection, and he loves the rich yellow and thin, twisted petals.

Growth habit

Spreading, moderate vigour, with fairly long arching branches, 3 m tall by 4 m wide.

Foliage

Leaves broadly elliptic, margin crenate in upper half, shallowly crenate below, apex blunt, base oblique, 110 mm long by 65 mm wide; petiole 10 mm long; young foliage a medium yellowish green; mature foliage glabrous, dark sage-green, in autumn turning butter-yellow.

Flowers

Petals 20 mm long by 1 mm wide, slightly twisted and crimped, golden yellow; calyx red-purple; overall effect of deep buttercup-yellow; scent faint but sweet; flowering in midwinter.

Hamamelis ×*intermedia* 'Amanon' (van Heijningen, 2001)

Comments

This plant was raised by J. H. M. van Heijningen, at Breda, The Netherlands. It is named for his granddaughter, whose name is Manon; however, he wanted all his cultivars to begin with the letter A, ensuring prominence at the top of any alphabetical list. He used the phrase "I love you, Manon," or in Italian "Amore Manon," which he then shortened to 'Amanon.' According to van Heijningen this is a distinct improvement on *Hamamelis* ×*intermedia* 'Pallida' because of the flowers, scent, and autumn colour of the foliage. In my opinion, although it is a good cultivar, it is not sufficiently distinct from many other cultivars available. It certainly does not have the flower power of *H.* ×*intermedia* 'Pallida' or as sweet a scent.

Growth habit

Upright, later making a rounded bush, moderately vigorous, 3 m tall by 3 m wide.

Foliage

Leaves ovate-orbicular, margin shallowly crenate in upper half, smooth to scarcely crenate below, apex blunt, base obliquely cordate, 105 mm long by 100 mm wide; petiole 10 mm long; young foliage a light yellowish green; mature foliage glabrous, medium green colour, in autumn has attractive tints of yellow, orange, and red.

Flowers

Petals 25 mm long by 1.5 mm wide, slightly twisted and crimped, primrose-yellow with light red tint at base; calyx light maroon-red; overall a good pale sulphur-yellow; sweet scent but faint; flowering in midwinter.

Hamamelis ×*intermedia* 'Andrea' (van der Werf, 2002)

Comments

This selection was raised by Wim van der Werf, Boskoop, The Netherlands, in 1971. It has been under observation in Wim's nursery for many years, under his number (71W). As a young plant it retained dead leaves but on maturity this tendency has diminished quite considerably. Named by Wim after his second daughter. Although not yet in commerce, this cultivar received one star in the Royal Boskoop Horticultural Society trial in 2002.

Growth habit

Spreading, vigorous, making a bush 3 m tall by 4 m wide.

Foliage

Leaves ovate-orbicular, margin shallowly crenate, apex acute, base oblique, 100 mm long by 75 mm wide; petiole 12 mm long; young foliage a medium green; mature foliage glabrous, dark green, in autumn yellow.

Flowers

Petals 20 mm long by 1.5 mm wide, slightly curled and crimped, good clear yellow, some red tint at base; calyx deep maroon-red; overall a good clear golden yellow, slightly scented; flowering mid through late winter.

Hamamelis ×*intermedia* 'Angelly' (van Heijningen, 1985)

Comments

This is an excellent and distinct witch hazel raised by J. H. M. van Heijningen in Breda, The Netherlands. It was exhibited at the Flora Nova Show, Boskoop, Holland, in 1987, where it received a gold medal. The name derives from a corruption of two of van Heijningen's daughter's names, Angeline and Elly. This is one of the finest introductions of recent years; the tight compact growth habit, good acid-yellow flowers, late flowering, and good scent make this a very worthwhile introduction. My regard for the good qualities of this plant increases each year. It is somewhat slow to grow in production in nurseries and is therefore unlikely to be produced in large numbers; the public will have to seek this plant out from specialist suppliers. In the Royal Boskoop Horticultural Society trial, this cultivar received one star in the special purposes category, indicating that it is unlikely to be readily available, at least from Dutch nurseries. Tim Brotzman comments that in North America, it is proving to be a much better plant in the south than *Hamamelis* ×*intermedia* 'Arnold Promise', which suffers from a foliage blight and a tendency to biennial flowering. He is very impressed with it, the best of the lemon yellows for catching one's eye. A slower growth rate can be a plus point, as is the reddish coppery tint to the new growth and long-lasting flowers.

Growth habit

Upright, compact twiggy habit, 2.5 m tall by 2 m wide.

Foliage

Leaves orbicular-obovate, margin shallowly crenate in upper half, smooth to scarcely crenate below, apex acute, base oblique, 90 mm long by 80 mm wide; petiole 10 mm long; young foliage a grey-green heavily flushed light maroon-purple; mature foliage glabrous, grey-green, some autumn colour, yellow with hint of orange.

Flowers

Petals 22 mm long by 2.5 mm wide, fairly straight, slightly curled and crimped, clear light yellow; calyx light green; overall a citron-yellow, sweet scent; flowering late winter through early spring.

Hamamelis ×*intermedia* 'Antoine Kort' (Kalmthout Arboretum, 2002)

Comments

A Kalmthout selection under the number K.982, raised by Antoine Kort at Kalmthout, this cultivar has long been admired at the turn of a bend in the witch hazel walk at the arboretum and features in many photographs taken of the walk, when the many witch hazels are in flower. Named by the committee which oversees the development of Kalmthout to honour the man responsible for starting the garden from what was previously Charles van Geert's nursery.

Growth habit

Spreading plant of strong vigorous growth, the branches making laterals quite readily, 3 m tall by 5 m wide.

Foliage

Leaves orbicular-obovate, margin crenate in upper half, shallowly crenate below, apex blunt, base oblique, 95 mm long by 85 mm wide; petiole 10 mm long; young foliage a medium grey-green heavily flushed light maroon; mature foliage glabrous, green, some autumn colour, orange-red in a good autumn.

Flowers

Petals 20 mm long by 1.5 mm wide, curled, twisted and crimped, a good clear red; calyx purple-red; overall a good bright red; scent sweet and fairly strong; flowering in midwinter.

Hamamelis ×*intermedia* 'Aphrodite' (van Heijningen, 1985)

Comments

This cultivar represents a colour breakthrough in the hybrids and is destined to become very popular. Raised by J. H. M. van Heijningen at Breda, The Netherlands, from seed collected off a plant of *Hamamelis* ×*intermedia* 'Vesna' growing close to *H.* ×*intermedia* 'Pallida', a case of two fine parents giving rise to a superb offspring. This cultivar, quite rightly in my opinion, received three stars in the Royal Boskoop Horticultural Society trial in 2002. Tim Brotzman comments that it has tended to exhibit biennial flowering in Ohio, this may be, however, following long hot, dry summers. The colour is certainly unique and the plant is vigorous.

Growth habit

Spreading, vigorous, with good lateral branching habit, 3 m tall by 4 m wide.

Foliage

Leaves ovate-orbicular, margin crenate in upper half, smooth to scarcely crenate below, apex acute, base oblique, 110 mm long by 85 mm wide; petiole 20 mm long; young foliage a light yellowish green; mature foliage glabrous, dull green, little or no autumn colour.

Flowers

Petals 24 mm long by 1.8 mm wide, fairly straight, slightly crimped, orange-red; calyx red-purple; overall a burnt orange colour; very faint scent; flowering late winter.

Hamamelis ×*intermedia* 'Arnold Promise' (Arnold Arboretum, 1963)

Synonym

Hamamelis ×*intermedia* 'Arnold's Promise'

Comments

Raised at the Arnold Arboretum, Massachusetts. A valuable plant because of its twiggy growth habit, late profuse flowering, and autumn colour, unusual in yellow-flowered cultivars. For a full background of this cultivar, see chapter 8. Received three stars in the Royal Boskoop Horticultural Society trial in 2002 and was given an Award of Garden Merit from the Royal Horticultural Society in 1993.

Growth habit

Vase-shaped, moderately vigorous, twiggy, 3 m tall by 2.5 m wide.

Foliage

Leaves broadly elliptic, margin crenate in upper half, shallowly crenate below, apex blunt, base oblique, 75 mm long by 55 mm wide; petiole 15 mm long; young foliage a light yellowish green; mature foliage glabrous, medium to dark green, in autumn shades of yellow, orange and red.

Flowers

Petals 18 mm long by 1.5 mm wide, petals curled and crimped, yellow; calyx brownish green; overall a lemon-yellow effect; scent is sweet and fairly strong; flowering late winter to early spring.

Hamamelis ×intermedia 'Aurora' (van Heijningen, 1985)

Comments

Raised by J. H. M. van Heijningen at Breda, The Netherlands, from the same parentage as 'Aphrodite', this cultivar has perhaps the largest flowers of any witch hazel to date. van Heijningen is to be congratulated, along with *Hamamelis ×intermedia* 'Angelly' and *H. ×intermedia* 'Aphrodite', in raising three quite unique cultivars. This plant received two stars in the Royal Boskoop Horticultural Society trial in 2002. Tim Brotzman reports that it has a tendency to retain its dead leaves in winter in Ohio.

Growth habit

Upright when young, ultimately vase-shaped, 3.5 m tall by 3.5 m wide.

Foliage

Leaves obovate, margin shallowly crenate in upper half, smooth to scarcely crenate below, apex acute to blunt, base oblique, 115 mm long by 70 mm wide; petiole 15 mm long; young foliage a medium yellowish green with a faint light purple flush; mature foliage glabrous, sage-green, in autumn yellow, orange with red tints.

Flowers

Petals 30 mm long by 2 mm wide, straight and crimped, yellow at tip grading through deep yellow with red tinting at base; calyx purple-red; overall a yellow-red bicolour effect; scent sweet and strong; flowering in midwinter.

Hamamelis ×*intermedia* 'Barmstedt Gold' (Hachmann, 1975)

Synonym

Hamamelis ×*intermedia* 'Barmstedt's Gold'

Comments

Raised by Heinrich Bruns, Westerstede, Germany, the plant was acquired by J. Hachmann, Barmstedt, Germany, and in time named and introduced by him. This cultivar is listed in Hachmann's catalogue as 'Barmstedt's Gold', but the first published reference to this plant lists as 'Barmstedt Gold', to which name it is universally known, at least outside of Germany. This is a superb cultivar, the best in its colour group, standing out in the landscape from a considerable distance. *Hamamelis* ×*intermedia* 'Barmstedt Gold' is just starting to become popular and be asked for—it is a slow process from raising a good witch hazel to it becoming mainstream in the nursery industry, a quarter of a century, in fact. This cultivar received only two stars in the Royal Boskoop Horticultural Society trial in 2002 and was given an Award of Garden Merit from the Royal Horticultural Society in 1997. In my opinion this is perhaps the finest cultivar of *H.* ×*intermedia* to date. Tim Brotzman agrees that in North America, this is probably one of the very best witch hazels.

Growth habit

Upright when young, later making a rounded bush, 3.5 m tall by 3.5 m wide.

Foliage

Leaves ovate-orbicular, margin crenate in upper half, shallowly crenate below, apex acute, base obliquely cordate, 110 mm long by 70 mm wide; petiole 12 mm long; young foliage a medium yellowish green; mature foliage glabrous, dark green, in autumn yellow.

Flowers

Petals 25 mm long by 1.5 mm wide, slightly twisted and crimped, yellow-orange tinted red at base; calyx red-purple; overall effect strong golden yellow; faint to medium-strength scent; flowering mid to late winter.

Hamamelis ×*intermedia* 'Bernstein' (Hachmann, 1999)

Synonym

Hamamelis ×*intermedia* 'Selektion Orange'

Comments

Another Heinrich Bruns selection acquired by Hachmann and grown for a long time as 'Selektion Orange', then named and introduced by them in 1999. This cultivar has more upright growth than *Hamamelis* ×*intermedia* 'Barmstedt Gold' and is more orange.

Growth habit

Upright, quite vigorous, 3.5 m tall by 3 m wide.

Foliage

Leaves ovate-orbicular, margin crenate in upper half, shallowly crenate below, apex blunt, base oblique, 90 mm long by 75 mm wide; petiole 10 mm long; young foliage a medium yellowish green; mature foliage glabrous, dark green, in autumn orange flushed red.

Flowers

Petals 27 mm long by 2 mm wide, twisted and crimped, pale straw-yellow suffused red from base to midway; calyx light maroon-red; overall light orange; no scent; flowering mid through late winter.

Hamamelis ×*intermedia* 'Birgit' (de Belder, 1986)

Comments

A Hemelrijk selection raised by de Belder under the number H.10568 and named by de Belder after one of Dr. de Clerck's daughters, a family friend. Although the flowers are relatively small, this is the darkest red-flowered cultivar to be introduced to date. The original plant grew on the edge of a ditch and was somewhat overgrown by other plants, but some of the branches overhung the ditch and could be admired from the road. This plant needs to be inspected from close quarters to enjoy its rich dark red flowers. Tim Brotzman says that he remembers it at Hemelrijk as a purple-red and definitely the darkest flowered selection he has seen.

Growth habit

Upright when young, later more rounded, vigorous, making a bush 4 m tall by 3 m wide.

Foliage

Leaves ovate-orbicular, margin crenate in upper half, shallowly crenate below, apex acute, base oblique, 95 mm long by 70 mm wide; petiole 10 mm long; young foliage a medium green heavily flushed maroon; mature foliage glabrous, dark green, in autumn butter-yellow suffused orange-red.

Flowers

Petals 16 mm long by 1.5 mm wide, twisted and crimped, red-purple; calyx dark purple; overall dark red; slight scent; flowering mid to late winter.

Hamamelis ×*intermedia* 'Böhlje's Feuerzauber' (Böhlje, ca. 1977)

Comments

Raised, named, and introduced by Böhlje, Westerstede, Germany. This cultivar is similar to *Hamamelis* ×*intermedia* 'Feuerzauber' but flowers more bicoloured, giving an overall lighter colour. This may also be one of Heinrich Bruns's seedlings.

Growth habit

Upright, ultimately vase-shaped, vigorous, making a bush 4 m tall by 3.5 m wide.

Foliage

Leaves ovate-orbicular, margin crenate, apex acute to blunt, base obliquely cordate, 95 mm long by 70 mm wide; petiole 12 mm long; young foliage a medium yellowish green; mature foliage glabrous, dark green, yellow-orange tints in autumn. Colouring a week to ten days earlier than *Hamamelis* ×*intermedia* 'Feuerzauber'.

Flowers

Petals 20 mm long by 1.5 mm wide, curled and crimped, yellow, heavily suffused with red; calyx purple-red; overall, a light reddish colour; faint but sweet scent; flowering throughout midwinter.

Hamamelis ×intermedia 'Brandis' (Helmers, 1985)

Synonym

Hamamelis ×intermedia 'Brandes'

Comments

A selection from Heinrich Bruns, named after the manor house he used to live in. I am indebted to Helmerich Helmers for pointing out the correct spelling, the cultivar had previously entered Holland as *Hamamelis ×intermedia* 'Brandes'. This overlooked cultivar was introduced by Helmers Nursery in Westerstede; it is vigorous with good yellow flowers. I collected my plant of this cultivar from the research station in Rostrup, and my friend Wim van der Werf obtained his from Helmers Nursery; his differs from my plant in having more curly and deeper yellow flowers. Further work is required to ascertain which is the correct plant. A lot of confusion took place when Bruns's plants were dispersed, with plants such as *H. ×intermedia* 'Old Copper' and *H. ×intermedia* 'Orange Beauty' receiving more than one name (see chapter 8).

Growth habit

Spreading, vigorous, making a bush 3 m tall by 4 m wide.

Foliage

Leaves ovate-orbicular, margin crenate in upper half, shallowly crenate below, apex acute, base obliquely cordate, 100 mm long by 80 mm wide; petiole 8 mm long; young foliage medium green heavily flushed maroon; mature foliage glabrous, medium to dark green, in autumn yellow.

Flowers

Petals 21 mm long 1.5 mm wide, curled and crimped, yellow with red-purple tint at base; calyx red-purple; overall good bright yellow; no scent; flowering mid through late winter.

Hamamelis ×intermedia 'Carmine Red' (Hillier Nurseries Ltd., 1934)

Comments

This was one of the first red cultivars to be introduced, selected by Hillier in

1934 from a batch of *Hamamelis japonica* var. *flavopurpurascens* seed-raised plants growing in the Chandler's Ford Nursery. 'Carmine Red' is now superseded by more recent cultivars.

Growth habit

Spreading, vigorous, sprawling growth making a bush wider than high, 3 m tall by 4.5 m wide.

Foliage

Leaves orbicular, margin crenate in upper half, shallowly crenate below, apex blunt, base obliquely cordate, 90 mm long by 90 mm wide; petiole 18 mm long; young foliage medium green heavily flushed maroon; mature foliage glabrous, a dark, shiny green, in autumn butter-yellow; tends to retain dead leaves during the winter, at least on young plants.

Flowers

Petals 18 mm long by 2 mm wide, twisted and crimped, red fading to coppery bronze at tips; calyx red-purple; overall dull red colour; scent sweet but faint; flowering throughout midwinter.

Hamamelis ×*intermedia* 'Citronella' (de Belder, 2002)

Comments

A Hemelrijk selection raised by de Belder under the number H.10578, this cultivar closely resembles *Hamamelis japonica* in flower, although a good yellow colour. There are several plants growing at Hemelrijk with similar flowers.

Growth habit

Vase-shaped when young, later more spreading, moderate vigour, making a bush 3.5 m tall by 3.5 m wide.

Foliage

Leaves obovate, margin crenate in upper half, shallowly crenate below, apex blunt, base oblique, 80 mm long by 55 mm wide; petiole 10 mm long; young foliage a greyish green; mature foliage glabrous, dark olive-green, in autumn yellow.

Flowers
Petals 17 mm long by 1.5 mm wide, curled, twisted and crimped, pale sulphur-yellow; calyx light maroon-red, heavily flushed green; overall an acid sulphur-yellow; no scent; flowering mid through late winter.

Hamamelis ×*intermedia* 'Copper Cascade' (de Belder, 1993)

Comments
A Hemelrijk selection raised by de Belder under the number H.10539. At de Belder's Arboretum, the original plant happens to be growing in the perfect situation—in an open glade among the trees—where its growth habit can be seen to perfect effect. Introduced by me in 1990. This cultivar is not of the first rank but interesting for its growth habit. If the flowers were larger, this would be a worthwhile cultivar.

Growth habit
Spreading, mushroom-shaped, much like an *Acer palmatum* 'Dissectum', slow growing, compact twiggy habit, 2 m tall by 4 m wide.

Foliage
Leaves orbicular-obovate, margin crenate in upper half, shallowly crenate below, apex blunt, base oblique, 75 mm long by 60 mm wide; petiole 12 mm long; young foliage medium green slightly bronze tinted; mature foliage glabrous, green with brownish tints, in autumn yellow-orange.

Flowers
Petals 15 mm long by 1.5 mm wide, curled at tip and crimped, yellow-orange grading to red at base; calyx red-purple; overall coppery red; scent faint; flowering throughout midwinter.

Hamamelis ×*intermedia* 'Cyrille' (de Belder, 2002)

Comments
A Hemelrijk selection raised by de Belder under the number H.20566; at Hemelrijk it is growing in an open area to the left of the road with the massive beech trees that leads to the *Hydrangea paniculata* plantings. This cultivar was one that David and Chantal Bömer liked, and they asked Jelena de Belder if they could name it after their recently born son, to which she

agreed. An interesting cultivar with its unusual flower colouring, best admired from close quarters.

Growth habit

Vase-shaped, later developing a more spreading habit, moderately vigorous, 3 m tall by 3 m wide.

Foliage

Leaves orbicular-obovate, margin crenate in upper half, shallowly crenate below, apex acute to blunt, base oblique, 95 mm long by 80 mm wide; petiole 20 mm long; young foliage a medium yellowish green; mature foliage glabrous, a dull green, no autumn colour.

Flowers

Petals 17 mm long by 2 mm wide, straight and crimped, straw-yellow, flushed strawberry red from base to midway; calyx maroon-red; overall a pale yellow-red bicolour effect; slight scent; flowering mid through late winter.

Hamamelis ×*intermedia* 'Diane' (de Belder, 1969)

Synonym

Hamamelis ×*intermedia* 'New Red'

Comments

A Kalmthout selection raised by de Belder under the number K.968. The original plant has died through being waterlogged in the winter; fortunately, however, this cultivar has been propagated in large numbers and is readily available. To date this has been the best red-flowered cultivar available. Some years it can look absolutely superb, others the colour is not as good, because of the factors mentioned in chapter 1. Sometimes fades to a brownish red colour at the end of the flowering period. Named after Robert and Jelena de Belders' daughter. Received two stars in the Royal Boskoop Horticultural Society trial in 2002 and was given an Award of Garden Merit by the Royal Horticultural Society in 1993. There is a superb example growing in the Valley Garden, Windsor.

Growth habit

Spreading, making a bush a little wider than high, 2.5 m tall by 3 m wide.

Foliage

Leaves ovate-orbicular, margin crenate in upper half, shallowly crenate below, apex acute to blunt, base obliquely cordate, 90 mm long by 75 mm wide; petiole 12 mm long; young foliage medium yellowish green, very faintly flushed maroon; mature foliage glabrous, dark green, in autumn turns maroon through yellow-orange to crimson.

Flowers

Petals 20 mm long by 2 mm wide, curled and crimped, red, claret at base; calyx purple-red; overall effect red; slight scent; flowering throughout mid-winter.

Hamamelis ×intermedia 'Double Gold' (van Gemeren, 1996)

Comments

A variegated sport of *Hamamelis ×intermedia* 'Westerstede' found in the nursery of J. M. van Gemeren, Hazerswoude, The Netherlands, and propagated and introduced by them.

Growth habit

Upright, making a bush 2.5 m tall by 2 m wide; less vigorous than *Hamamelis ×intermedia* 'Westerstede'.

Foliage

Leaves ovate-orbicular, margin crenate in upper half, shallowly crenate below, apex acute, base oblique, 90 mm long by 70 mm wide; petiole 12 mm long; young foliage medium green with lemon yellow variegated margin; mature foliage glabrous, dark green with a broad, irregular margin of creamy yellow, this colour also extending irregularly towards centre of leaf, no autumn colour.

Flowers

Petals a bit smaller than *Hamamelis ×intermedia* 'Westerstede', 14 mm long by 1 mm wide, curled and crimped, pale sulphur-yellow; calyx green, overlaid a dull maroon; overall a pale sulphur-yellow; faint scent; flowering late winter.

Left: 1 Jelena and Robert de Belder
Courtesy of Kalmthout Arboretum

Below: 2 *Hamamelis vernalis* (*Journal of the Arnold Arboretum* 1963, Vol. 44, pl. 198).

Archives of the Arnold Arboretum, Cambridge, Massachusetts, USA

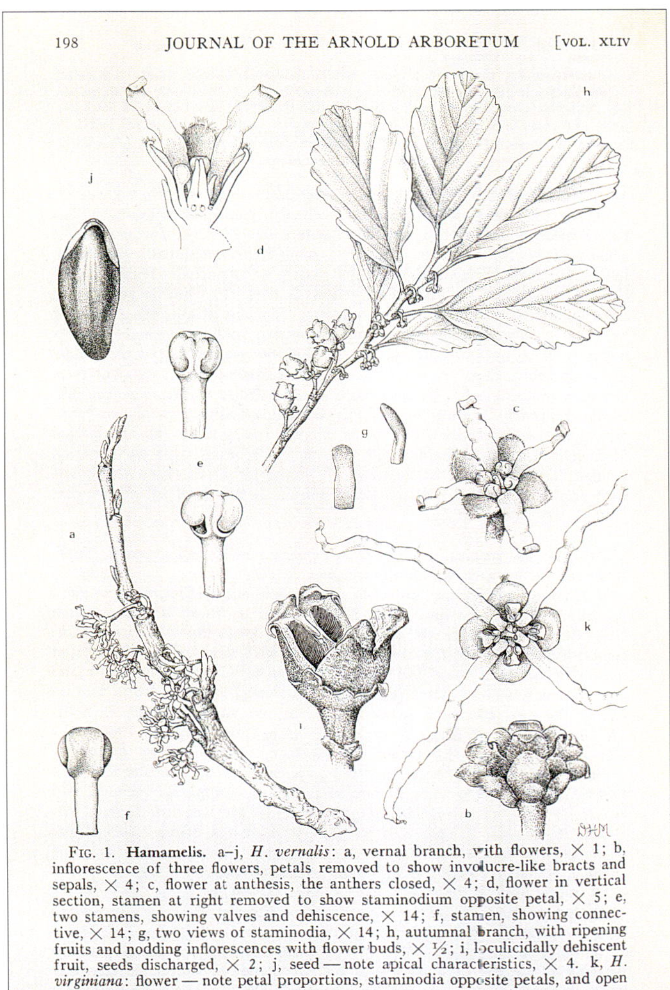

198 JOURNAL OF THE ARNOLD ARBORETUM [VOL. XLIV

FIG. 1. **Hamamelis.** a–j, *H. vernalis*: a, vernal branch, with flowers, × 1; b, inflorescence of three flowers, petals removed to show involucre-like bracts and sepals, × 4; c, flower at anthesis, the anthers closed, × 4; d, flower in vertical section, stamen at right removed to show staminodium opposite petal, × 5; e, two stamens, showing valves and dehiscence, × 14; f, stamen, showing connective, × 14; g, two views of staminodia, × 14; h, autumnal branch, with ripening fruits and nodding inflorescences with flower buds, × ½; i, loculicidally dehiscent fruit, seeds discharged, × 2; j, seed — note apical characteristics, × 4. k, *H. virginiana*: flower — note petal proportions, staminodia opposite petals, and open anthers, × 5.

Left: 3 *Hamamelis mollis* (*Curtis's Botanical Magazine* 1903, Vol. 129, pl. 7884).
Courtesy of the Royal Horticultural Society

Opposite: 5 *Hamamelis virginiana* (Sargent, 1893, *The Silva of North America*, Vol. 2, pl. 198).
Courtesy of the Royal Horticultural Society

Right: 4 *Hamamelis japonica* (*Curtis's Botanical Magazine* 1882, Vol. 108, pl. 6659).
Courtesy of the Royal Horticultural Society

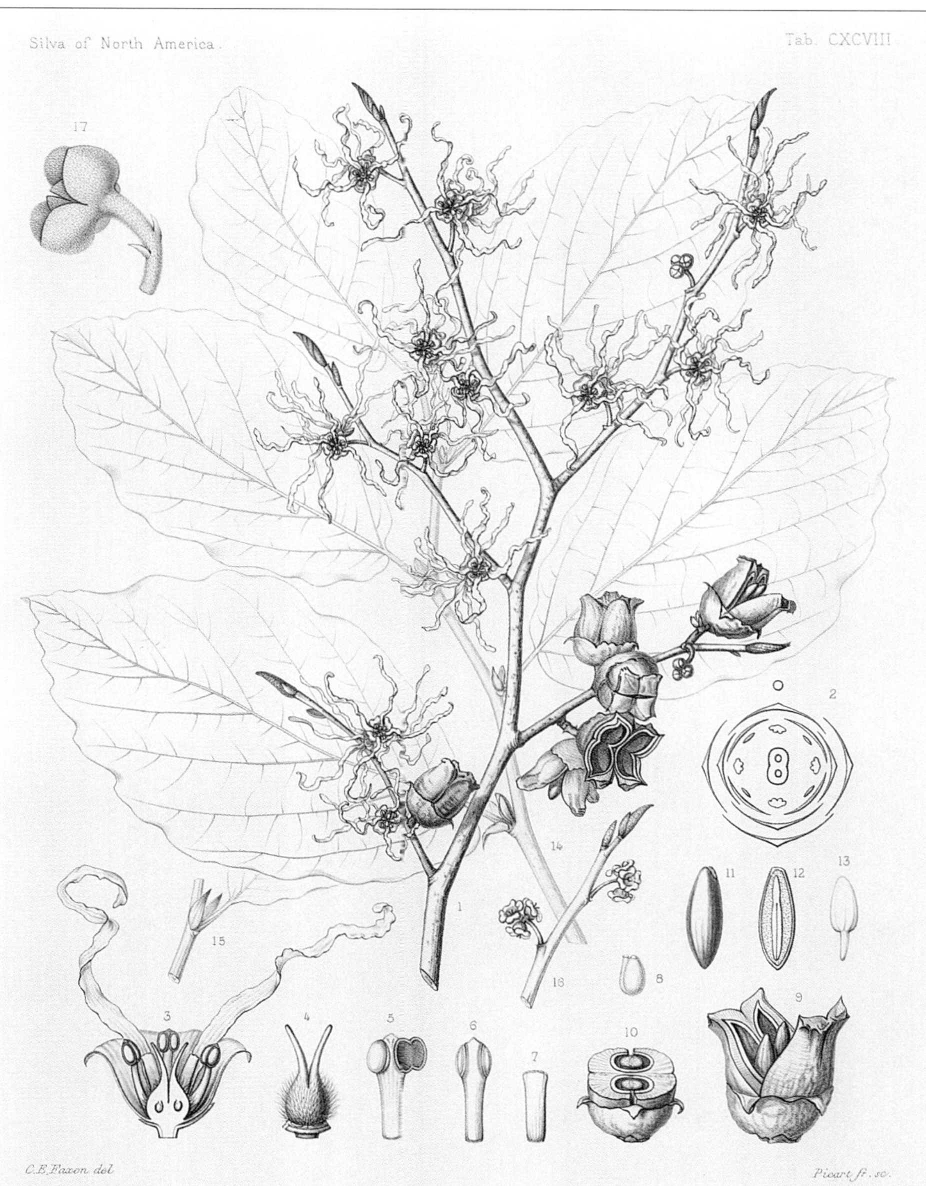

C. E. Faxon del. Picart ft. sc.

HAMAMELIS VIRGINIANA, L.

A. Riocreux direx.t Imp. R. Taneur, Paris.

6 Antoine Kort

8 Charles S. Sargent

7 Ernest Henry Wilson

9 Alfred Rehder

10 Charles Maries

11 Philipp Franz von Siebold

12 Augustine Henry

Above: 13 *Hamamelis virginiana* var. *virginiana* L.

Right: 14 *Hamamelis virginiana* var. *virginiana* L.

Left: 15 *Hamamelis virginiana* var. *henryi*

Below: 16 *Hamamelis virginiana* var. *mexicana*

Right: 17 *Hamamelis virginiana* 'Mohonk Red'

Below: 18 *Hamamelis virginiana* var. *virginiana* L. growing in Ohio

19 *Hamamelis vernalis* 'Autumn Embers'

20 Autumn colour of *Hamamelis vernalis* 'Autumn Embers' at Witch Hazel Nurseries, Kent, England

21 *Hamamelis vernalis* 'Christmas Cheer'

22 *Hamamelis vernalis* 'Holden'

23 *Hamamelis vernalis* 'January Pride'

24 *Hamamelis vernalis* 'Kohankie Red'

25 *Hamamelis vernalis* 'Lombarts Weeping'

26 *Hamamelis vernalis* 'New Year Gold'

27 *Hamamelis vernalis* 'Orange Glow'

28 *Hamamelis vernalis* 'Orange Spangles'

Below: 29 *Hamamelis vernalis* 'Red Imp'

Right: 30, 31 *Hamamelis vernalis* 'Sandra'; autumn colour at Witch Hazel Nurseries, Kent, England

32 *Hamamelis vernalis* 'Sashet'

33 *Hamamelis vernalis* 'Squib'

34 *Hamamelis vernalis* 'Washington Park'

35 *Hamamelis japonica* 'Arborea'

36 *Hamamelis japonica* 'Brentry'

37 *Hamamelis japonica* 'Paleface'

38 *Hamamelis japonica* 'Rubra'

39 *Hamamelis japonica* 'Sulphurea'

40 *Hamamelis japonica* 'Zuccariniana'

41 *Hamamelis mollis* 'Coombe Wood'

42 *Hamamelis mollis* 'Emily'

43 *Hamamelis mollis* 'Fred Chittenden'

44 *Hamamelis mollis* 'Goldcrest'

45 *Hamamelis mollis* 'Iwado'

46 *Hamamelis mollis* 'Jermyns Gold'

47 *Hamamelis mollis* 'Kort's Yellow'

48 *Hamamelis mollis* 'Princeton Gold'

49 *Hamamelis mollis* 'Wisley Supreme'

50 *Hamamelis* ×*intermedia* 'Adieu'

51 *Hamamelis* ×*intermedia* 'Advent'

52 *Hamamelis ×intermedia* 'Agnes'

53 *Hamamelis ×intermedia* 'Alexander'

54 *Hamamelis ×intermedia* 'Allgold'

55 *Hamamelis ×intermedia* 'Angelly'

56 *Hamamelis* ×*intermedia* 'Antoine Kort'

57 *Hamamelis* ×*intermedia* 'Aphrodite'

58 *Hamamelis* ×*intermedia* 'Arnold Promise'

59 *Hamamelis* ×*intermedia* 'Aurora'

60 *Hamamelis ×intermedia* 'Barmstedt Gold'

61 *Hamamelis ×intermedia* 'Bernstein'

62 *Hamamelis ×intermedia* 'Birgit'

63 *Hamamelis ×intermedia* 'Böhlje's Feuerzauber'

64 *Hamamelis* ×*intermedia* 'Carmine Red'

65 *Hamamelis* ×*intermedia* 'Copper Cascade'

66 *Hamamelis* ×*intermedia* 'Cyrille'

67 *Hamamelis* ×*intermedia* 'Diane'

68 *Hamamelis ×intermedia* 'Early Bird'

69 *Hamamelis ×intermedia* 'Feuerzauber'

70 *Hamamelis ×intermedia* 'Frederic'

71 *Hamamelis ×intermedia* 'Friesia'

72 *Hamamelis* ×*intermedia* 'Georges'

73 *Hamamelis* ×*intermedia* 'Gimborn's Perfume'

74 *Hamamelis* ×*intermedia* 'Gingerbread'

75 *Hamamelis* ×*intermedia* 'Glowing Embers'

76 *Hamamelis ×intermedia* 'Harlow Carr'

77 *Hamamelis ×intermedia* 'Harry'

78 *Hamamelis ×intermedia* 'Heinrich Bruns'

79 *Hamamelis ×intermedia* 'Hiltingbury'

80 *Hamamelis ×intermedia* 'Jelena'

81 *Hamamelis ×intermedia* 'John'

82 *Hamamelis ×intermedia* 'Limelight'

83 *Hamamelis ×intermedia* 'Livia'

84 *Hamamelis ×intermedia* 'Luna'

85 *Hamamelis ×intermedia* 'Moonlight'

86 *Hamamelis ×intermedia* 'Nina'

87 *Hamamelis ×intermedia* 'Ninotchka'

88 *Hamamelis ×intermedia* 'Old Copper'

89 *Hamamelis ×intermedia* 'Orange Beauty'

90 *Hamamelis ×intermedia* 'Orange Encore'

91 *Hamamelis ×intermedia* 'Orange Peel'

92 *Hamamelis ×intermedia* 'Ostergold'

93 *Hamamelis ×intermedia* 'Pallida'

94 *Hamamelis ×intermedia* 'Parasol'

95 *Hamamelis ×intermedia* 'Primavera'

96 *Hamamelis* ×*intermedia* 'Ripe Corn'

97 *Hamamelis* ×*intermedia* 'Robert'

98 *Hamamelis* ×*intermedia* 'Rubin'

99 *Hamamelis* ×*intermedia* 'Rubinstar'

100 *Hamamelis ×intermedia* 'Ruby Glow'

101 *Hamamelis ×intermedia* 'Sarah'

102 *Hamamelis ×intermedia* 'Savill Starlight'

103 *Hamamelis ×intermedia* 'Sunburst'

104 *Hamamelis ×intermedia* 'Spanish Spider'

105 *Hamamelis ×intermedia* 'Strawberries and Cream'

106 *Hamamelis ×intermedia* 'Treasure Trove'

107 *Hamamelis ×intermedia* 'Twilight'

108 *Hamamelis ×intermedia* 'Vesna'

109 *Hamamelis ×intermedia* 'Westerstede'

110 *Hamamelis ×intermedia* 'Wiero'

111 *Hamamelis ×intermedia* 'Winter Beauty'

112 *Hamamelis ×intermedia* 'Zitronenjette'

113 *Hamamelis* 'Brevipetala'

114 *Hamamelis* 'Danny'

115 *Hamamelis* 'Dishi'

116 *Hamamelis* 'Doerak'

117 *Hamamelis* 'Fire Blaze'

118 *Hamamelis* 'Girard Orange'

119 *Hamamelis* 'Rochester'

Above: 120 *Hamamelis ×intermedia* at Kalmthout Arboretum, Antwerp, Belgium, with 'Jelena' and 'Pallida' on the left

Right: 121 *Hamamelis ×intermedia* at Kalmthout Arboretum, Antwerp, Belgium

Left: 122 *Hamamelis ×intermedia* at Hemelrijk, Essen, Belgium

Above: 123 *Hamamelis ×intermedia* at Hemelrijk, Essen, Belgium

Above: 124 Stock plants at Witch Hazel Nurseries, Kent, England

Right: 125 *Hamamelis mollis* 'Wisley Supreme' showing juvenilty in leaf retention on young shoots but not older ones

Left: 126 *Hamamelis mollis* in Valley Garden, Windsor, England

Left: 127 Tim Brotzman and Chris Sanders examining *Hamamelis mollis* 'Coombe Wood' at the RHS Garden Wisley, Surrey, England

Left: 128 *Hamamelis mollis* in Valley Garden, Windsor, England

Right: 129 Various *Hamamelis* at Valley Garden, Windsor, England

Right: 130 *Hamamelis* 'Fire Blaze' at Hemelrijk, Essen, Belgium

Below left: 131 *Hamamelis ×intermedia* 'Sunburst' at the RHS Garden Wisley, Surrey, England

Below right: 132 *Hamamelis ×intermedia* 'Robert' at Hemelrijk, Essen, Belgium

Above: 133 *Hamamelis* ×*intermedia* 'Pallida' at Valley Garden, Windsor, England

Right: 134 *Hamamelis* ×*intermedia* 'Livia' and a yellow witch hazel at Hemelrijk, Essen, Belgium

Right: 135 *Hamamelis* ×*intermedia* 'Jelena' at Valley Garden, Windsor, England

Above: 136 *Hamamelis* ×*intermedia* 'Barmstedt Gold' at Witch Hazel Nurseries, Kent, England

Left: 137 *Hamamelis* ×*intermedia* 'Agnes' at Hemelrijk, Essen, Belgium

Above: 138 *Hamamelis* ×*intermedia* 'Sunburst' before pruning

Right: 139 Pruning *Hamamelis* ×*intermedia* 'Sunburst'

Above: 140 Close-up of pruning showing cutting back of the previous year's growth to two buds

Above: 141 *Hamamelis* ×*intermedia* 'Sunburst' after pruning

Left: 142 Mildew on *Hamamelis*

Below left: 143 Fruit gall caused by the weevil *Pseudonanthomus hamamelidis*

Below right: 144 Cone gall caused by the aphid *Hormaphis hamamelidis*

Hamamelis ×*intermedia* 'Early Bird' (de Belder, 1984)

Comments

A Hemelrijk selection raised by de Belder under the number H.10583 and introduced by me in 1985. Although not the first cultivar to come into flower, it gets its name from its early-flowering habit. At my nursery in Kent, England, this is usually the second cultivar to come into flower after *Hamamelis* 'Rochester'; 'Early Bird' is, however, the first *H.* ×*intermedia* hybrid to come into flower and valuable on that count.

Growth habit

Upright, twiggy habit, only of moderate vigour, 3 m tall by 2.5 m wide.

Foliage

Leaves orbicular-obovate, margin shallowly crenate in upper half, smooth to scarcely crenate below, apex blunt, base obliquely cordate, 85 mm long by 80 mm wide; petiole 10 mm long; young foliage light green; mature foliage glabrous, dark shiny green, in autumn yellow suffused with light maroon.

Flowers

Petals 20 mm long by 1.5 mm wide, twisted, curled and heavily crimped, sulphur-yellow; calyx maroon-red; overall a clear deep sulphur-yellow; no scent; flowering early through midwinter.

Hamamelis ×*intermedia* 'Feuerzauber' (Hesse, 1958)

Synonyms

Hamamelis ×*intermedia* 'Fire Charm', *H.* ×*intermedia* 'Firecracker', *H.* ×*intermedia* 'Magic Fire'

Comments

A selection raised, named, and introduced by H. A. Hesse, Weener, Germany. This is a good reliable cultivar, although not a clear red, and it is stronger growing than *Hamamelis* ×*intermedia* 'Diane'. It received one star in the Royal Boskoop Horticultural Society trial in 2002.

Growth habit

Upright in growth when young, ultimately vase-shaped, a strong grower, 3.5 m tall by 3.5 m wide.

Foliage

Leaves ovate-orbicular, margin crenate in upper half, shallowly crenate below, apex blunt, base obliquely cordate, 120 mm long by 80 mm wide; petiole 12 mm long; young foliage a medium yellowish green; mature foliage glabrous, medium sage-green, in autumn orange-red shades.

Flowers

Petals 23 mm long by 1.5 mm wide, slightly twisted and crimped, coppery orange suffused red; calyx purplish red; overall coppery red; sweet but faint scent; flowering mid to late winter.

Hamamelis ×intermedia 'Frederic' (de Belder, 2000)

Synonym

Hamamelis ×intermedia 'Frederique'

Comments

A Hemelrijk selection raised by de Belder under the number H.18641. The original plant is growing with several other witch hazels under high tree canopy. It stood out, however, when I first saw it and has performed well at my nursery in Kent, England, being one of the best cultivars for combining both quality of flower and autumn foliage colour. Named after Robert and Jelena de Belders' grandchild, the son of Jean-Louis and Diane van Strydonck. I grew this cultivar in my collection for several years prior to it being named, and it continues to impress.

Growth habit

Upright when young, ultimately a rounded bush, with vigorous strong-growing branches, 4 m tall by 4 m wide.

Foliage

Leaves ovate-orbicular, margin crenate in upper half, shallowly crenate below, apex acute, base obliquely cordate, 90 mm long by 80 mm wide; petiole 8 mm long; young foliage a light greyish green; mature foliage glabrous, dark green, in autumn yellow, orange, and red; one of the most reliable cultivars for a good display.

Flowers

Petals 21 mm long by 1.5 mm wide, curled and slightly crimped, golden yellow, suffused red at base to midway; calyx deep purple-red; overall orange; no scent; flowering midwinter.

Hamamelis ×*intermedia* 'Friesia' (Sanstede, ca.1975)

Comments

I know very little of the background to this cultivar, except that it was raised by Friedrich Sanstede, Bad Zwischenahn, Germany. The plant made its way from Germany into Holland, which is where I obtained it; possibly another Heinrich Bruns seedling. The flowers are rather dull in colour and remain fairly curled; growth habit is not very good and there is little to recommend this cultivar to the reader.

Growth habit

Spreading, moderate vigour, making a bush 3 m tall by 4 m wide.

Foliage

Leaves ovate-orbicular, margin crenate in upper half, shallowly crenate below, apex acute, base oblique, 95 mm long by 85 mm wide; petiole 12 mm long; young foliage a medium yellowish green; mature foliage glabrous, light sage-green, no autumn colour.

Flowers

Petals 14 mm long by 2.5 mm wide, curled and crimped, petal red; calyx purple-red; overall reddish; no scent; flowering late winter.

Hamamelis ×*intermedia* 'Georges' (de Belder, 1999)

Comments

A Hemelrijk selection raised by de Belder under the number H.20487. It was named after Robert de Belder's brother George and grandson George, son of Danny and Barbara de Belder, hence 'Georges'. For many years this plant retained its dead leaves but has recently lost this tendency, so the plant has been named. As with *Hamamelis* ×*intermedia* 'Copper Cascade', the original plant is growing in a fairly open position to the right of the road with the huge beech trees. With a background of trees including some pines, this uniquely coloured plant is awe inspiring at around 7 m tall by 4 m wide. Tim Brotzman notes that this year (2003), his plant growing in Ohio has had the best autumn colour of any in his collection.

Growth habit

Very upright, vigorous strong growing branches, making a bush 4 m tall by 2 m wide.

Foliage

Leaves ovate-orbicular, margin shallowly crenate in upper half, apex acute, base obliquely cordate, 120 mm long by 80 mm wide; petiole 8 mm long; spring foliage a medium green; mature foliage glabrous, dark green, in autumn starting maroon then turning through yellow-orange to crimson.

Flowers

Petals 18 mm long by 2 mm wide, straight, curled at tip and crimped, light red at base fading to coppery red at tip; calyx deep purple-red; overall a crushed strawberry red; no scent; flowering midwinter.

Hamamelis ×intermedia 'Gimborn's Perfume' (von Gimborn Arboretum, 1984)

Synonyms

Hamamelis ×intermedia 'Perfume', *H. mollis* 'Perfume'

Comments

Selected from a plant of unknown origin at the von Gimborn Arboretum, Doorn, Holland, and introduced by Wim van der Werf. This cultivar could be from the same seed lot as *Hamamelis ×intermedia* 'Sunburst' as it has the same unfortunate habit of the leaves developing yellow interveinal chlorosis in midsummer, the patches ultimately becoming necrotic and brown. This phenomenon is worse in some seasons more than others. Tim Brotzman notes that it often retains its old leaves in winter.

Growth habit

Rounded bush of medium vigour, making a plant 3 m tall by 3 m wide.

Foliage

Leaves ovate-orbicular, margin crenate in upper half, shallowly crenate below, apex acute, base obliquely cordate, 90 mm long by 70 mm wide; petiole 8 mm long; spring foliage medium yellowish green; mature foliage glabrous, medium to dark green, in autumn yellow.

Flowers

Petals 21 mm long by 1.5 mm wide, slightly twisted and crimped, yellow tinted red at base; calyx red; overall pale yellow; scent sweet and strong; flowering mid to late winter.

Hamamelis ×*intermedia* 'Gingerbread' (de Belder, 1995)

Synonyms

Hamamelis ×*intermedia* 'Fiery Orange', *H.* ×*intermedia* 'Ginger Bread'

Comments

A Hemelrijk selection raised by de Belder under the number H.10659 and named by Jelena de Belder and me in 1995, when I mentioned that the dark orange flowers were reminiscent of gingerbread cake. This is a very distinct cultivar for several reasons, namely the intense dark orange flowers, purple-flushed young foliage, and good bushy growth in the nursery. It will I think become quite popular in the future.

Growth habit

Spreading, moderately vigorous, making a bush 2.5 m tall by 3.5 m wide.

Foliage

Leaves ovate-orbicular, margin crenate in upper half, shallowly crenate below, apex acute, base obliquely cordate, 100 mm long by 65 mm wide; petiole 8 mm long; young foliage is a medium to dark green heavily flushed maroon-purple which is retained for several weeks; mature foliage glabrous, dark green, in autumn yellow.

Flowers

Petals 19 mm long by 1.5 mm wide, quite curled and remaining so; deep burnt orange, suffused red at base; calyx deep purple-red; overall a clear burnt orange; scent slight; flowering in late winter.

Hamamelis ×*intermedia* 'Glowing Embers' (Lane, 1999)

Synonym

Hamamelis ×*intermedia* 'Iwado'

Comments

Raised by Kochiro Wada, of the Hakoneya Nursery, Japan, although the precise identity and name of this plant is uncertain (for comments, see chapter 8). To avoid any confusion and because the plant is worthwhile, I decided to rename it in 1999. This excellent cultivar has one fault of being somewhat sensitive to late spring frost damage as a young plant.

Growth habit

Spreading bush of moderate vigour, making a plant 2.5 m tall by 4 m wide.

Foliage

Leaves ovate-orbicular, margin shallowly crenate in upper half, smooth to scarcely crenate below, apex blunt, base obliquely cordate, 110 mm long by 80 mm wide; petiole 8 mm long; young foliage a medium greyish green; mature foliage glabrous, dark, almost glossy green, no autumn colour.

Flowers

Petals 27 mm long by 1.5 mm wide, fairly straight, slightly crimped, golden yellow, suffused red at base, fading to tip; calyx deep purple-red; overall a coppery orange; scent slight; flowering throughout midwinter.

Hamamelis ×*intermedia* 'Golden' (Hohman, ca. 1963)

Comments

Raised, named, and introduced by Henry Hohman of the Kingsville Nursery, Maryland. Despite continued attempts by me and friends in the United States, we have not been able to track this plant down. Description is scant; Mike Dirr found reference to this cultivar for his article in the *American Nurseryman* (1983) from a student named David Lofgren, who was working at Longwood Gardens in 1976. The reference to this cultivar was in a thesis he was preparing, and the only information available is to the flowers. The U.S. National Arboretum had a plant under accession number 53EW.NA.23880, received from the Kingsville Nursery in 1963. According to Ruth Dix the plant was still alive in the late 1970s, but it slowly died due to canker problems. All she can remember is that it was very tall and had golden yellow flowers.

Growth habit
Not known.

Foliage
Not known.

Flowers
Petals 16 mm long, heavily crimped and slightly twisted, colour a good clear yellow with deep blush-pink tint at base.

Hamamelis ×intermedia 'Harlow Carr' (Bond, 1990)

Synonym
Hamamelis ×intermedia 'Newington'

Comments
Selected by me from a plant growing at the RHS Garden Harlow Carr, Harrogate, Yorkshire, England; it was labelled as 'Copper Beauty'. This is a name that has been used for *Hamamelis ×intermedia* 'Jelena' in the past. Realizing it was not this cultivar but something different, I asked for propagation material. Subsequently, I gave a plant to John Bond, keeper of the garden at Great Windsor Park, who decided to name it after the garden from which it arose. This cultivar is very similar in colour to the well-known *H. ×intermedia* 'Barmstedt Gold', but the petals are more curled. Received one star in the Royal Boskoop Horticultural Society trial in 2002.

Growth habit
Rounded bush of moderate vigour, 3 m tall by 3 m wide.

Foliage
Leaves ovate-orbicular, margin crenate in upper half, shallowly crenate below, apex acute, base obliquely cordate, 110 mm long by 80 mm wide; petiole 15 mm long; young foliage a medium yellowish green; mature foliage glabrous, sage-green, in autumn turning yellow.

Flowers

Petals 20 mm long by 2 mm wide, curled and crimped, light golden yellow, red at base; calyx a bright maroon-red; overall a deep golden yellow; slight scent; flowering mid through late winter.

Hamamelis ×intermedia 'Harry' (de Belder, 1988)

Comments

A Hemelrijk selection raised by de Belder under the number H.10590. Raised and named by de Belder after Harry van Trier, one time curator of the Kalmthout Arboretum in Belgium. Robert and Jelena de Belder told Harry to pick his favourite witch hazel growing at Hemelrijk to be named after him. Although the original plant is growing close to a pine tree and cannot be seen to best advantage, I think he has picked the best plant from the one hundred or more that are growing in Hemelrijk. The longer I grow the plant, the more convinced I am that it is, along with *Hamamelis ×intermedia* 'Sunburst', the top plant for visual display (if only they had the scent of *H. ×intermedia* 'Pallida'). This selection only received two stars in the Royal Boskoop Horticultural Society trial in 2002, possibly because Boskoop's plants were smaller than mine and there is a tendency for some dead leaves to be retained through the winter on young plants.

Growth habit

Upright when young, moderate vigour, making a compact rounded bush with age, 2.5 m tall by 2.5 m wide.

Foliage

Leaves orbicular, margin shallowly crenate in upper half, apex acute, base obliquely cordate, 110 mm long by 85 mm wide; petiole 6 mm long; young foliage a medium greyish green; mature foliage glabrous, dark green, no autumn colour.

Flowers

Petals 25 mm long by 3 mm wide, straight, slightly crimped, yellowish orange; calyx greyish purple; overall a pale orange; scent faint; flowering in midwinter.

Hamamelis ×intermedia 'Heinrich Bruns' (Lane, 2003)

Synonym

Hamamelis ×intermedia 'Orange Glow'

Comments

Another selection from Heinrich Bruns, possibly in the early 1970s; the information regarding the naming and introduction is scant. I collected this particular clone in the research station in Rostrup, near Westerstede, Germany. The people there were unsure of its precise origin, stating that it was received from Heinrich Bruns. In the station it was labelled as *Hamamelis ×intermedia* 'Orange Glow', which has posed a problem as there is already an *H. vernalis* 'Orange Glow' in existence, most likely raised prior to this clone. Neither the research station nor Helmerich Helmers could be absolutely sure who named the plant. Unfortunately, I am unable to prove conclusively which was named first; the *H. vernalis* clone has almost certainly been distributed more extensively than the Bruns-raised *H. ×intermedia*. I have therefore decided to change the name of this plant, by bestowing it with his name, in memory of a great witch hazel breeder.

Growth habit

Upright when young, later becoming vase-shaped, 3.5 m tall by 3.5 m wide.

Foliage

Leaves orbicular, margin crenate in upper half, shallowly crenate below, apex acute, base obliquely cordate, 80 mm long by 80 mm wide; petiole 10 mm long; young foliage light green; mature foliage glabrous, dark green, no autumn colour.

Flowers

Petals 23 mm long by 1.5 mm wide, slightly curled and crimped, straw-yellow suffused red from base to midway; calyx purple-red; overall a pale orange-red; no scent; flowering in midwinter.

Hamamelis ×intermedia 'Hiltingbury' (Hillier, ca. 1945)

Comments

Raised by Hillier Nurseries Ltd. from the same seed batch as *Hamamelis ×intermedia* 'Carmine Red'. The original plant used to grow in the

Hiltingbury Nursery, but both plant and the nursery site are no longer in existence. This selection is perhaps worth growing for its autumn colour, but it is inferior in flower to other red-flowered cultivars. Tim Brotzman relates that the plant at the Arnold Arboretum is famous for the intense red autumn colour.

Growth habit

Rounded bush, 3 m tall by 3 m wide.

Foliage

Leaves ovate-orbicular, margin crenate in upper half, shallowly crenate below, apex acute, base obliquely cordate, 90 mm long by 70 mm wide; petiole 15 mm long; young foliage a medium yellowish green; mature foliage glabrous, dark green, superb in autumn, lovely shades of orange, red, and finally scarlet.

Flowers

Petals 18 mm long by 1.5 mm wide, pale copper suffused red; calyx purple-red; overall a muddy red colour; scent sweet but faint; flowering mid to late winter.

Hamamelis ×intermedia 'Jelena' (de Belder, 1954)

Synonym

Hamamelis ×intermedia 'Copper Beauty'

Comments

A Kalmthout selection under the number K.978. The original plant has perished but, as with *Hamamelis ×intermedia* 'Diane', has been propagated extensively and is readily available. This selection was raised by Antoine Kort and named by Robert de Belder in 1954 after his wife Jelena. The story goes that Robert was showing at the Royal Horticultural Society in London the new plant, which had not as yet received a name. People were so taken by the beauty of this witch hazel, that it was causing quite a stir, and they were pressing Robert with regard to the name of it. As he was recently married, he decided there and then to name it in honour of his wife Jelena. One or two Dutch nurseries (including W. J. Hooftman, who offered the plant in his 1958 catalogue), had distributed it in small numbers under the name

H. ×*intermedia* 'Copper Beauty'. The cultivar soon became popular under the correct name and was produced in numbers by the Dutch nursery trade. Today *H.* ×*intermedia* 'Jelena' is deservedly one of the best cultivars. It is such a warm coppery orange colour that, on cold days, you feel you could warm your hands against its flowers. Received two stars in the Royal Boskoop Horticultural Society trial in 2002 and was given an Award of Garden Merit by the Royal Horticultural Society in 1993.

Growth habit

Vase-shaped, vigorous shrub with ascending branches, making a shrub 4 m tall by 4 m wide.

Foliage

Leaves ovate-orbicular, margin crenate in upper half, shallowly crenate below, apex acute, base obliquely cordate, 115 mm long by 80 mm wide; petiole 12 mm long; young foliage a yellowish green with a light bronze flush; mature foliage glabrous, dark green, in autumn shades of yellow, orange, and red.

Flowers

Petals 24 mm long 1.5 mm wide, red at base becoming ochre-yellow at tip; calyx claret-red, slightly glossy; overall effect is a warm coppery orange; no scent; flowering early to midwinter.

Hamamelis ×*intermedia* 'John' (de Belder, 1996)

Comments

A Hemelrijk selection raised by de Belder under the number H.10575 and named after John Schnieder, a good friend of the de Belders. The original plant is in poor condition, growing among hardy hybrid rhododendrons and close to a pine tree. It consists of a single shoot of about 3 m with a few flowering branches in the top 1 m or so. As the flowers showed a lot of potential, Jelena asked me to propagate it, which I did from a couple of shoots—all there was of the previous years growth. It looks to be a bushy plant with rather upright growth. This cultivar is not yet introduced to the trade.

Growth habit

Upright, vigorous, ultimately making a rounded bush 3.5 m tall by 3.5 m wide.

Foliage

Leaves orbicular-obovate, margin shallowly crenate in upper half, apex blunt, base obliquely cordate, 95 mm long by 85 mm wide; petiole 10 mm long; young foliage medium yellowish green; mature foliage glabrous, dark green, no autumn colour.

Flowers

Petals 25 mm long by 2 mm wide, slightly twisted and crimped, golden yellow, tinted red at base fading to midway; calyx bright reddish maroon; overall a golden-orange; no scent; flowering in midwinter.

Hamamelis ×*intermedia* 'Limelight' (de Belder, 1984)

Comments

A Kalmthout selection under the number K.980, raised and named by de Belder in 1984. Introduced by Adrian Bloom and by me in 1995. It is inferior to other yellow-flowered cultivars and is not likely to be generally grown. It is interesting though, as, along with *Hamamelis ×intermedia* 'Wiero', probably has the palest yellow flowers among the hybrids. At the Kalmthout Arboretum, the original plant grows to the left of the path on the witch hazel walk.

Growth habit

Vase-shaped, later more spreading, moderately vigorous, making a bush 2.5 m tall by 2.5 m wide.

Foliage

Leaves ovate-orbicular, margin shallowly crenate in top half, smooth to scarcely so below, apex blunt, base oblique, 90 mm long by 75 mm wide; petiole 12 mm long; young foliage a dark yellowish green; mature foliage glabrous, light to medium green, in autumn yellow.

Flowers

Petals 18 mm long by 1.5 mm wide, heavily twisted and crimped, pale acid-yellow; calyx bright purplish maroon; overall a pale yellow; no scent; flowering late winter.

Hamamelis ×intermedia 'Livia' (de Belder, 1993)

Comments

A Hemelrijk selection raised by de Belder under the number H.10653, It was named by Robert and Jelena de Belder after their first granddaughter, Livia, daughter of Jean-Louis and Diane van Strydonck. Introduced to the nursery trade by Bevers en Zn. BV, Wernhout, Holland. This is, in my opinion, the best red cultivar raised to date. The original plant grows by a ditch at Hemelrijk alongside an unnamed yellow witch hazel and in front of a large hardy hybrid rhododendron, a perfect backdrop. At the end of January 2003, Chris Sanders and I saw this plant in Hemelrijk to perfection, on what was a dull drizzly afternoon with not enough light to photograph, but the memory of that breathtaking vision permanently etched in our minds. Tim Brotzman comments that in the southern United States it suffers with the same blighting of foliage that has attacked *Hamamelis ×intermedia* 'Arnold Promise', other than that he is impressed with the red flowers, which do not change colour as they fade.

Growth habit

Spreading with twiggy branches, moderate vigour, making a shrub 2.5 m tall by 3 m wide.

Foliage

Leaves broadly elliptic, margin crenate in upper half, shallowly crenate below, apex acute, base oblique, 110 mm long by 65 mm wide; petiole 10 mm long; spring foliage a medium yellowish green heavily flushed maroon-purple; mature foliage glabrous, dark green, faint orange-red autumn tints.

Flowers

Petals 22 mm long by 1.5 mm wide, deep red; calyx purple-red; overall a strong carmine-red colour; quite a good scent; flowering late autumn to late winter. This cultivar, together with *Hamamelis* 'Rochester' and *H.* 'Doerak', has one of the longest flowering periods of any witch hazel.

Hamamelis ×intermedia 'Luna' (de Belder, 1954)

Comments

A Kalmthout selection under the number K.954. This cultivar was raised by Antoine Kort and selected and named by Robert and Jelena de Belder. It is a sister to *Hamamelis* ×*intermedia* 'Ruby Glow'. I introduced this cultivar to the trade in the United Kingdom in 1980, but it had been in the nursery trade in North America for a long time. *Hamamelis* ×*intermedia* 'Luna' is no longer grown to any extent.

Growth habit

Rounded bush, moderate vigour, making a plant 3.5 m tall by 3.5 m wide.

Foliage

Leaves orbicular-obovate, margin crenate in upper half, shallowly crenate below, apex acute, base obliquely cordate, 95 mm long by 85 mm wide; petiole 12 mm long; young foliage a light yellowish green; mature foliage glabrous, medium green, in autumn has light yellowish orange tints.

Flowers

Petals 20 mm long by 1.5 mm wide, curled and slightly crimped, pale yellow tinted red-purple at base; calyx red-purple; overall a bicolour effect, does not stand out from a distance; little scent; flowering midwinter.

Hamamelis ×*intermedia* 'Moonlight' (Hillier, ca. 1960)

Comments

A selection from Hillier Nurseries Ltd. that they obtained from Exbury Gardens, Hampshire, as *Hamamelis mollis* 'Pallida'. This selection is not widely grown any more, as it has a habit of retaining dead leaves during the winter. Compared to *H.* ×*intermedia* 'Pallida', the flowers are more twisted and paler. In the past, it has been sold incorrectly as *H.* ×*intermedia* 'Pallida' both in the United Kingdom and, according to Tim Brotzman, also in North America.

Growth habit

Vase-shaped with vigorous, ascending branches, ultimately making a more spreading bush 3.5 m tall by 4 m wide.

Foliage

Leaves ovate-orbicular, margin crenate in upper half, shallowly crenate below, apex acute, base obliquely cordate, 100 mm long by 80 mm wide; petiole 10 mm long; young foliage a medium yellowish green; mature foliage glabrous, medium green, in autumn a deep butter-yellow, unfortunately the leaves then turn brown and hang through the winter.

Flowers

Petals 23 mm long by 1.5 mm wide, curled and crimped, very pale sulphur-yellow; calyx deep claret-red; overall a pale sulphur-yellow; scent sweet and strong; flowering midwinter.

Hamamelis ×*intermedia* 'Nina' (Lange, 1953)

Synonym

Hamamelis ×*japollis* 'Nina'

Comments

A selection from Chartottenlund Botanic Garden, Denmark, named in 1953 by Johan Lange. Unfortunately, when it entered the Dutch nursery trade, propagation material of three other witch hazels plus the true *Hamamelis* ×*intermedia* 'Nina' all growing very close together were propagated and distributed (see chapter 8). These other plants are inferior to the true 'Nina', so it was many years before the value of this cultivar was realized. The original plant of the true 'Nina' grew in the Forest Botanical Garden, Charlottenlund, Denmark, until it died in 1990. It had, however, been propagated several times by grafting onto *H. virginiana*. I am indebted to Poul Sondergaard, who sent me genuine material from a plant growing in the Horsholm Arboretum.

Growth habit

Rounded bush, vigorous plant with strong shoots, ultimately making a bush 4 m tall by 4 m wide.

Foliage

Leaves ovate-orbicular, margin crenate in upper half, shallowly crenate below, apex acute, base obliquely cordate, 120 mm long by 85 mm wide; petiole 15 mm long; young foliage a medium yellowish green; mature foliage glabrous, dark green, in autumn a deep butter-yellow.

Flowers

Petals 23 mm long by 1.5 mm wide, twisted and crimped, yellow; calyx greyish purple; overall a good clear yellow; flowering period mid to late winter.

Hamamelis ×*intermedia* 'Ninotchka' (de Belder, 2002)

Comments

A Hemelrijk selection raised by de Belder under the number H.10601. This plant has recently been named for Jean-Louis and Diane van Strydonck's second daughter.

Growth habit

Rounded bush, later more spreading, moderate vigour, making a plant 3 m tall by 3 m wide.

Foliage

Leaves obovate, margin crenate in upper half, shallowly crenate below, apex blunt, base oblique, 95 mm long by 60 mm wide; petiole 12 mm long; young foliage a medium green; mature foliage glabrous, dark green, in autumn turning yellow.

Flowers

Petals 17 mm long by 1.5 mm wide, curled, twisted and crimped, clear sulphur-yellow; calyx light maroon-red; overall a clear primrose-yellow; fairly strong and sweet scent; flowering late winter.

Hamamelis ×*intermedia* 'Old Copper' (Bruns, ca.1970)

Synonym

Hamamelis ×*intermedia* 'Robin'

Comments

A selection from Heinrich Bruns, Westerstede, Germany, which was not available in the nursery trade until introduced by me in 1998. I obtained this cultivar from the research station in Rostrup; they knew very little of the background except that it was a Bruns seedling. My observations so far are that, although the flowers are not very large, they are extremely profuse, in colour similar to 'Jelena' but a bit darker.

Growth habit

Upright when young, later vase-shaped, moderate vigour with twiggy branches, making a bush 3 m tall and 2.5 m wide.

Foliage

Leaves broadly elliptic, margin crenate in upper half, shallowly crenate below, apex acute, base oblique, 95 mm long by 55 mm wide; petiole 12 mm long; young foliage a medium green, heavily flushed maroon; mature foliage glabrous, dark green, in autumn yellow.

Flowers

Petals 18 mm long by 1.5 mm wide, curled and crimped, light orange, heavily suffused red; calyx dark purple-red; overall a dark burnished coppery red colour; no scent; flowering mid to late winter.

Hamamelis ×*intermedia* 'Orange Beauty' (van Nes, 1965)

Synonyms

Hamamelis ×*intermedia* 'August Lamken', *H.* ×*intermedia* 'Aurora' (wrongly applied), *H.* ×*intermedia* 'Orange'

Comments

Another selection from Heinrich Bruns raised around 1955. It was also in the past listed as *Hamamelis* ×*intermedia* 'Orange', until it was renamed and introduced to the nursery trade in 1965 by Vuyk van Nes Nursery, Boskoop, Holland. *Hamamelis* ×*intermedia* 'August Lamken', a cultivar which I have obtained from Westerstede in Germany, appears to be identical. *Hamamelis* ×*intermedia* 'Orange Beauty' has also been sold in The Netherlands incorrectly as *H.* ×*intermedia* 'Aurora'. This cultivar is now perhaps somewhat overlooked for newer introductions; it does, however, perform well every year with a good display and is wonderfully scented.

Growth habit

Somewhat spreading shrub, vigorously strong growing branches, making a plant 3 m tall by 4 m wide.

Foliage

Leaves broadly elliptic, margin crenate in upper half, shallowly crenate below, apex acute, base oblique, 120 mm long by 65 mm wide; petiole 15 mm long; young foliage a medium yellowish green flushed maroon-purple; mature foliage glabrous, dark green, in autumn shades of yellow and orange.

Flowers

Petals 22 mm long by 1.5 mm wide, twisted, slightly crimped, yellow-orange, tinted red-purple at base; calyx dark purple-red; overall effect a good strong orange colour; good scent; flowering in mid to late winter.

Hamamelis ×intermedia 'Orange Encore' (Brotzman, 1995)

Comments

Raised, named, and introduced by Tim Brotzman, of Madison, Ohio. This represents a breakthrough in selection—not because of its flowers which are very late, even into midspring some years—but for the incredibly long display of foliage colour from spring through to autumn. Brotzman relates that his original plant grows in the shade at the edge of a wood, and he has so far not been as excited as I have about the foliage colour; my plants are fully out in the open.

Growth habit

Spreading, vigorous growth, ultimately making a bush 3 m tall by 3.5 m wide.

Foliage

Leaves ovate-orbicular, margin shallowly crenate in upper half, smooth to scarcely crenate below, apex acute, base oblique, 95 mm long by 70 mm wide; petiole 12 mm long; young foliage pale green heavily flushed maroon; mature foliage glabrous, dark green heavily flushed maroon, autumn colour starting deep maroon-purple finally turning crimson. This is the only witch hazel I know of that maintains this foliage colour throughout the growing season.

Flowers

Petals 12 mm long by 1.5 mm wide, very curled, not always opening fully, crimped, deep golden yellow; calyx brownish red; overall a light orange; early to midspring; the leaves start to emerge at the end of the flowering period which gives it a messy look.

Hamamelis ×intermedia 'Orange Peel' (de Belder, 1988)

Comments

A Hemelrijk selection raised by de Belder under the number H.10640. Along with *Hamamelis ×intermedia* 'Harry' and *H. ×intermedia* 'Sunburst', this selection has wide petals (around 3 mm). Unlike the other two, however, the petals remain more curled and consequently look less impressive. The name is a good one, and it performs well in the nursery so is likely to become popular. This cultivar was introduced by Bevers en Zn. BV, Wernhout, Holland, and it received one star in the Royal Boskoop Horticultural Society trial in 2002. Tim Brotzman notes that the young shoots have an attractive rusty colour, not quite an indumentum, but distinctive. He also has commented on the attractive foliage, both in summer and autumn.

Growth habit

Upright when young, making a rounded bush 3.5 m tall by 3.5 m wide.

Foliage

Leaves orbicular, margin shallowly crenate in upper half, smooth to scarcely crenate below, apex acute to blunt, base obliquely cordate, 95 mm long by 85 mm wide; petiole 8 mm long; young foliage a medium yellowish green; mature foliage somewhat pubescent, dark green, in autumn taking on yellow, orange, and red tints.

Flowers

Petals 22 mm long by 3 mm wide, slightly curled and crimped, yellow-orange; calyx greyish purple; overall effect is a clear orange; sweet scent; flowering period is mid to late winter.

Hamamelis ×intermedia 'Ostergold' (Böhlje, ca.1977)

Comments

Raised, named, and introduced by Böhlje Nursery, Westerstede, in 1977. The original plant in their nursery is large and vigorous, late flowering, and always puts on a good display. Although virtually unknown outside of Germany, this is a worthwhile cultivar.

Growth habit

Spreading, strong, vigorous, making a bush 3.5 m tall by 4.5 m wide.

Foliage

Leaves ovate-orbicular, margin crenate in upper half, shallowly crenate below, apex acute, base oblique, 115 mm long by 70 mm wide; petiole 20 mm long; young foliage totally flushed a bright maroon-purple, retaining this characteristic for several weeks; mature foliage glabrous, dark green, in autumn yellow.

Flowers

Petals 20 mm long by 1.5 mm wide, slightly curled and crimped, golden yellow; calyx bright maroon-red; overall a buttercup-yellow; no scent; flowering in late winter.

Hamamelis ×*intermedia* 'Pallida' (RHS Garden Wisley, 1958)

Synonym

Hamamelis mollis 'Pallida'

Comments

Raised at the RHS Garden Wisley, this is still the best sulphur-yellow cultivar available for garden use, so it is important here to document as accurately and as near completely as possible the origin of this fine cultivar. It was known for a long time as *Hamamelis mollis* 'Pallida' before it was realized that this plant was an ×*intermedia* type. When I first started to study witch hazels, I began to question whether in fact *H. mollis* 'Pallida' was indeed a form or cultivar of *H. mollis*, as all its characteristics suggested an *H.* ×*intermedia* type. Other people started to do the same, and it is now accepted that it is a cultivar of *H.* ×*intermedia*.

It received an RHS First Class Certificate in 1958, when exhibited by Crown Estates Commissioners, Windsor. Both Mike Grant and I have been unable to trace any published reference to *Hamamelis mollis* 'Pallida' prior to this date. It was known to a few individuals before this date, however, among them L. Russell of Richmond Nurseries, Windlesham, Surrey. It was first offered for sale in their Autumn 1953 catalogue, his father John Russell having obtained graft wood from Wisley in 1946. The original plant must therefore have been planted on Battleston Hill between 1941 and 1946. A

1941 inventory of trees and shrubs at Wisley shows that there were no witch hazels on Battleston Hill at that time. Plants were given to the Royal Botanic Gardens, Kew, the RHS Garden Wisley, and the Savill Garden, Windsor, the plant in the Savill Garden most likely being one of the first propagations from the original Wisley plant. The original plant still grows on Battleston Hill at Wisley. It is a seed-raised plant or a layer because any suckers that come up prove to be the same as the top, so obviously the plant is on its own roots. This is the plant that has been propagated and generally distributed not just through Europe but worldwide.

The origin of *Hamamelis* ×*intermedia* 'Pallida' is not precisely recorded, as previously stated, the original plant still grows on Battleston Hill at the RHS Garden Wisley. According to the garden's staff, it came from seed sent from a neglected nursery in the south of Holland. Robert de Belder suggests that this may in fact have been Kalmthout Arboretum. My feeling is that this is not very plausible—if seed had been sent, one would have expected several plants on Battleston Hill. So, either there was very poor germination or other plants were disposed of before flowering had been observed.

A more plausible origin is that it arose as a spontaneous seedling from the *Hamamelis mollis* var. *pallida* (now called *H. mollis* 'Fred Chittenden) which was growing in Severn Acres, pollinated by perhaps *H. japonica* 'Superba' or *H. japonica* 'Arborea' growing nearby and the resultant seedling being moved to Battleston Hill. The true origin will now never be known for sure, but we can be thankful it arose at Wisley, is still there, has been distributed and propagated more than any other cultivar of *H.* ×*intermedia.* It sets the standard on which to judge all others. Received three stars in the Royal Boskoop Horticultural Society trial in 2002, the highest award, and it was given an Award of Garden Merit from the Royal Horticultural Society in 1993.

Growth habit

Spreading shrub, 3 m tall by 4 m wide.

Foliage

Leaves ovate-orbicular, margin crenate in upper half, shallowly crenate below, apex acute, base oblique, 120 mm long by 85 mm wide; petiole 15 mm long; young foliage a medium yellowish green; mature foliage glabrous, medium green, in autumn turning yellow.

Flowers

Petals 25 mm long by 1.8 mm wide, curled and crimped, sulphur-yellow; calyx red-purple; overall a good clear sulphur-yellow, standing out well from a distance; scent sweet and strong; flowering early to midwinter.

Hamamelis ×*intermedia* 'Parasol' (de Belder, 1995)

Comments

A Kalmthout selection raised by de Belder under the number K.7525. This selection was named 'Parasol' because the branch tips weep slightly on a spreading plant, similar in habit to *Hamamelis* ×*intermedia* 'Copper Cascade'. This cultivar was introduced by me in 1995, but it is unlikely to become popular because the flowers are not all that impressive.

Growth habit

Spreading plant, branch tips weep slightly, twiggy growth, 2 m tall by 3.5 m wide.

Foliage

Leaves broadly elliptic, margin crenate in upper half, smooth to scarcely crenate below, apex acute, base oblique, 80 mm long by 55 mm wide; petiole 18 mm long; young foliage a medium yellowish green; mature foliage glabrous, grey-green, in autumn slight yellow-orange tints.

Flowers

Petals 19 mm long by 1.5 mm wide, curled and crimped, straw-yellow, heavily suffused red at base, less so towards tip; calyx dark maroon-red; overall a reddish yellow to light red effect; no scent; flowering in midwinter.

Hamamelis ×*intermedia* 'Primavera' (de Belder, 1969)

Comments

A Kalmthout selection under the number K.977, raised and named by de Belder, and introduced by the Dutch nursery trade soon after it was named. The name comes from the Spanish word for spring. Its main fault is the flowers tend to face downwards, so the plant needs to attain a fair size before they can be fully appreciated. Once the plant has achieved some size, it can look very good indeed, as it is free flowering and a clear yellow colour. Received one star in the Royal Boskoop Horticultural Society trial in 2002.

Growth habit

Upright when young, ultimately vase-shaped, 3 m tall by 3 m wide.

Foliage

Leaves orbicular, margin crenate in upper half, shallowly crenate below, apex acute, base obliquely cordate, 110 mm long by 100 mm wide; petiole 10 mm long; young foliage medium green with light bronze flush; mature foliage glabrous, sage-green, in autumn yellow.

Flowers

Petals 21 mm long by 1.8 mm wide, curled at tip and crimped, clear bright yellow tinted purple-red at base; calyx claret-red, slightly glossy; overall a warm yellow; scent faint; flowering mid to late winter.

Hamamelis ×intermedia 'Ripe Corn' (de Belder, 1995)

Synonym

Hamamelis ×intermedia 'Aureolin'

Comments

A Hemelrijk selection raised by de Belder under the number H.10548, named by de Belder and introduced to the trade by Bevers, en Zn. BV, Wernhout, Holland. The original plant grows in a group of others close to a pine tree and was slightly damaged in the storm of October 2000. It is a fine, large specimen, 6 m tall by 10 m wide.

Growth habit

Rounded shrub, 3.5 m tall by 3.5 m wide.

Foliage

Leaves ovate-orbicular, margin shallowly crenate, apex acute, base obliquely cordate, 120 mm long by 75 mm wide; petiole 15 mm long; young foliage a light yellowish green; mature foliage glabrous, medium green, in autumn butter-yellow.

Flowers

Petals 21 mm long by 1.5 mm wide, fairly straight and crimped, yellow; calyx red-purple; overall a bright yellow; faint scent; flowering in mid-winter.

Hamamelis ×*intermedia* 'Robert' (de Belder, 2000)

Comments

A Hemelrijk selection raised by de Belder under the number H.10617 and raised at Hemelrijk by de Belder. Chris Sanders and I had both long admired this witch hazel at Hemelrijk; after Robert de Belder's death in 1998, we talked it over and decided it would be a fitting tribute to name this plant in his memory. Two winters later, we broached the subject with Jelena and she agreed. The original plant grows close to *Hamamelis* ×*intermedia* 'Orange Peel' and a large rhododendron and looks superb every year. On my first visit to Hemelrijk, I noticed this plant straight away. On enquiring the name, I found it did not have one. The following summer I was allowed to have propagation material, so enabling me to admire the plant in my collection.

Growth habit

Upright when young, later vase-shaped, 3.5 m by 3 m.

Foliage

Leaves orbicular-obovate, margin shallowly crenate, apex blunt, base obliquely cordate, 100 mm long by 75 mm wide; petiole 8 mm long; young foliage a medium green; mature foliage glabrous, medium to dark green, in autumn yellow-orange turning to crimson.

Flowers

Petals 23 mm long by 2 mm wide, straight, lightly curled and crimped, light red grading to coppery orange at tip; calyx bright maroon-red; overall a warm reddish, coppery orange; sweet scent; flowering early through midwinter.

Hamamelis ×*intermedia* 'Rubin' (Böhlje, ca. 1967)

Synonym

Hamamelis japonica 'Rubin'

Comments

Raised, named, and introduced by Böhlje Baumschulen, this is an excellent addition to the range of red-flowered cultivars and likely to prove to be one of the best. Received three stars in the Royal Boskoop Horticultural Society trial in 2002, which only goes to endorse my opinion of this plant. Tim

Brotzman agrees that this plant shows excellent red colour in the flowers and performs well in Ohio.

Growth habit

Rounded, growth vigorous yet twiggy, making a bush 4 m tall by 4 m wide.

Foliage

Leaves obovate, margin crenate in upper half, shallowly crenate below, apex acute, base oblique, 100 mm long by 65 mm wide; petiole 10 mm long; young foliage medium yellowish green, lightly flushed maroon; mature foliage glabrous, dark green, in autumn yellow flushed orange.

Flowers

Petals 18 mm long by 2 mm wide, curled and crimped, red; calyx red-purple; overall a good clear red; little scent; flowering mid to late winter.

Hamamelis ×*intermedia* 'Rubinstar' (Helmers, 1980)

Comments

Raised, named, and introduced by Helmerich Helmers, Westerstede, Germany, because of the really good autumn foliage, although the flowers are not too much to write home about.

Growth habit

Rounded bush when young, later more spreading, 3 m tall by 3.5 m wide.

Foliage

Leaves ovate-orbicular, margin shallowly crenate, apex blunt, base obliquely cordate, 90 mm long by 75 mm wide; petiole 15 mm long; young foliage light to medium green; mature foliage glabrous, dark green, in autumn brilliant crimson.

Flowers

Petals 18 mm long by 1.5 mm wide, curled, twisted and crimped, clear red; calyx purple-red; overall colour red; no scent; flowering mid to late winter.

Hamamelis ×*intermedia* 'Ruby Glow' (de Belder, 1953)

Synonyms

Hamamelis ×*intermedia* 'Adonis', *H. japonica* 'Flavopurpurascens Superba', *H. japonica* 'Rubra Superba'

Comments

A Kalmthout selection under the number K.981. Raised in 1935 from seed of *Hamamelis japonica* f. *flavopurpurascens* pollinated by *H. mollis* by Antoine Kort. Selected and named by de Belder in conjunction with the Boskoop nurserymen F. J. Grootendorst & Zonen and W. J. Hooftman. This was the first significant red-flowered cultivar to be raised, superseding *H.* ×*intermedia* 'Hiltingbury' and *H.* ×*intermedia* 'Carmine Red'; it is now eclipsed by other red cultivars, however. Received one star in the Royal Boskoop Horticultural Society trial in 2002. The original plant is still in Kalmthout alongside its sister *H.* ×*intermedia* 'Luna', obviously still in position from the nursery row when first planted out. Both plants are very large and probably represent some of the oldest hybrids in existence. There is also an excellent plant in the Wild Garden at the RHS Garden Wisley.

Growth habit

Bushy and upright, medium vigour, twiggy, making a bush 4 m tall by 3 m wide.

Foliage

Leaves orbicular, margin crenate in upper half, shallowly crenate below, apex blunt, base obliquely cordate, 70 mm long by 70 mm wide; petiole 10 mm long; young foliage medium green; mature foliage glabrous, dark green, in autumn yellow-orange tinted red.

Flowers

Petals 19 mm long by 1.5 mm wide, slightly curled and crimped, red lighter towards tip; calyx red-purple; overall a dull red; scent very faint; flowering mid to late winter.

Hamamelis ×*intermedia* 'Sarah' (de Belder, 1987)

Synonym

Hamamelis ×*intermedia* 'Sara'

Comments

A Hemelrijk selection under the number H.10555, raised by de Belder, and introduced by me in 1995. This particular cultivar is close to *Hamamelis japonica* in appearance, growth habit, flowers, and autumn colour.

Growth habit

Upright to a rounded bush, vigorous with many twiggy shoots, 4 m tall by 3.5 m wide.

Foliage

Leaf obovate, margin crenate in upper half, smooth to scarcely crenate below, apex acute, base oblique, 85 mm long by 60 mm wide; petiole 12 mm long; young foliage medium yellowish green; mature foliage glabrous, dark sage-green, in autumn yellow flushed orange-red; one of the few yellow-flowered cultivars to give autumn colour.

Flowers

Petals 19 mm long by 1 mm wide, twisted, curled and crimped, yellow flushed red-purple at base; calyx purple; overall a yellow lightly flushed red; scent fairly strong; flowering late winter to early spring.

Hamamelis ×*intermedia* 'Savill Starlight' (Bond, 1994)

Comments

Raised at the Savill Gardens, Windsor, England, named by John Bond, and introduced by me in 1995. This selection arose as a spontaneous seedling, not far from a plant of *Hamamelis japonica* 'Zuccariniana' probably pollinated by a nearby plant of *H.* ×*intermedia* 'Pallida'.

Growth habit

Spreading bush, moderate vigour, twiggy, 2.5 m tall by 3.5 m wide.

Foliage

Leaves broadly elliptic, margin shallowly crenate, apex blunt, base obliquely cordate, 90 mm long by 70 mm wide; petiole 6 mm long; young foliage a medium green; mature foliage glabrous, sage-green, in autumn yellow.

Flowers

Petals 18 mm long by 1.5 mm wide, slightly curled and crimped, pale yellow; calyx green with maroon flush; overall a pale sulphur-yellow; no scent; flowering in late winter.

Hamamelis ×intermedia 'Sister Jelena' (de Belder, 1998)

Synonym

Hamamelis ×intermedia 'Jelena's Sister'

Comments

A Kalmthout selection raised by de Belder under the number K.977. This selection has dull burnt orange flowers and the unfortunate habit of retaining dead leaves in the winter. It has long been known by those familiar with the witch hazels in Kalmthout as 'Jelena's Sister', this plant being similar to though duller than *Hamamelis ×intermedia* 'Jelena'. In most people's opinion, this plant is not worthy of naming but appeared in the book *Het Arboretum van Kalmthout*, by Jelena de Belder, Anne Verhaeghe, and Bie Wouters (1998), so has therefore been validly published.

Growth habit

Rounded, moderate growth, 3 m tall by 3 m wide.

Foliage

Leaves ovate-orbicular, margin shallowly crenate, apex blunt, base oblique, 115 mm long by 85 mm wide; petiole 10 mm long; young foliage a medium green; mature foliage glabrous, dark grey-green, little autumn colour of yellow, quickly going brown.

Flowers

Petals 24 mm long by 2 mm wide, slightly twisted and crimped, greyish orange; calyx greyish purple; overall colour of a dull burnt orange; scent faint; flowering mid through late winter.

Hamamelis ×*intermedia* 'Spanish Spider' (Kalmthout Arboretum, 2001)

Comments

A Kalmthout selection raised by Antoine Kort under the number K.7513 (since naming and the recataloguing of the plants in the arboretum, it has been renumbered). The name was chosen by the Scientific Committee of the Kalmthout Arboretum. Visitors to the arboretum, coming to see the witch hazel collection during the opening period of January and February 2001, were asked to give suggestions as to a name for this plant. One of the suggestions was 'Rusty Spider'; the committee liked this name but decided to change this proposal to the definitive name 'Spanish Spider'. "Spanish" was chosen because of the colour of the petals, according to the *RHS Colour Chart* as Spanish orange, the colour is not rusty. The form of the petals resembles the legs of a spider; a single petal looks like a single leg and a cluster of flowers a walking spider. The name was first published in June 2001 in *Nervatuur*, the magazine of Kalmthout Arboretum.

Growth habit

Upright, vigorous growth, 4 m tall by 3 m wide.

Foliage

Leaves orbicular, margin crenate in upper half, shallowly crenate below, apex acute, base obliquely cordate, 90 mm long by 80 mm wide; petiole 10 mm long; young foliage a medium yellowish green heavily flushed bronze; mature foliage glabrous, a light green, in autumn yellow quickly turning brown.

Flowers

Petals 26 mm long by 1 mm wide, narrow twisted and crimped, straw-yellow, flushed red fading from base to tip; calyx reddish maroon; overall colour crushed strawberry-yellow bicolour; no scent; flowering throughout midwinter.

Hamamelis ×*intermedia* 'Strawberries and Cream' (de Belder, 1986)

Synonym

Hamamelis ×*intermedia* 'Strawberry and Cream'

Comments

A Hemelrijk selection raised by de Belder under the number H.11140. This cultivar received its name because of the bicolour effect resembling strawberries splashed with cream and was introduced by me in 1990. The original plant grows to the left of one of the roads by the entrance gate to Hemelrijk. Received one star in the Royal Boskoop Horticultural Society trial in 2002.

Growth habit

Rounded, vigorous growth, making a bush 3.5 m tall by 3.5 m wide.

Foliage

Leaves orbicular, margin shallowly crenate, apex acute, base obliquely cordate, 115 mm long by 100 mm wide; petiole 12 mm long; young foliage a medium yellowish green flushed bronze; mature foliage glabrous, medium to dark green, in autumn yellow.

Flowers

Petals 20 mm long 2 mm wide, curled, slightly crimped, tip yellow grading to red-purple at base; calyx purple; overall a pale yellow-red bicolour; scent faint; flowering period mid through late winter.

Hamamelis ×*intermedia* 'Sunburst' (Veerman, 1967)

Synonym

Hamamelis mollis 'Sunburst'

Comments

Raised by Albert Doorenbos, one time superintendent of parks for The Hague, Holland. He sowed seeds of *Hamamelis mollis*, most probably in the 1950s, and this 'Sunburst' plant can still be seen growing in the Suiderpark, The Hague. Originally listed as *H. mollis* 'Sunburst' but this plant is obviously a hybrid. It is outstanding for its large yellow flowers but unfortunately suffers from interveinal necrosis on the leaves, some years hardly affected, others more so. Also retains dead leaves in winter, but grows out of this habit with age. Named and introduced to the trade by D. Veerman Jr., Boskoop, Holland, in 1967. Received two stars in the Royal Boskoop Horticultural Society trial in 2002, almost certainly downgraded because of the foliage problem.

Growth habit

Vase-shaped, vigorous growth, making a shrub 4 m tall by 3 m wide.

Foliage

Leaves ovate-orbicular, margin shallowly crenate, apex acute, base obliquely cordate, 90 mm long by 70 mm wide; petiole 10 mm long; young foliage dark yellowish green; mature foliage glabrous, dark green, leaves are often affected by interveinal necrosis leading to dead brown patches, early leaves affected, later ones not as much, no autumn colour.

Flowers

Petals 26 mm long by 2.5 mm wide, fairly straight, slightly crimped, yellow; calyx light claret-red; overall a clear pale yellow; no scent; flowering mid to late winter.

Hamamelis ×intermedia 'Swallow Hayes' (Edwards, 2000)

Comments

Named and introduced by Pat Edwards, one of the National Collection holders of *Hamamelis* in England. This particular plant was distributed out of Holland as *H. ×intermedia* 'Pallida'; although having nice yellow flowers and scented, it is inferior to the true 'Pallida' and not likely to be grown to any extent.

Growth habit

Vase-shaped when young, later more spreading, moderately vigorous, making a shrub 3 m tall by 3.5 m wide.

Foliage

Leaves ovate-orbicular, margin crenate in upper half, shallowly crenate below, apex acute, base obliquely cordate, 90 mm long by 70 mm wide; petiole 10 mm long; young foliage medium yellowish green; mature foliage glabrous, sage-green, in autumn yellow.

Flowers

Petals 17 mm long by 1.5 mm wide, slightly twisted and crimped, clear sulphur- to lemon-yellow with faint red tinting at base; calyx maroon-red; overall pale yellow, good scent but not as sweet or strong as *Hamamelis ×intermedia* 'Pallida'; flowering in midwinter.

Hamamelis ×intermedia 'Treasure Trove' (de Belder, 2002)

Comments

A Hemelrijk selection, raised by de Belder, under the number H.11419. Named by Jelena de Belder, Maurice Foster, Chris Sanders, and me in February 2002 after being admired for several years. The original plant grows in the open to the left of the road leading down to the *Hydrangea paniculata* collection; it has a spread of a good 9 m and is less than 3 m tall.

Growth habit

Horizontal spreading, vigorous, making a bush 2 m tall by 4 m wide.

Foliage

Leaves broadly elliptic, margin crenate in upper half, shallowly crenate below, apex acute, base oblique, 110 mm long by 65 mm wide; petiole 15 mm long; young foliage a light greyish green; mature foliage glabrous, sage-green, in autumn yellow.

Flowers

Petals 21 mm long by 1.5 mm wide, curled and crimped, bright yellow tinted red at base; calyx maroon-red; overall a deep golden yellow; no scent; flowering late winter.

Hamamelis ×intermedia 'Twilight' (van der Werf, 1997)

Comments

Raised, named, and introduced by Wim van der Werf, getting its name from the contrasting red and yellow flowers. It has an unfortunate habit of retaining dead leaves in winter, although this tendency reduces with age.

Growth habit

Rounded bush, vigorous growth, making a shrub 4 m tall by 4 m wide.

Foliage

Leaves ovate-orbicular, margin crenate in upper half, shallowly crenate below, apex acute, base oblique, 100 mm long by 80 mm wide; petiole 12 mm long; young foliage a medium yellowish green; mature foliage glabrous, dark green, no autumn colour.

Flowers

Petals 21 mm long by 2 mm wide, straight and slightly crimped, yellow with nearly complete red suffusion, on older plants the flower colour is a more uniform crimson-red with less yellow in the petals; calyx purple-red; overall an unusual effect with some flowers bicoloured and others clear red, from a distance crimson-red; no scent; flowering throughout midwinter.

Hamamelis ×intermedia 'Vesna' (de Belder, 1954)

Synonym

Hamamelis ×intermedia 'Vezna'

Comments

A Kalmthout seedling under the number K.957, raised by Antoine Kort, named by de Belder. Vesna is the Russian goddess of spring. This cultivar was introduced to the trade around 1970 by nurserymen in Boskoop, Holland. The original plant at Kalmthout is growing in a position which does not show this plant to best effect, just past the plants of *Hamamelis ×intermedia* 'Ruby Glow' and *H. ×intermedia* 'Luna'. The *H. ×intermedia* 'Vesna' is to the right of the path, with trees overhead, up against the boundary fence, and possibly best viewed from the road outside the arboretum. To my mind, this excellent cultivar has been overlooked by the nursery trade; I think it is one of the best in its colour group and should be more widely produced by nurseries. Received one star in the Royal Boskoop Horticultural Society trial in 2002.

Growth habit

Upright, ultimately making a vase-shaped bush, 4 m tall by 3 m wide.

Foliage

Leaves ovate-orbicular, margin shallowly crenate, apex blunt, base oblique, 95 mm long by 75 mm wide; petiole 10 mm long; young foliage medium yellowish green; mature foliage glabrous, dark green, in autumn shades of yellow, orange, and red.

Flowers

Petals 26 mm long by 1.5 mm wide, twisted and slightly crimped, yellow-orange, slight red tinting at base; calyx deep claret-red, slightly glossy; overall effect light orange; scent quite strong and sweet; flowering mid to late winter.

Hamamelis ×*intermedia* 'Westerstede' (Helmers, 1977)

Comments

Raised by Heinrich Bruns and named after the town in which he had his nursery; it was introduced by Helmers Baumschulen in 1977. This selection is similar in many respects to *Hamamelis* ×*intermedia* 'Arnold Promise', but in my opinion nowhere near such a good plant. *Hamamelis* ×*intermedia* 'Westerstede' is not to be dismissed, however, particularly in North America, where it outperforms *H.* ×*intermedia* 'Arnold Promise' in resistance to mildew in the south and cold hardiness in the north. Received one star in the Royal Boskoop Horticultural Society trial in 2002.

Growth habit

Upright bush, good vigour, making a shrub 3.5 m tall by 2.5 m wide.

Foliage

Leaves orbicular-obovate, margin shallowly crenate, apex acute, base oblique, 100 mm long by 80 mm wide; petiole 10 mm long; young foliage a light green; mature foliage glabrous, dull green, in autumn yellow.

Flowers

Petals 15 mm long by 1.5 mm wide, curled and crimped, yellow; calyx greenish brown; overall pale yellow; scent faint; flowering late winter to early spring.

Hamamelis ×intermedia 'Wiero' (van der Werf, 1989)

Comments

Raised and introduced by Wim van der Werf and named after his father. This cultivar is interesting because of its late, very pale yellow flowers. It is a plant that improves with age and it needs to be viewed closely or have a good background to show the flowers to best advantage. Tim Brotzman relates that in Ohio there is almost a shade of light green to the flowers; no others have this shade, to his knowledge, and it does stand out. It received two stars in the Royal Boskoop Horticultural Society trial in 2002.

Growth habit

Rounded to spreading bush, twiggy growth, compact 2.5 m tall by 3 m wide.

Foliage

Leaves orbicular-obovate, margin shallowly crenate, apex acute, base oblique, 100 mm long by 60 mm wide; petiole 10 mm long; young foliage a medium grey-green; mature foliage glabrous, dark green, in autumn yellow.

Flowers

Petals 17 mm long by 1.5 mm wide, curled, crimped, yellow; calyx yellow-green; overall very pale yellow; scent faint; flowering mid through late winter.

Hamamelis ×intermedia 'Winter Beauty' (Wada, 1962)

Comments

Raised, named, and introduced by Kochiro Wada, a nice cultivar, but somewhat susceptible to late spring frost damage; for this reason not propagated. *Hamamelis ×intermedia* 'Winter Beauty' was imported into Boskoop by Otto en Zonen in 1963, but only grown for a short while by the Dutch nursery trade because of its susceptibility to spring frost damage. According to Tomoo Wada, son of Kochiro Wada, this was a cross between *H. mollis* and *H. japonica* 'Zuccariniana', selected from many seedlings; he mentions that it is floriferous, with good yellow blossoms, and it flowers earlier than *H. mollis*.

Growth habit
Rounded bush, later more spreading, vigorous, making a shrub 3.5 m tall by 4 m wide.

Foliage
Leaves ovate-orbicular, margin shallowly crenate, apex blunt, base obliquely cordate, 100 mm long by 85 mm wide; petiole 10 mm long; young foliage a medium yellowish green; mature foliage glabrous, sage-green, in autumn yellow but not reliably so.

Flowers
Petals 24 mm long by 1.5 mm wide, twisted and crimped, yellow-orange flushed pale rose; calyx red-purple; overall a deep golden yellow; no scent; flowering mid to late winter.

Hamamelis ×*intermedia* 'Zitronenjette'

Comments
A cultivar of unknown origin, which I collected from Kalmthout Arboretum, Belgium, who had received it from a nursery in Germany.

Growth habit
Spreading, vigorous, making a shrub 3 m tall by 4 m wide.

Foliage
Leaves ovate-orbicular, margin shallowly crenate, apex blunt, base oblique, 95 mm long by 85 mm wide; petiole 15 mm long; young foliage medium yellowish green; mature foliage glabrous, light green, in autumn yellow.

Flowers
Petals 20 mm long by 1.5 mm wide, twisted and crimped, sulphur-yellow; calyx light maroon-red; overall colour a strong sulphur-yellow; no scent; flowering in late winter.

Other Hybrids

As well as hybrids between *Hamamelis mollis* and *H. japonica*, there are a few named hybrids which have *H. vernalis* as a parent. It is evident from work carried out at the Holden Arboretum, Kirtland, Ohio, that *H. vernalis* crosses very easily with other witch hazels that may be in flower at the time. As some are crosses of *H. vernalis* with *H.* ×*intermedia*, the parentage starts to become a little complex. I have therefore decided not to give them a hybrid epithet.

Tim Brotzman has this to say about these hybrids, "One of the things I find fairly distinctive with them is the overall floriferousness of the plants. If the number of flowers per stem were evaluated, irrespective of the size of individual flower, there is no doubt that these hybrids are much more profuse. Just think of *Hamamelis* 'Fireblaze' and *H.* 'Girard Orange' for instance." He also likes them for the cut flower market; they tend to grow faster, more slender stems and display more blooms than the Asian hybrids.

Hamamelis 'Amethyst' (Shadow, 2003)

Synonyms

Hamamelis vernalis 'Brotzman Purple', *H. vernalis* 'Purple Seedling'

Comments

In the early 1980s Tim Brotzman, of Madison, Ohio, collected seeds from the plants he had, namely *Hamamelis vernalis* 'Sandra', *H.* ×*intermedia* 'Ruby Glow', *H.* ×*intermedia* 'Arnold Promise', *H.* ×*intermedia* 'Pallida', and *H.* 'Brevipetala'. The resultant plants were subsequently planted out and, judging by their character, it was obvious many were pollinated by *H. vernalis* 'Sandra'. These plants had extreme variability: three or four had no stamens and looked like paint brushes, two were lavender-purple, one was prostrate, two were very late flowering, one was a yellow, and one he named 'Orange Encore'. Tim was quite amazed to see such variation in fewer than a hundred seedlings. The first of the two plants with lavender-purple flowers has been named 'Amethyst' by Don Shadow. The plant retains some foliage in winter and is somewhat prone to mildew in Ohio, according to Tim.

Growth habit

Upright, later a more rounded bush, moderately vigorous, twiggy, 3 m tall by 2.5 m wide.

Foliage

Leaves ovate-orbicular, margin crenate in upper half, shallowly crenate below, apex blunt, base oblique, 85 mm long by 60 mm wide; petiole 8 mm long; young foliage grey-green; mature foliage, dark grey-green, in autumn a brilliant scarlet.

Flowers

Petals 14 mm long by 1.5 mm wide, fairly straight, crimped, reddish purple with a hint of violet; calyx dark purplish maroon; overall a light purple-red colour; spicy scent; flowering midwinter.

Hamamelis 'Brevipetala' (Chenault, 1935)

Synonyms

Hamamelis mollis 'Aurantiaca', *H. mollis* 'Brevipetala'

Comments

Raised and introduced by the Chenault Nursery, Orleans, France, in 1935. I had long suspected this as being a hybrid between *Hamamelis mollis* and *H. vernalis* because of the glaucous underside to the leaves. The statement by Chenault that it was raised from seed, brought from China by a French missionary, led me to be cautious in pronouncing it a hybrid. To my knowledge, until quite recently seed of *H. mollis* has not been introduced from China since E. H. Wilson's introductions. Isozyme work at the Holden Arboretum, Kirtland, Ohio, has now proved beyond all reasonable doubt that it is a hybrid between *H. vernalis* and *H. mollis.* The name 'Brevipetala' first appears in a bulletin of the Morton Arboretum dated 1938. Most plants in cultivation suffer from a virus which causes leaf distortion. I have managed to find a plant which seems to be virus free. Propagations from this plant have so far remained free from visible signs of virus with me for eight years now. Tim Brotzman recounts that his oldest plant is now twenty-seven years old and continues to throw the occasional virus-plagued limb every year.

Growth habit

Upright when young, becoming a rounded bush with age, moderate vigour, making a shrub 3.5 m tall by 3.5 m wide.

Foliage

Leaves ovate-orbicular, margin shallowly crenate, apex acute, base obliquely cordate, 115 mm long by 90 mm wide; petiole 20 mm long; young foliage a yellowish green; mature foliage, somewhat pubescent medium green, glaucous underneath, in autumn yellow.

Flowers

Petals 12 mm long by 1.5 mm wide, straight, slightly crimped, yellow-orange; calyx reddish purple; overall a deep golden yellow; strong and spicy scent; flowering early to midwinter.

Hamamelis 'Danny' (de Belder, 1983)

Synonyms

Hamamelis 'Dany', *H.* ×*intermedia* 'Danny', *H.* ×*intermedia* 'Dany'

Comments

A Kalmthout selection under the number K.7511, raised and named by Robert and Jelena de Belder after their son. This is one of the first *Hamamelis vernalis* hybrids to receive a name. The original plant still grows at Kalmthout, positioned at the apex of a bed where two paths converge. It can look spectacular when the sun shines through the red flowers.

Growth habit

Vase-shaped, with age becoming a more spreading bush, moderate vigour, making a shrub 3.5 m tall by 3.5 m wide.

Foliage

Leaves ovate-orbicular, margin crenate in upper half, shallowly crenate below, apex acute, base obliquely cordate, 100 mm long by 75 mm wide; petiole 10 mm long; young foliage a light grey-green; mature foliage glabrous, dark grey-green, in autumn some orange-red tints.

Flowers

Petals 13 mm long by 1 mm wide. Slightly twisted, curled and crimped, dark red at base paling towards tip; calyx purple-red; overall good dark red; spicy scent; flowering throughout midwinter.

Hamamelis 'Dishi' (de Belder, 2003)

Synonym

Hamamelis ×*intermedia* 'Dishi'

Comments

A Hemelrijk selection raised by de Belder under the number H.10688, this cultivar was named using the Slovenian word for fragrant. Apart from the very good scent, there is little merit with the flowers in this cultivar; autumn colour of the foliage is good, however. The original plant grows to the right of the road leading out from the houses and buildings at Hemelrijk, overhanging the ditch, where the scent can be enjoyed from the road.

Growth habit

Spreading, moderate vigour, making a shrub 3 m tall by 3.5 m wide.

Foliage

Leaves broadly elliptic, margin crenate in upper half, smooth to scarcely crenate below, apex acute, base oblique, 120 mm long by 70 mm wide; petiole 10 mm long; young foliage a medium yellowish green faintly flushed bronze; mature foliage glabrous, sage-green, glaucous beneath, in autumn orange-red.

Flowers

Petals 17 mm long by 1.5 mm wide, straight, slightly crimped, yellow-orange suffused red at base to midway; calyx maroon-red; overall a coppery orange-red; scent strong and spicy yet sweet; flowering throughout midwinter.

Hamamelis 'Doerak' (van der Werf, 1991)

Synonym

Hamamelis mollis 'Doerak'

Comments

Raised from a seed sown in 1980 and named and introduced by Wim van der Werf in 1991, this interesting cultivar has an extraordinary intensity of flower colour but unfortunately has a tendency to retain dead brown leaves during the winter. Received two stars in the Royal Boskoop Horticultural Society trial in 2002.

Growth habit

Rounded bush, making a shrub 3 m tall by 3 m wide.

Foliage

Leaves orbicular, margin shallowly crenate, apex blunt, base obliquely cordate, 75 mm long by 75 mm wide; petiole 5 mm long; young foliage medium green; mature foliage somewhat pubescent, dark green, glaucous beneath, no autumn colour.

Flowers

Petals 15 mm long by 2 mm wide, curled and crimped, celandine-yellow; calyx pale maroon-red flushed green; overall a deep golden yellow; sweet scent; flowering mid through late winter, this cultivar has the longest flowering period of any witch hazel I have come across.

Hamamelis 'Fire Blaze' (de Belder, 1993)

Synonym

Hamamelis ×intermedia 'Fire Blaze'

Comments

A Hemelrijk selection raised by de Belder under the number H.10630. The original plant grows near *Hamamelis ×intermedia* 'Agnes'; it is a large spreading plant. Each year this cultivar flowers late and profusely with a glowing orange colour, and is hence aptly named. It is one of Jelena de Belder's favourites. The *H. vernalis* in its parentage shows in the intensity of the warm orange flower colour.

Growth habit

Vase-shaped when young, later more spreading, vigorous, making a shrub 3 m tall by 3.5 m wide.

Foliage

Leaves ovate-orbicular, margin crenate in upper half, smooth to scarcely crenate below, apex acute, base oblique, 100 mm long by 70 mm wide; petiole 8 mm long; young foliage a light yellowish green; mature foliage glabrous, medium green, in autumn yellow.

Flowers

Petals 15 mm long by 2 mm wide, fairly straight, very slightly crimped, red at base fading to straw-orange at tip; calyx bright maroon-red; overall a bright coppery orange; strong spicy scent; flowering late winter through early spring.

Hamamelis 'Girard Orange' (Girard, ca. 1980)

Synonym

Hamamelis ×*intermedia* 'Girard's Orange'

Comments

Raised by Peter Girard Jr. of Saybrook, Ohio, and named in 1990. Many years ago Girard imported some witch hazels from Holland and planted several varieties in a row. The row contained *Hamamelis vernalis* types, *H.* ×*intermedia* cultivars and *H. mollis.* It was from these that he saved open-pollinated seed, which was subsequently sown and from which this selection was made.

Growth habit

Rounded bush becoming more spreading, vigorous, making a shrub 3 m tall by 3.5 m wide.

Foliage

Leaves orbicular-obovate, margin crenate in upper half, smooth to scarcely crenate below, apex blunt, base oblique, 95 mm long by 70 mm wide; petiole 12 mm long; young foliage light green with faint bronze flush; mature foliage glabrous, dark green, shiny and glaucous underneath, in autumn purple and finally red.

Flowers

Petals 13 mm long by 1.5 mm wide, straight and crimped, pale straw colour suffused red at base fading towards tip; calyx bright maroon-red; overall a pale orange; faint scent; flowering mid through late winter.

Hamamelis 'Kim' (de Clerck, 1983)

Comments

A selection raised by de Belder at Hemelrijk and given to Wardje de Clerck and named by him after his daughter. This cultivar has not been introduced to the trade as yet and was only seen by me recently. I include this cultivar here as it looks more like a *Hamamelis vernalis* hybrid, rather than *H.* ×*intermedia*. Close observation in the next year or two will confirm whether this is true.

Growth habit

Vase-shaped when young, tending to spread later, moderate vigour, 3 m tall by 3 m wide.

Foliage

Leaves ovate-orbicular, margin crenate in top half, shallowly crenate below, apex acute, base oblique, 95 mm long by 70 mm wide; petiole 10 mm long; young foliage a grey-green; mature foliage glabrous, sage-green, in autumn orange-red.

Flowers

Petals 15 mm long by 1.5 mm wide, slightly twisted and curled, crimped, dark red, slightly paler at tip; calyx deep maroon-red; overall a good clear red; scent strong like *Hamamelis vernalis*; flowering mid to late winter.

Hamamelis 'Lansing' (van der Werf, 1988)

Synonym

Hamamelis vernalis 'Lansing'

Comments

Raised and named by Wim van der Werf after the road in Boskoop where he lives. This is a seedling of *Hamamelis* 'Brevipetala', which has obviously backcrossed with *H. vernalis*, in my opinion.

Growth habit

Rounded bush, moderately vigorous, making a shrub 3.5 m tall by 3.5 m wide.

Foliage

Leaves orbicular-obovate, margin crenate in upper half, smooth to scarcely crenate below, apex acute, base oblique, 110 mm long by 65 mm wide; petiole 15 mm long; young foliage light yellowish green; mature foliage glabrous, dull sage-green, in autumn yellow.

Flowers

Petals 11 mm long by 1.5 mm wide, slightly curled, strongly crimped, dull coppery red; calyx maroon-red; overall a deep coppery red colour; scent faint; flowering throughout midwinter.

Hamamelis 'Rochester' (Fennichia, ca. 1960)

Synonyms

Hamamelis mollis 'Rochester Superba', *H. mollis* 'Superba', *H. mollis* superbum

Comments

A selection raised at Rochester Park, New York, first mentioned by Richard Fennichia in 1960 as *Hamamelis mollis superbum*, a form with reddish flowers. Like *H.* 'Brevipetala', this is a hybrid between *H. mollis* and *H. vernalis.* Tim Brotzman comments that it often retains its dead leaves and can get mildew; it is probably, however, the most overpowering with its scent of any that he grows. A very useful cultivar in that it has a strong sweet scent and is the first hybrid to come into flower, usually the first week of December at my nursery in Kent, England.

Growth habit

Spreading, moderate vigour, making a shrub 3 m tall by 3.5 m wide.

Foliage

Leaves ovate-orbicular, margin shallowly crenate, apex acute, base obliquely cordate, 110 mm long by 85 mm wide; petiole 12 mm long; young foliage a light yellowish green; mature foliage somewhat pubescent, grey-green, underside of leaf glaucous, in autumn yellow; can also suffer from the same virus problem as *Hamamelis* 'Brevipetala'.

Flowers

Petals 13 mm long by 1.5 mm wide, mainly straight, slightly crimped, red at base grading to light orange at tip; calyx dull light red; overall a coppery orange; strong and spicy scent; flowering early through midwinter.

Chapter 8

The Development of Hybrid Witch Hazels

Hamamelis ×*intermedia* is a hybrid group between *H. mollis* Oliv. and *H. japonica* Sieb. & Zucc. which has occurred spontaneously only in cultivation, the two species being widely separated in their natural distribution. *Hamamelis* ×*intermedia* arose initially at three sites, the Arnold Arboretum, United States; the Kalmthout Arboretum, Belgium; and Charlottenlund Botanic Garden, Denmark. Since the first recorded hybrids arose, others have occurred at various places, mainly in Europe but also in Japan. As breeding programmes have progressed, many of these hybrids are not primary (from the two species) but are second, third, and even fourth generation progeny of *H.* ×*intermedia* cultivars. Several of these are much closer in appearance to the original parents and may be mistaken for forms of either *H. mollis* or *H. japonica*.

Hybrids of other parentage have also arisen in cultivation. *Hamamelis vernalis*, for instance, has naturally crossed with *H. mollis*, *H.* ×*intermedia*, *H. japonica*, and possibly *H. virginiana*. Some selections of crosses of *H. vernalis* with *H. mollis* and *H.* ×*intermedia* have been named. In North America there has been some successful crosses of *H. virginiana* with the Asian hybrids. In this chapter I chronicle the times and places of introductions and the people responsible for them.

Arnold Arboretum

This is where the first recorded *Hamamelis* ×*intermedia* hybrid arose. This hybrid was first raised in 1929, from seed collected the previous year by William Judd, the Arnold Arboretum's propagator at the time. The seed came from two *H. mollis* plants growing in the arboretum, one a plant received from Veitch, from the Maries introduction, and the other from a plant raised from seed collected by E. H. Wilson in 1907. These seeds were sown and seven seedlings survived to flowering. None of these plants proved to be true *H. mollis*, instead being intermediate between *H. mollis* and *H. japonica* (several plants of which were growing nearby in the arboretum). The plants showed considerable variation in the amount of pubescence and size and shape of leaves. The flowers varied in colour from reddish through coppery orange to yellow. Some bloomed sparsely, others retained their dead leaves. The epithet ×*intermedia* was applied to the hybrids by Alfred Rehder in 1945, after observing the plants for some years.

One proved to be outstanding and was given the cultivar name 'Arnold Promise' in 1963. The identity of the male parent was not precisely recorded, but plants of *Hamamelis japonica* var. *flavopurpurascens* and *H. japonica* 'Zuccariniana' were all growing near the maternal *H. mollis* plants. The growth habit and leaf shape of *H.* ×*intermedia* 'Arnold Promise' would suggest *H. japonica* 'Zuccariniana' as being the likely parent. After initial assessment, the original plant was planted to the side of the administration building, and after forty-seven years it measured 5.1 m tall by 5.4 m wide. It is no longer there, unfortunately, as it was sacrificed when the building was extended.

Hybrids between *H. mollis* and *H. japonica* 'Zuccariniana' appeared elsewhere in Rehder's own garden, where the two parent species were growing alongside each other. Spontaneous seedlings appeared almost every year and always proved to be hybrids. Nothing is recorded as to the fate of these seedlings; presumably they were not of sufficient merit to be grown on.

Charlottenlund Botanical Garden

Johan Lange of the Charlottenlund Botanical Garden noted that seeds of *Hamamelis mollis* were sown in the garden as early as the 1920s, but no record ensues as to their fate. The only seedlings that were successfully grown resulted from a sowing in 1934. After World War II one of these seedlings (number T40) was selected by Lange as being superior to the others. The female parent was a *H. mollis* that was planted in the gardens, which originated from Hesse's Nursery in Germany. Growing close by were three plants of *H. japonica*, one of which was undoubtedly the male parent. In 1953 Lange named the plant *H. japollis* 'Nina' (a synonym of *H.* ×*intermedia* 'Nina'), for the wife of Dr. C. Syrach Larsen, who was responsible for sowing the seeds. Unfortunately, during the late 1970s and early 1980s four different clones were distributed from Denmark to Holland, all purported to be 'Nina'. It was not until 1990 that Wim van der Werf and I obtained true stock from Denmark and were subsequently able to identify the correct clone among the four available in the trade.

Kalmthout Arboretum

In 1856 a Belgian nurseryman named Charles van Geert moved his nursery from the growing city of Antwerp to Kalmthout, on a 1.5-ha piece of land. The soil, being sandy and acid, was ideal for growing ericaceous plants and conifers (a few of which can still be seen today). After van Geert died in 1896, Antoine Kort took over in 1897 and was in charge of the nursery until his death in 1951.

In 1902 Kort started the arboretum, calling it the Société Horticole de Clampthout, and he extended the nursery, which was run successfully until the beginning of World War I. During this period up to the war, the nursery flourished and Kort had thirty-six employees, with much of the production of woody plants going to Germany and the United States. Things started to go wrong after the war, however. Germany was bankrupt, so that market dried up, and the United States was very concerned about importing plant diseases, which meant that Kort had lost most of his customer base by 1918. Some parts of the nursery were sold off to enable the nursery to survive. The recession of the 1930s led to further decline; ornamentals were not in demand, as people wanted useful plants such as fruit trees. During World War II, German tanks damaged much of the nursery. After the war Kort was getting old and the nursery fell into a dilapidated state.

With the help of his head gardener, Piet van Ginderen, Kort raised some seedlings from a plant of *Hamamelis japonica* var. *flavopurpurascens* after World War I. In 1935 he made some tentative descriptions of the seedlings, but did not name any. He selected a hybrid, which was initially called *H. japonica* var. *rubra superba*, and this was introduced by the Moerheim Nursery of Dedemsvaart, Holland, in 1946. This plant was later given the name *H. ×intermedia* 'Ruby Glow' by H. J. Grootendorst and W. J. Hooftman.

In 1952 George and Robert de Belder took over the dilapidated Kalmthout Arboretum. Nearly twenty years after Kort's initial attempts to describe the seedlings, Robert found his notes. From these Robert was able to identify the plants in the garden, and he named four of them: *Hamamelis ×intermedia* 'Adonis' (soon changed to 'Ruby Glow', 1953) and, in conjunction with the Boskoop nurserymen F. J. Grootendorst & Zonen and W. J. Hooftman, *H. ×intermedia* 'Jelena', 'Luna', and 'Vesna' (all 1954). The only original plant not alive today is 'Jelena'.

Jelena Kovacic had a particular interest in witch hazels. After studying agriculture in her native Slovenia and qualifying as an agronomist, she decided to travel and worked for a nursery in Elmshorn, Germany. In January 1954 a delivery of *Hamamelis* arrived from Boskoop, and when she saw the spidery flowers opening in the winter, she was struck by their beauty and hardiness. At that moment a lifelong interest in the plants was kindled. Six months later, as a student at Kalmthout, she met George and Robert de Belder. Robert and Jelena fell in love and married soon after.

At that time Kalmthout was still in a neglected state and very overgrown in parts. Robert, however, was able to show Jelena some of the large plants, two *Hamamelis mollis*, one near the house and the other in a part of the garden called the arboretum. A plant of *H. japonica* 'Zuccariniana' was close to the *H. mollis*, and several seedlings were raised from it. On the east side of the garden there was a large plant of *H. japonica* 'Aborea' and a plant of *H. japonica* var. *flavopurpurascens*. It was from this plant that Antoine Kort had raised his seedlings before World War II. There were thirteen sizeable hybrids planted down the eastern boundary of the arboretum. Robert and Jelena found these and started to clear the weeds and scrub from around them.

After they returned from a January honeymoon in Slovenia, her wish was fulfilled to see the witch hazels in full bloom. From this point on, Robert and Jelena were very keen on sowing seeds of *Hamamelis*, and within two years they had around 2500 seedlings growing in nursery beds. Some were planted on the eastern side of the garden with Kort's hybrids; the majority, however, were taken to Hemelrijk in 1961, shortly after Robert and Jelena bought the estate. Over the years, the best hybrids were selected and planted in their current locations in Hemelrijk.

Selections were made from both Kort's hybrids and their own. Of the seedlings raised by Kort and the de Belders and planted at Kalmthout, around forty or so remain today. From these, besides 'Ruby Glow', 'Luna', and 'Vesna' already mentioned, the following seven have been named by the de Belders: *Hamamelis* ×*intermedia* 'Diane' (1969), 'Primavera' (1969), 'Danny' (1983), 'Limelight' (1984), 'Adieu' (1992), 'Parasol' (1995), and 'Sister Jelena' (1998). More recently, the Scientific Committee for Kalmthout Arboretum, which meets to advise on all aspects of running and planning future developments for the garden, have named two cultivars, *H.* ×*intermedia* 'Spanish Spider' (2001) and 'Antoine Kort' (2002), the latter in recognition of the man who first raised hybrid seedlings at Kalmthout.

Hemelrijk

This unique place is a private arboretum started by Robert and Jelena de Belder in the 1960s, when they acquired the estate in Essen, Belgium. The name Hemelrijk means "Kingdom of Heaven," very appropriate for such a wonderful place. They moved to live at Hemelrijk after deciding to hand over Kalmthout and the running of it to the city of Antwerp in 1993. In the 1960s and 1970s they planted around 2500 plants of *Hamamelis* at Hemelrijk that had resulted from seed saved from the best clones in Kalmthout. In addition, around 1970 they moved some sizeable plants from Kalmthout when they were fifteen years old. As the plants began to flower the inferior ones were weeded out; today there are around a hundred hybrid witch hazels from thirty to forty-five years of age.

Twenty-two *Hamamelis ×intermedia* raised at Hemelrijk have been named: 'Early Bird' (1984), 'Birgit' (1986), 'Strawberries and Cream' (1986), 'Sarah' (1987), 'Harry' (1988), 'Orange Peel' (1988), 'Copper Cascade' (1993), 'Livia' (1993), 'Fire Blaze' (1993), 'Ripe Corn' (1995), 'Gingerbread' (1995), 'Agnes' (1996), 'John' (1996), 'Georges' (1999), 'Robert' (2000), 'Frederic' (2000), 'Citronella' (2002), 'Cyrille' (2002), 'Ninotchka' (2002), 'Treasure Trove' (2002), and 'Dishi' (2003), as well as *H. japonica* 'Canary Yellow' (2001). Some of these hybrids are destined to be the leading cultivars of the future.

The following is an account of Jelena de Belder's thoughts on selecting *Hamamelis* cultivars: "To select *Hamamelis* takes time and uses a lot of space. It is best to start evaluating seedlings after twenty-five years, although they start to flower well after ten years. They reach their typical growth habit after twenty-five years and a final selection should be made after forty years." Mrs. de Belder took her time in making selections, and in recent years five valuable new cultivars have been named: 'Ripe Corn', 'Robert', 'Frederic', 'Georges', and 'Gingerbread'. She also asks the question, "Is there room for more, perhaps a compact cultivar for modern gardens or a good treelike selection?" Whatever the future, growing and selecting *Hamamelis*, has given her a lot of pleasure over the years.

Hakoneya Nursery

The late Kochiro Wada was responsible for selecting at least two excellent clones of *Hamamelis mollis*, namely 'Iwado' and 'Imperialis', besides many other plants. He was an exceptional breeder and raiser of new plants. Two hybrids came from this nursery and were raised by Wada. The first of these was called *Hamamelis* ×*intermedia* 'Winter Beauty' (1962) and was introduced into Holland, whence it soon made its way to England. A second cultivar, 'Improved Winter Beauty', was introduced to England in 1975 by Chris Sanders. This cultivar was not propagated and is thought to have been lost to cultivation in England. Attempts to trace the five plants to where they were sold indicated they were no longer in existence.

In 1980, however, Tim Brotzman of Madison, Ohio, imported from Japan graft material of three plants, 'Winter Beauty', 'Iwado', and an unnamed plant. David Leach, a good friend of Tim, had known Kochiro Wada well but Wada had recently died. Through another of Leach's friends in Japan, Dr. Hideo Suzuki, propagation material of the abovementioned plants was obtained through the good auspices of Kochiro Wada's son, Toomoo. The scion material came in late winter, almost too late for grafting, from Dr. Suzuki—Toomoo had been prevented from collecting them because of deep snow in the mountains where the mother plants were situated.

Toomoo Wada is a chemist, but he continued to sell plants for a period of time after his father's retirement and subsequent death. Initially he sold plants from the abandoned Hakoneya Nursery; when they ran out he sourced plants from other nurseries in Japan and exported for a few years, then ceased all trading. Had it not been for this importation, however, the fine witch hazel *Hamamelis* ×*intermedia* 'Glowing Embers' would have been lost. 'Iwado' and the unnamed plant proved to be the same clone. The name 'Iwado' had been given to a clone of *H. mollis* by Wada and was imported into the United States by the U.S. National Arboretum (see chapter 6). This means the clone that Tim Brotzman has could possibly be 'Improved Winter Beauty', agreeing as it does with the limited description given by Toomoo Wada. As the situation is quite confused and the full story is unlikely to be unravelled, I have given this plant the cultivar name 'Glowing Embers' (1999).

Hillier Nurseries Ltd.

This famous nursery was started by Edwin Hillier in 1864 with 0.8 ha (2 acres) of land in Winchester, Hampshire, England. This nursery was known for supplying the largest range of woody and herbaceous plants available anywhere. This particularly was the case when Sir Harold Hillier was running the nursery; he collected plants on his travels around the world and started the arboretum, now run by Hampshire County Council, which contains one of the largest collections of woody plants found in one location.

Four generations on from Edwin Hillier and still a family run business, the nursery is currently one of the largest in the United Kingdom and today mainly supplies plants to garden centres and landscapers.

Five hybrids have been raised or selected at Hillier Nurseries Ltd. *Hamamelis ×intermedia* 'Carmine Red' (1934) and 'Hiltingbury' (ca. 1945) were selected from a batch of seedlings of *H. japonica* which had been lined out in the Chandlers Ford Nursery. Three yellow-flowered plants were named and introduced later, 'Moonlight' (1960), received from Exbury Gardens as *H. ×intermedia* 'Pallida'; 'Allgold' (ca.1973); and 'Advent' (1979). The origins of the latter two are unknown.

Westerstede, Germany

In the development of *Hamamelis ×intermedia* cultivars, the importance of this area in Germany has not been fully recognized and needs to be mentioned here. The information I have is not as complete as I would wish, but the output of named cultivars is, in my reckoning, second only in importance to Kalmthout and Hemelrijk.

One nurseryman in the area stands out as a raiser of *Hamamelis*, Heinrich Bruns. Until the late 1970s a nursery was operating in Westerstede called Gebr. Bruns (the Brothers Bruns). One of the brothers in the firm won a few million marks in the lottery, which changed his lifestyle and caused problems with the partnership, and the nursery was wound up. The brother responsible for raising the witch hazel hybrids was Heinrich. After World War II he raised many plants from seed, and perhaps forty or so grew to maturity. The stock of hybrids was sold to other nurserymen in the Westerstede area (notably Böhlje, Helmers, and Wieting) and Hachmann in Pinneberg. Some hybrids were also sold to the public, and large unnamed plants can be seen in gardens in the city. I can recall seeing some large examples in people's gardens while being driven around Westerstede by Helmerich Helmers. As far as I can ascertain, Heinrich Bruns died around 1990 and was quite ill for some years before that. All breeding and selection work was almost certainly done prior to 1985. He has left a superb legacy of witch hazel cultivars for people to enjoy, and we are grateful to him for that.

Some of Bruns's hybrids were named and introduced by the abovementioned nurseries or Dutch nurseries. The following cultivars are attributable to Bruns: *Hamamelis ×intermedia* 'Orange Beauty' (1965), 'Old Copper' (1970), 'Barmstedt Gold' (1975), 'Westerstede' (1977), 'Brandis' (1985), 'Bernstein' (1999), and 'Heinrich Bruns' (2003). Six or seven other cultivars were raised by other nurserymen in the area, namely Böhlje, 'Rubin' (1967), 'Böhlje's Feuerzauber' (1977) and 'Ostergold' (1977); Helmers, 'Rubinstar' (1980); Sanstede, 'Friesia' (1975); Hesse, 'Feuerzauber' (1958); and 'Zitronenjette' (nursery unknown).

The RHS Garden Wisley

This garden in Surrey, England, is one of the most famous in the United Kingdom. It houses probably the largest collection of plants, of all types, grown at any one location. Witch hazels are an important feature of the garden and a reasonably comprehensive collection is planted mainly on Battleston Hill and in the wild garden. Very little raising or breeding has been carried out here. However, this garden will always be remembered as the source of *Hamamelis* ×*intermedia* 'Pallida', the most famous hybrid cultivar, and the original plant still grows on Battleston Hill. Originally called *H. mollis* 'Pallida', it has now been shown to be an *H.* ×*intermedia* cultivar. The origin of the plant was not recorded, but for the most likely explanation, see chapter 7.

Albert Doorenbos

Doorenbos was superintendent of parks for The Hague, Holland. In the late 1950s he sowed seeds of *Hamamelis mollis*. From this *H.* ×*intermedia* 'Sunburst' (still growing in The Hague) was named, and subsequently introduced by D. Veerman Jr. in 1967. *Hamamelis* ×*intermedia* 'Gimborn's Perfume' (1984) is most likely to have come from the same source.

Wim van der Werf

He is a nurseryman in Boskoop, The Netherlands, who is a good friend of mine and holds the National Collection for The Netherlands. This collection is planted on a piece of land surrounded by canals, and to visit the collection one has to go on a boat from the main nursery site. The collection was used for the recent trial (2002) of witch hazel cultivars by the Judging Committee of the Royal Boskoop Horticultural Society. Wim has sown seeds and raised and named the following four cultivars: *Hamamelis* ×*intermedia* 'Wiero' (1989), 'Doerak' (ca. 1991), 'Twilight' (1997), and 'Andrea' (2002).

Johan van Heijningen

A retired schoolteacher living in Breda, Holland, van Heijningen has raised some exceptional cultivars by sowing seed from *Hamamelis ×intermedia* 'Arnold Promise', 'Jelena', 'Vesna', and 'Pallida' in the main. To date, the following have been introduced: *H. ×intermedia* 'Angelly' (1985), 'Aphrodite' (1985), 'Aurora' (1985), 'Alexander' (1995), and 'Amanon' (2001). After the de Belders and Bruns, van Heijningen is the most important individual in the development of witch hazel hybrids. His nursery site contains many hundreds of seedlings, which he has been evaluating over the last 30 years, and he consistently has adhered to his selection criteria of good flowers, growth habitat, and good scent.

Brotzman Nursery

In 1980 Tim Brotzman sowed seeds of mainly *Hamamelis vernalis* 'Sandra', *H. ×intermedia* 'Ruby Glow', *H. ×intermedia* 'Pallida', *H. ×intermedia* 'Jelena', and *H.* 'Brevipetala'. From the resultant seedlings, the following two cultivars have been selected: *H. ×intermedia* 'Orange Encore' (1995) and *H.* 'Amethyst' (2003).

Future Developments in Witch Hazel Breeding

With more than 120 named cultivars of *Hamamelis* already in existence, one could argue that there is no further need to raise and name new cultivars. Fortunately, because of time and space required and the fact that witch hazels are not as popular as, say, roses, rhododendrons, camellias, and magnolias in the woody plant world or hostas and hemerocallis in the herbaceous world, where far too many plants have been named, I do not think there will be an explosion of new cultivars. It is my feeling that the popularity and demand for witch hazels is unlikely to warrant more than twenty-five cultivars being produced by the nursery industry. That number would be for those nurseries that specialize to some extent in certain genera; the average retail nursery outlet or garden centre is unlikely to stock more than six to ten cultivars.

All existing named cultivars have derived from the process of raising quantities of seedlings from seed saved from open-pollinated plants; then a selection process takes place and plants are named. Precise breeding programmes are few and far between. The U.S. National Arboretum, Washington, D.C., and the Holden Arboretum, Kirtland, Ohio, have started specific breeding programmes, but as yet no named selections have arisen.

Any breeding and selection work must be undertaken with specific goals or aims in mind. With so many named cultivars already in existence, the last thing that is required is a host of new names for plants similar to existing cultivars. Flooding the market with new cultivars only dilutes the impact and popularity of the few really worthwhile ones that come out. Breeders must be careful about what is named and released, with any potential new cultivar undergoing trials and being tested and assessed by the breeders.

Having said this, however, there is always room for improvement. The following aims may prove useful for anyone wanting to raise and name new cultivars of witch hazels. First, the plant must be distinct from existing cultivars. If similar to existing cultivars, the plant must be an improvement in one or more characteristics. Points to consider are:

Morphology

Leaves: Size; shape; good colour; young, mature, and senescent stages; no retention of leaves in winter; yellow and purple foliage should be achievable.

Plant structure: Compact, weeping, treelike.

Floral traits: Colour, purple and white in addition to existing colours; floriferousness; extension of flowering season from midautumn through early winter; good flower size; strong, sweet scent.

Physiology

Propagation: Easily rooted from cuttings, responds to stool bed layering, can be successfully tissue cultured.

Pest and disease resistance: Particularly for mildew, certainly a goal in parts of North America.

The gene pool in witch hazels is wider than one may think initially. The possibilities with *Hamamelis vernalis* are good—purple flowers and rooting capability are two that spring to mind. *Hamamelis japonica* var. *megalophylla* could be used for healthier, glossy green foliage and good autumn colour. Repeating the original cross for *H.* ×*intermedia* using different *H. mollis* and *H. japonica* selections would give interesting results.

To date most, if not all, *Hamamelis* ×*intermedia* selections derive from *H. mollis* ('Jermyns Gold', Boskoop types) and *H. japonica* ('Rubra', 'Sulphurea', and 'Zuccariniana'). Second generation hybrids from *H.* ×*intermedia* do not extend the gene pool but merely recombine existing genes, which can in itself bring good results. Witness what we have already. The possibilities for future breeding are endless. What is important, however, is that selection and evaluation is critical and is judged by others, as well as the raiser, before naming and introducing new cultivars.

Breeding Procedures

New hybrid witch hazels can be produced in two ways. First, seed may be collected from good cultivars, sown, planted out, and evaluated. This is mainly what has happened so far, and worthwhile cultivars have arisen using this method. Second, plants may be intentionally cross-pollinated. This method allows breeders to work with the healthiest and most interesting parent plants. I am indebted to Ruth Dix at the U.S. National Arboretum for outlining to me her method used to obtain crosses of *Hamamelis virginiana* with Asiatic species and *H.* ×*intermedia* hybrids.

The flowers are usually harvested just as they are opening, before the anthers dehisce. On some cultivars the anthers dehisce before the flower opens. In that case, for pollen collection only, Dix goes ahead and uses them. If the anthers are too green or not mature enough, they will not dehisce as they dry—a thing to avoid. The flowers should be put in a moist container in the refrigerator until the anthers can be picked out, which is best done as soon as possible.

Dix picks the anthers out onto a piece of waxed weighing paper and then stores them in gelatine capsules in a refrigerator. The anthers usually dehisce as they dry, and the gelatine capsules tend to help by absorbing moisture. The capsules could be dried over silica gel or some such drying agent. The pollen can be stored in the gelatine capsules in a refrigerator (5°C, 40°F) for quite a time. Peter Dummer suggests warming up the flowers to dehisce the pollen. He removes the pollen and places it in a tube with a small quantity of silica gel, then stores the tubes in a vacuum flask.

For the actual pollination process, Dix emasculates the flowers as they are opening. The important thing is to emasculate before the anthers shed pollen. The branches or inflorescences are bagged before the flowers open and are kept bagged until the stigmas are no longer receptive. The flowers should be checked on a daily basis to see which need emasculation, as they do not all open at the same time. If some are missed and start to dehisce, then the whole flower should be removed to prevent contamination. When pollinating outdoors, the temperature needs to be above freezing and the sky sunny, as this is the only time pollinators would be visiting the flowers. A small camel-hair paintbrush is used to dip the stored pollen out of the gelatine capsule and paint it on the stigmas. The process is discontinued when the stigmas and styles turn brown. Using this method, Dix has produced hybrids of *Hamamelis virginiana* and *H.* ×*intermedia*.

Pollinating in the field is not an easy process when the weather is unpredictable and often inclement. When possible, Bob Marquard prefers to use plants in containers, which can be brought into a glasshouse for pollinating or pollen collection. In his experience, attempts at self-pollinating various selections of *Hamamelis* have not yielded mature fruits, which indicates that there must be some mechanism that prevents self-pollination. If *Hamamelis* are indeed self-incompatible, breeding can be conducted without emasculating the flowers.

The size and proximity of the stigma, being very close to the anthers, make emasculation a precise and tedious process. It should be possible to bring two potted plants together in a controlled environment and allow them to cross-pollinate naturally. This could be achieved by placing two plants in a netting-covered cage in a glasshouse and introducing blowflies to pollinate the flowers. This procedure would save a lot of work in manually transferring pollen with a camel-hair paintbrush.

Chapter 9

Propagation

As with all plants, there are two basic methods of propagation of witch hazels: sexual (regenerative) propagation from seed and vegetative propagation (for instance, cuttings, grafting, budding, layering, division, and micropropagation). Of the two methods, sexual reproduction brings the genes from both parents to combine in the offspring that are raised from seed. This can prove to be very interesting, with new and different forms being produced from the combination of genes of both parents. This may result in plants judged to be superior in many respects to the parents. Equally, however, the resultant plants can be disappointing, showing no improvement on either of the parents.

Sexual Propagation

There are three circumstances when one might want to raise witch hazels from seed. First, seedlings are raised for the production of grafting rootstocks by specialist production nurseries which sell the plants to other growers for budding or grafting. After stratifying the seed with a warm period followed by a cold period, it is sown on outdoor seedbeds with the aim of producing a population of 250 seedlings per square metre. The seed is then covered with a layer of grit to keep the seed in place, prevent capping of the soil, allow for gaseous exchange, allow water to percolate into the soil more easily, keep the seed cooler, and enable weeds to be pulled out more easily. During the first year in the United Kingdom, seedlings only make 20–30 cm of growth with a stem diameter, measured at the hypocotyl, of 3–4 mm. They are left in the seedbed for another year to make plants of 6–8 mm stem diameter, a more useful size for potting, grafting, or planting in the field for budding.

Raising plants of known wild provenance is important. If you have the opportunity, collect seed from the wild or obtain seed from other plant collectors or botanic gardens which have had plant collecting expeditions. The gene bank in cultivation, particularly with *Hamamelis japonica* and *H. mollis*, is not very great, and I am certain there are many interesting forms still to be collected in the wild.

Finally, sexual propagation techniques can be used to raise new cultivars. Before introduction, new cultivars need to be judged against existing cultivars so breeders can ensure what they have is distinct, or a definite improvement, if of the same type as an existing cultivar. However, by widening the gene pool, using *Hamamelis vernalis*, *H. virginiana*, and different forms of *H. mollis* and *H. japonica*, there is room to raise new, distinct, and interesting or showy cultivars.

Procedure for raising witch hazels from seed

The fruits should be collected in early autumn before natural seed dispersal occurs in mid to late autumn. The fruits should be placed in a thin layer in trays in a light airy place and covered with netting or newspaper to prevent the ejected seed from being lost. Once all the seed has been ejected, the fruits and seed can be sieved to obtain a clean seed sample.

When following a natural stratification period, seed can be sown any time after extraction, until the following early spring. The seed will then be exposed to a warm period during the summer, which breaks down the hard waxy seed coat, and during the following winter will receive a cold period to ripen the embryo before germination takes place the following spring (that is, eighteen months after harvesting). If sowing seed for the first time, there is an initial eighteen-month wait period; from then on, however, if sowing each year, there will be germination on a yearly basis.

The germination process can be speeded up by giving the seed a warm moist stratification for eight to ten weeks at 20°C (68°F) followed by a cold moist period of twenty weeks at 4°C (39°F). Special facilities are not required; in the home, the cupboard containing the hot water tank can be used for the warm treatment and a refrigerator for the cold treatment. Peat (or a peat alternative such as coir) is a good medium for this stratification treatment. The peat must be just moist, not wet. If you can squeeze moisture out of the peat, it is too wet. Mix the seed with the moist peat at 1 part seed to 3 parts peat by volume, place it in a polythene bag, and tie with a label describing the contents round the top of the bag. Because oxygen is vital to the stratification process, the bags should be opened every couple weeks; blow air inside, close the top, and vigorously shake. Once the stratification treatment has been carried out, the seed can be sown to germinate that summer. It should be noted, however, because the treatment takes more than six months, sowing may not take place until late spring. Subsequent germination and growth may not be all one would hope for unless grown in glasshouse conditions.

When sowing seed of small samples, such as wild collected seed, or if trying to raise new cultivars, it pays to sow into pans or seed trays or use the protection of a cold frame. It is important to net against birds taking the seed and to use traps to catch mice. Once a source of seed is found, it won't take long for it all to disappear.

Vegetative Propagation

All forms of vegetative propagation allow the reproduction of plants identical to the parent from which the propagation material is taken. This can be a great advantage in maintaining a particular plant which has proved to be outstanding. Such plants are usually given cultivar status and propagated up by nurseries for the public to purchase and enjoy. For the nurseryman, the only practical method at the moment is by grafting or budding the particular cultivar onto seed-raised rootstocks. Other vegetative methods are either too slow or unreliable for the nursery. For the gardener, who perhaps only requires to reproduce one new plant, layering is a good practical solution. Patience is required, however, as it takes a couple of years before the layer can be severed from the parent plant and grown on as an individual in its own right.

Cuttings

Witch hazels can be propagated by softwood cuttings, although they are not easy to root. Rooting, however, is not such a problem as successful overwintering of the cutting. The first winter is difficult, and even if successfully overwintered, plants from cuttings take much longer to make a saleable plant than from grafting or budding (see discussions of these techniques below).

Healthy stock plants are required for producing cutting material. The plants should be fed in the spring with a compound fertilizer to promote active vegetative growth. Make tip cuttings with three to four nodes, remove the lower leaves, and give the base of the cutting a slice wound. Cuttings are best taken before late spring to ensure good rooting and the build up of sufficient carbohydrate reserves for overwintering. A hormone treatment of 2500 ppm indolebutyric acid (IBA) in the form of a liquid dip or 0.8 per cent IBA in the form of a powder should be applied. The cuttings are then stuck in an open propagation media, something like 40 per cent peat moss, 30 per cent composted bark, and 30 per cent perlite. Root the cuttings in cell trays to avoid disturbance and damage to the roots when potting off the next spring.

Cuttings can be placed in several different environments. One commonly used technique is mist propagation, where nozzles above the propagation bench produce short bursts, misting and wetting the leaf surface of the cuttings. Control mechanisms are available to ensure that as the leaf of the cutting dries out, the nozzles will burst again to rewet the leaf. Alternatively, cuttings can be covered with a layer of clear polythene film, similar to that which covers clothes that have been to the dry-cleaners. Usually a tent is formed over the propagation bench and covered with milky polythene or shade material to prevent scorching from the sun. The polythene creates high humidity around the cutting. Once cuttings have formed roots, they are gradually weaned from the misting system or contact polythene film.

In both environments, a basal temperature of 20°C (68°F) is optimal. Rooting will take eight to ten weeks. Cuttings should be left in situ to overwinter. Keep them on the dry side, and do not pot them up until growth commences in the spring.

Grafting

The most important factor in any type of grafting or budding is to have a healthy, well-established rootstock. Scion material is ideally sourced from stock plants growing in the nursery. It is also possible to take material from the growing crop. The following grafting techniques are those most universally used in Europe.

To establish rootstocks, two-year-old plants of *Hamamelis virginiana* with a stem diameter of 4–6 mm should be raised or purchased. During the winter and early spring, pot up into 9-cm containers and place in a cold frame to establish a good root system. Some pruning of the roots is likely to be required to enable easy potting, and low side shoots should also be removed. Use a well-drained growing media; witch hazel roots dislike poor drainage conditions, which can only lead to root death. An approved pesticide should be incorporated in the growing media as a precaution against vine weevil damage. The following is a useful growing media:

3 parts medium-grade moss peat
1 part composted bark
2500 g controlled-release fertilizer per cubic metre
2400 g dolomitic limestone per cubic metre
300 g fritted trace elements per cubic metre
granular vine weevil pesticide at the approved rate

Other *Hamamelis* rootstocks have been used, namely *H. vernalis*. This is an undesirable rootstock, however, due to its inherent propensity to sucker. Plants grafted onto this stock will eventually be overgrown. The Isu tree, *Distylium racemosum*, another member of the *Hamamelidaceae*, has also been used. One advantage of this rootstock is a reduction in vigour, which is useful for small gardens. Because this plant is an evergreen, grafting can be carried out as late as midautumn, thus extending the grafting season. The rootstock is fairly easily raised from cuttings and is of sufficient size for grafting after two years. Rootstock of *D. racemosum* will sucker, but any sucker growth is easily seen from the top growth and is not as vigorous or strong. The main disadvantage of *D. racemosum* is that there is no reliable information available as to how long-lived the plants are on this rootstock.

Bench grafting can be carried out at two times of year: the dormant season and summer. Dormant season grafting is carried out in mid to late winter. The first operation is to bring the potted rootstocks into the glasshouse to dry off the containers. This is done with gentle heat and should commence about three weeks prior to grafting. The stocks should be brought inside in early winter to be ready for midwinter grafting. Drying off with gentle heat stimulates some root development.

Scion material should be collected from the stock plants and brought inside for the grafting operation. The normal type of graft for winter bench grafting onto pot-grown rootstocks is an apical whip graft. The stock is cut down to 6–8 cm above compost level. A three- to four-bud scion is prepared and the graft tied in with a rubber strip. The completed grafts can be waxed and stood on an open bench in the glasshouse or, if not waxed, placed in a low polythene tent. The most important instructions for dormant season grafting are:

Expose rootstock to gentle heat only (18–20°C, 65–70°F).
Control the moisture content in the container; the medium needs to be just moist, if too wet, flooding of the graft union can occur.
Do not begin serious watering until the scion is starting to make reasonable growth.
Minimize the risk of flooding the union by employing a side veneer or modified side veneer graft.

I personally have never been able to achieve as good results with winter grafting of witch hazels as those achieved with summer grafting, which is preferred by most people in the nursery trade. Sometimes dormant season grafting is necessary, however, if you are receiving material through the post. It is much easier and safer to send material in winter, as green material in summer can deteriorate rapidly. Material that is received from gardens and arboretums in the winter may have been taken from old plants and be thin, even the shoots two to three years old, with flower buds—a far cry from the well-grown young material from nursery stock plants. In this case, plants should be top worked, that is, take three- or four-year-old plants either lifted and rootballed from the field or specimens in containers and graft in the tips of the shoots using a side veneer or modified side veneer graft. Top working is always more successful because the higher up the stem, the more even the sap flow, so there is hardly any risk of flooding the graft union.

Summer grafting of witch hazels is carried out during late summer; some success can be obtained until the third week of September, but August is the optimum time. The mother plants and rootstocks will have completed their major growth phase by late summer and there is a natural lowering of sap rise, which makes for safer grafting with less risk of flooding the union than with winter grafting.

Bring the rootstocks inside, cut back to a manageable height of 20 cm, and remove any low side shoots. Scion material—well ripened shoots of the current season's growth—should be collected from the stock plants. Prepare the scion material by using the lower part of the shoot, making it three to four buds long, cutting flush above the topmost bud, and removing the lower leaf. If the leaves are particularly large, they can be reduced in size by half. Remember, however, that any wound is a possible entry point for disease, particularly botrytis. The scion material should be kept damp and cool until being used.

Next perform a side veneer or modified side veneer graft, low down on the rootstock. The grafts should be sprayed with clean water until placed in a low polythene tent, which just covers the grafts. High humidity is important to stop the leaves on the scion from wilting, thus the low polythene tent. It is possible to cut the leaves off the scion to reduce the risk of wilting; however, this procedure may stimulate the buds on the scion to grow. This resultant growth is very soft and prone to botrytis, which is difficult, if not impossible, to control in the confines of the low polythene tent. At this time of the year the polythene tent should be heavily shaded; often a second larger tent of milky polythene is useful.

Callusing should take place in about four weeks, from which time gradual weaning should take place by giving air for periods of time, particularly on overcast days. After a time the polythene can be removed and replaced with shade netting. Do not cut the rootstock back to the scion until the following mid to late winter, prior to bud break in the spring.

Chip budding

Instead of using a three- to four-bud scion and side grafting, a one-bud graft and the chip budding method can be carried out (see field budding for details). This works well; the only real problem with this method is that it is somewhat awkward to tie the bud in. All other aspects for aftercare are as for side grafting.

Field budding

This technique works very well and produces much bushier plants than grafting. In fact, plants behave very much in the same way as roses, with adventitious side buds growing as well as the main bud giving usually three or four shoots from the base.

The warmer the climate the better the result. Field budding works exceptionally well in New Zealand, where I first heard of this technique and later saw it in operation. The warm summers in North America and the mainland of Europe also suit the method well. Nurserymen in the United Kingdom are dependent on having a warm August for good results. I have used this method in Kent for the last fifteen years. Kent, along with East

Anglia, has as near a continental climate as you can get in the United Kingdom, particularly North Kent, where my nursery is located.

When preparing the land, the soil should be free from perennial weeds, as they will be much more difficult to control after planting. Organic matter is beneficial, and this can be added prior to planting. The soil should then be ploughed and then knocked down to a planting tilth with a power harrow. Raise or purchase two-year-old plants of 6–8 mm stem diameter. Plant these in rows, 1 m apart, with 40–50 cm between plants in the row. Prepare rootstock by lightly trimming the roots and removing low side shoots.

In the United Kingdom and North America the optimum time for the actual budding operation is during the first three weeks of August. The budwood is fairly well ripened at that time, and there is still enough activity in the rootstocks. If there has been a fairly prolonged period of dry weather, the rootstocks should be irrigated beforehand. It is important that the rootstocks are actively growing at the time of budding.

Take scion material from carefully maintained stock plants. I only use the two basal buds on a shoot, the four or five further up not being ripe enough. If you use unripe buds, the chip may take but the bud can fall off. Tie the buds in with 25-mm wide polythene tape, taking care to go around the long bud and not damage it. Remove the ties at six to eight weeks, when the buds have taken. It is important to check the buds before untying all of them.

In midautumn shorten the rootstocks back to 45 cm to prevent wind rock during the winter. In midwinter head plants back to the bud, and apply a bud guide to the chips. During the summer, remove sucker growth, control nearby weeds, and feed and irrigate the plants.

Bare root bench and field grafting

Because conventional techniques of grafting onto pot-grown rootstocks did not fit well with his other nursery operations, Harald Neubauer of The Hidden Hollow Nursery, Belvidere, Tennessee, has experimented with several methods. If the scion material is thin, Harald uses a side veneer graft; if more substantial, an apical whip graft is used. The graft is then waxed and plunged into moist peat until planting time; some callus will form during this period. Planting takes place just prior to bud burst. If there is a snag because the side veneer method has been used, this needs to be removed in midsummer. This grafting method also can be used in early spring on established rootstocks growing in the field.

T-budding

This method can be quite successful in the more southern regions of United States, which experience warmer climate and higher rainfall during the summer. In the United Kingdom, however, results are not as good as chip budding. In T-budding, the buds are tied in with a rubber strip in late summer, and the following spring the rootstock is cut down to just above the bud. During the growing season, all sucker growth should be removed.

Layering

Although not a commercial method, for the propagation of only one or two plants, layering is a good method. It has the added advantage of the plant being on its own roots. The principals of layering are etiolation and restriction. Etiolation is achieved by placing the shoot into a trench made in the soil, thus excluding light from the stem. Restriction is done by bending, twisting, cutting into, or girdling the stem to restrict the sap flow; roots will begin to form above the point of restriction. Layering is carried out in the spring; select a suitable shoot and make a sloping cut into the stem. The stem should be bent down in a 15-cm-deep trench and pegged into place. The shoot should be buried for two years before severing it from the parent plant.

Micropropagation

This is a specialised method of vegetative propagation, which needs laboratory type facilities. Micropropagation involves taking very small pieces of plant tissue and regenerating these on agar containing sugars, minerals, and plant hormones in sterile conditions. With woody plants it is mainly the meristem tissue at the shoot tip which is used; axillary buds are also often cultured. Once shoot proliferation takes place on the agar medium in the growth rooms, the shoots are divided and numbers increased until sufficient numbers are produced. These small shoots are then usually taken from the growth room and rooted in conventional composts and carefully controlled propagation facilities.

To date *Hamamelis* have not been reliably produced by this method. A major problem seems to be adequately cleaning up the material for culture. In addition, once the material is in culture, the explants produce an abundance of phenolic oxidation which causes loss of the explants. Weaning plants from culture to a growing media outside has also proved to be difficult. It would certainly be a bonus if a reliable and not-too-expensive method could be developed for witch hazels. The benefit of having them on their own roots would be tremendous.

Chapter 10

Cultivation

In this chapter I provide some simple basic rules of cultivation to help the gardener achieve success. The witch hazels have deservedly become some of the most popular winter-flowering shrubs. With the exception of *Hamamelis virginiana*, they all flower in the winter months, unperturbed by bad weather, bearing their flowers on leafless branches. Those plants that have a good scent can be appreciated from quite a distance, especially on mild and still days. During the summer months the hazel-like foliage blends in well with European and North American native trees and shrubs, an advantage in rural settings where plants with exotic foliage can look obtrusive. Finally, many selections have excellent autumn colours.

Purchasing Plants

For the nurseryman the only really economic way of producing plants is by grafting or budding onto rootstocks of *Hamamelis virginiana*. As with any other plant, purchasing grafted plants makes them more expensive than cutting raised plants. In addition, suckers can arise from below the graft union. If suckers are evident on plants, you should avoid purchasing them. Another point to look out for is how bushy the plants are. They can often be seen with just one or two shoots; but good-quality plants will have been pruned in the nursery to promote a well-shaped bushy plant.

You should also examine the root system in the container. *Hamamelis* will not tolerate impeded drainage, which can result in root death. In certain situations with container-grown plants (the majority are sold this way) the basal quarter to third of a container can become waterlogged, particularly over the winter period. This can lead to death of some roots, which can give rise to fungal infection that spreads further through the root system.

Therefore, check to see that the container-grown plant has a healthy root system throughout.

In the United Kingdom nurseries and garden centres usually sell witch hazels in 3-L (two years old from grafting), 5-L (three years old), and 10-L containers (three to four years old). According to Tim Brotzman, the sizes usually sold in the United States are 10-inch pots (an 18- to 24-inch, bushy plant at a reasonable price) and 14-inch pots (a 24- to 36-inch plant). Although the largest plants are quite a bit more expensive, they are easier to establish in the garden with less incidence of loss than with smaller plants. In summary, then, purchase bushy plants with good growth, healthy root systems, and as large as one can afford.

Siting

The selection of a good site is important. It is a good idea to site plants to have a clear foreground, a lawn or path where close inspection of the flowers can be undertaken. It is also uplifting on dull winter days if plants can easily be observed from within the house, through patio doors or from a conservatory.

A background of evergreen shrubs or conifers will show the flowers off to a much better effect, especially the cultivars with pale to golden yellow flowers. If there is a deciduous tree canopy in the garden, hollies (*Ilex*) and yews (*Taxus*) can be successively grown underneath them to give an evergreen background. The cultivars with coppery orange to red flowers are seen at their best when the low winter sun can shine through the branches, lighting the flowers up.

Although witch hazels will grow under a light tree canopy, they tend to have straggly growth and they flower less than those grown in a more open situation. It is also important to ensure they are planted sufficiently well away (3–4 m) from the background evergreens, which have thirsty roots, such as hollies, laurels (*Prunus laurocerasus*), and conifers. The competition will be too much for them, as will that from surface-rooting trees such as birch (*Betula*) and cherry (*Prunus*).

One of the most important points with regard to site for witch hazels is the avoidance of frost pockets. The plants are fully hardy as far as winter cold is concerned, but are susceptible to damage from late spring frosts. If a frost occurs at the critical period when sap is rising and buds are bursting, bark split can occur, which can result in a severe check to the plant. This check often manifests itself in little or no growth the following summer and possibly some branch death. Young plants are more susceptible than older ones, and newly planted witch hazels can be killed before they get a chance to establish. If a frost pocket is unavoidable and growing a witch hazel is desired, then the gardener must be prepared to protect the plant with horticultural fleece on frosty nights in the spring until the plant is several years old and well established. Older plants can still be damaged, but their powers of recovery are much stronger.

Soils

Witch hazels require that utopia of soils, that is, one which is freely drained but moisture retentive. Impeded drainage is the worst problem with any soil, whether it is a heavy clay soil or sandy soil with ironstone or sandstone pans. Witch hazels can be difficult to grow in clay soils because of the closely packed particles, which can impede drainage, so it is important to aerate these soils. Humus is the most important constituent for opening up the soil. Work in garden compost or well-rotted manure together with annual mulches of the same, and let the worms do the work for you. Witch hazels will grow quite happily on soils with a pH range of 4.5 to 6.5. Shallow soils overlying chalk can be a problem, when lime-induced chlorosis can be evident. This can be overcome to some degree by applying sequestered iron.

Planting

The most important aspect with regard to planting is soil preparation. If a completely new border is being started, it should be thoroughly dug, breaking up the second spit, if necessary. The size of the planting hole is then not critical, as all the new plants are starting afresh. If a plant is going into a gap or in place of a plant that has been removed from a border, then an area up to ten times the diameter of the root ball or container should be prepared. Do not plant too deeply, the rootball or surface of the container should be only just covered with soil. Firm the soil, apply some general fertilizer around the plant, and mulch with compost to a depth of 5 cm. I believe mulching with garden compost is better than incorporating it into the soil.

Roots should be encouraged to spread and search for food and moisture, and feeding becomes more important once the root system becomes established.

Cultivation

It is important to keep witch hazels growing well. If they slow down or stop, flowering will be reduced in both quantity and quality. They flower mainly on wood produced the previous year, either short spurlike growths or longer extension growth. Poor growth will lead to less foliage cover during the growing season, poorer autumn colour, poorer flower bud formation, and less robust flower buds.

Once a plant becomes old wooded and restricted, it is often difficult to encourage it into good growth again. Suckering of the rootstock also can start and become troublesome. Sucker growth should be removed as soon as seen—on young plants cut off as close to the stem as possible, on older plants the suckers can be pulled away from the base of the plant. On no account should one cut back and leave stumps of the rootstock, as they will grow more vigorously the following year.

It is important that witch hazels have sufficient moisture during the summer months. Drought conditions have the most serious effects on the health of witch hazels. *Hamamelis mollis* is the first to suffer, with plants showing symptoms of marginal leaf scorch. It is therefore beneficial to water during dry periods, particularly when establishing young plants. After planting container plants which have been grown in a soil-free media, it is vital to water the first summer to ensure roots move out of the media into the surrounding soil. The same applies if a plant is lifted and transplanted; expect little growth the first season as it needs to make new roots and establish itself before making sensible new extension growth. The older the plant, the greater the shock, so watering the first and possibly the second summer is vital to get them re-established.

On some occasions it is also possible to have problems with lack of moisture in the winter. If it has been particularly dry, flowers can abort before properly opening. This is not a common occurrence but can happen. It is surprising how much water is required during the flowering period.

Conserving moisture is also very important, and the application of well-rotted manure or garden compost on an annual basis is decidedly beneficial.

Mulching conserves moisture in the ground for plant roots to take up, rather than evaporating from the bare soil surface. It is important to apply the mulch in the late winter when the soil is moist, rather than wait until spring when the soil can be starting to dry out. Mulching also keeps the soil cool, a condition most plants from the woodland understory prefer. Lastly, but importantly, mulches keep down weeds, which compete for moisture and nutrients.

Young plants are at risk of late spring frost damage, particularly when they are newly planted and have not established an extensive root system and built up a branch framework. It is therefore a good idea to have some horticultural fleece available to cover the plants on frosty nights in the spring when the sap is starting to rise in the plants. This is the vulnerable period, and a little effort to protect at this stage will reap dividends later. Older plants can still suffer some damage but, because of a well-established root system and branch framework, they can recover from the frost damage.

Pruning

Most books have stated that *Hamamelis* require little pruning apart from the removal of dead wood. This is fine if you have sufficient room to let the plants develop naturally. I have developed a system of pruning, however, which keeps the plant more compact and more suited to the smaller garden.

The first operation after leaf fall is to remove any sucker growth as close to the stem as possible, when it is easily seen. It should be an annual operation to check for and remove any suckers. From the second year after planting, once the plant is established, it should be pruned after flowering has finished. The technique is to prune all the previous season's growth back to two growth buds—simple, straightforward, and entirely effective. The previous season's growth will usually have a couple of flowers at the base, with the remainder of the shoot containing growth buds.

This annual regime of pruning encourages good extension growth for the following season, plus spur growth at the base, which will always bud up unless the plant is under severe stress. This leads to a dense bushy plant with prolific flowering. I have plants in my collection fifteen years old but only 1.5 m by 1.5 m in size. It pays to start with bushy young plants and reject any with only one or two shoots. Even these, however, can be brought back to a bushy framework given light and air and using this pruning method. As plants get older there will be a certain amount of dead twigs and branches in the centre of the plant. This will be particularly the case if it has been receiving the annual prune to keep it compact. Removal of this dead material should be carried out as well, at the same time as pruning the previous year's growth.

Witch hazels can also be fan trained, making optimum use of space and enabling several cultivars to be grown. My friend Chris Sanders, who has a fairly small back garden yet is very keen on witch hazels, has used panelled fencing to grow about twelve cultivars. These are planted about 2 m apart. It is important to start with a bushy plant with several shoots, which can be tied in to horizontally placed wires. All side shoots of substantial growth should be cut back to two growth buds, as in pruning a specimen grown as a bush. This should be carried out after flowering has finished. Short spur growth will also be formed and will bud up well for flowering the following year. This training gives Chris plants with a profusion of flowers set against a good background, a range of cultivars, and much pleasure during the winter months.

Hardiness and Heat Tolerance

In the United Kingdom and Western Europe all *Hamamelis* species and hybrids are winter hardy, withstanding temperatures as low as -20°C (-1°F). However, late spring frosts after bud burst can be devastating, particularly to young plants, causing shoot tip death and bark split from which they may or may not recover. In North America *Hamamelis* species and hybrids are hardy to zone 4.

In the southern United States, summer heat can be detrimental to effective growth. Even more of a problem, however, is the lack of cold in the winter. If witch hazels do not get sufficient winter chill, their flowering is erratic and late. Tim Brotzman has plans to evaluate many witch hazel cultivars for short chill-hour requirements, which will produce more useful plants for southern regions.

Pests and Diseases

Fortunately, witch hazels do not suffer from many pests or diseases and are generally trouble free once established. Apart from mild feeding by the larvae of various *Lepidoptera* and two specific pests of *Hamamelis virginiana*, there are few pests that attack witch hazels. In fact, for all the *Hamamelis* species in cultivation in Europe there is little problem as far as pests are concerned; witch hazels seem to be immune from aphid attack, and the amount of damage by caterpillars is minimal.

For gardeners in rural areas, particularly if the area is at all wooded, rabbits and deer can be significant problems. The only way of reducing damage here is to fence the property or the beds to keep them out.

For young plants in containers, particularly in the nursery situation, vine weevil (*Otiorhynchus sulcatus*) is a severe problem. It can also be a problem for gardeners who may wish to grow a witch hazel in a container on the patio, so the plant may be more readily enjoyed during the winter. Adult weevils are black and about 12 mm long. They are nocturnal, feeding on the leaves of plants at night and by day hiding under the pot or among leaf litter or rubbish. Eggs are laid on the compost after the adult females emerge in early summer. The grubs feed from late summer until the following mid and late spring on the roots of the plant. When fully grown, the grubs are white with a brown head and about 12 mm long. This discrete life cycle does not apply when plants are under the protection of glass or polythene, however, when adults may emerge in autumn and overwinter before laying eggs in spring and early summer. Only a few larvae are required to kill small plants in containers. The larvae can be controlled in container-grown plants by using an insecticide or biological control with the nematode *Steinernema kraussei*. Either treatment should be watered in with the compost in late summer.

In North America *Hamamelis virginiana* suffers from attack by the witch hazel leaf gall aphid (*Hormaphis hamamelidis*). Several generations may exist, alternating between the primary host plant, *H. virginiana*, and a secondary host, the river birch *Betula nigra*. The aphid attacks the young leaves and injects a substance while feeding. This substance causes abnormal cell differentiation, resulting in raised narrow galls on the upper leaf surface, commonly called "cone galls." The problem is rarely severe enough to cause the plant to be badly damaged.

The second problem with *Hamamelis virginiana* in North America is more serious, in that in some years it can cause an almost total failure in seed production. The witch hazel weevil (*Pseudonanthomus hamamelidis*) attacks the developing fruit in late spring and early summer, damaging its proper development and causing the fruit to become a misshapen gall. In years of bad attack by the weevil seed loss is often as high as 80–100 per cent, in other years as low as 30–40 per cent.

The most serious diseases which affect witch hazels are those which attack the roots. In the southern and eastern United States, the leaves of *Hamamelis japonica*, *H. mollis*, and their hybrids can be quite badly affected by powdery mildew. This appears as a white powdery coating of short-lived summer spores on stems and mostly the upper leaf surfaces. In dry conditions affected parts usually have a mealy or dusty white growth present, whereas in humid conditions this becomes powdery. Because the fungus can overwinter on diseased shoots, it is important to spray with a suitable fungicide at ten-day intervals from late spring to midsummer. Try to ensure there is sufficient air movement around plants, as still and damp conditions encourage the disease.

The leaf spotting fungus *Phyllosticta hamamelidis* can be troublesome in humid conditions with some cultivars in North America. I have seen mild attacks of what could prove to be this disease on a few cultivars in Europe, but as yet I know of no confirmed occurrence. This infects the leaves of witch hazels, causing small spots which grow into large reddish brown blotches. In severe infestation, the fungus often causes considerable leaf drop. The disease is favoured during wet seasons, the spores being spread by rain splash. Infected plant debris lying around the nursery provides a source of inoculum. The only control measures are hygiene and suitable fungicide sprays, beginning when the leaves are just unfurling and then at ten- to fourteen-day intervals after that.

Honey fungus (*Armillaria mellea*) is the most troublesome of diseases affecting *Hamamelis* and many other trees and shrubs in gardens. The older the garden, the more likely is the presence of the disease. Plants that have been weakened by disease or drought are most susceptible, as are old plants. Affected plants have symptoms of gradual leaf deterioration before eventually succumbing to the disease and dying. Eradication of honey fungus is virtually impossible, and the best way to counteract it is by trying to avoid stress to the plants. Watering, mulching, and feeding to keep the plants healthy is vital.

Diseases such as *Phytophthora cinnamomi*, *Phytophthora cryptogea*, *Cylindrocarpon radicicola*, and *Thielaviopsis basicola* (black root rot) are all indicative of poor drainage. These diseases are fatal to young plants in containers that become waterlogged in winter and in soils prone to waterlogging. It is vital to provide a free-draining soil to give young witch hazels a good start. These water- and soil-borne pathogens can be introduced to a crop through contaminated water supplies, propagation material, infected plants, or infested soil or compost. Once disease gets into a few roots, it can soon spread; with young plants having a small root system, they can be killed easily.

Chapter 11
Companion Plants

The way that witch hazels can be grown in the garden and how they can associate with other plants will very much depend on the size of the garden and the preferences of the gardener. In this chapter, I present my thoughts on how witch hazels may best be used in the garden.

Witch hazels lend themselves to being grown in woodland gardens, in partial shade afforded by species of oak (*Quercus*) and pine (*Pinus*), which should be limbed up to 7–8 m to let in light and air. In the United Kingdom, particularly, *Quercus robur* and *Pinus sylvestris* are the obvious choice to plant. The great gardens of southern England such as Borde Hill, Nymans, Leonardslee, Wakehurst, and the RHS Garden Wisley, all provide these conditions, epitomized in that pinnacle of woodland gardens, the Savill Garden, and in particular the Valley Garden in Windsor Great Park. In North America gardens such as the Arnold Arboretum, Bernheim Arboretum, Brookside Gardens, University of British Columbia Botanical Garden, and Washington Park Arboretum provide these conditions.

In this situation witch hazels can be allowed to grow freely and develop their natural growth habit, associating with other trees and shrubs. The genus *Betula*, for instance, provides many excellent companion plants, with selections such as *Betula pendula* 'Tristis', with its white bark and very graceful, pendulous branches. *Betula utilis* 'Grayswood Ghost' has superb glowing white bark and, along with other white-barked *B. utilis* selections, is a favourite in Europe. *Betula ermanii* 'Grayswood Hill' has beautiful creamy white bark, with pale brown lenticels contrasting on the trunk. The lovely, creamy white, flushed pink, newly exposed bark of *Betula albosinensis* 'China Ruby', which matures to a coppery red, makes this an altogether different and exciting birch for the garden. In North America the birch bark borer is a problem in the eastern and southern states. Resistant *Betula nigra* cultivars such as 'Heritage' and 'Duraheat', with their fawny pink exfoliating bark, and other somewhat resistant clones with white bark such as *B. platyphylla* 'Whitespire' should be used.

The mountain ashes are superb small trees. They have attractive foliage, often colouring well in the autumn, and the bunches of fruits range in colour from white through yellow, orange, and red. *Sorbus hupehensis*, which has long-lasting white fruits, and the pink-fruited *S. hupehensis* 'Pink Pagoda' are absolute musts. *Sorbus* 'Rose Queen', with bright rose red fruits, is a very worthwhile cultivar. Three other *Sorbus* selections, besides having attractive fruits and very reliable for autumn colour, can unhesitatingly be recommended for the garden: *Sorbus commixta* 'Embley, with orange red fruits, *Sorbus* 'Joseph Rock', with yellow fruits and superb autumn colour, and *S. sargentiana*, with small red fruits and perhaps the most spectacular autumn colour.

The genus *Acer* provides some excellent plants for woodland gardens, and the snake bark maples fit in admirably. In the wild they are understory trees, so they enjoy shelter from strong winds and exposure to strong sunlight. A cool moist root run is important during the summer for these plants. Again, in the eastern and southern United States the climate can prove to be too hot in summer. If they are able to be grown successfully, the following selections are worth considering: *Acer capillipes* 'Honey Dew', *Acer* ×*conspicuum* 'Phoenix', *A.* ×*conspicium* 'Silver Vein', *Acer davidii* 'Serpentine', *Acer rufinerve* 'Wintergold', and *Acer* 'White Tigress'. All of these have pronounced white striations on the bark, most noticeable on branches of two to ten years of age. Snake bark maples also exhibit good autumn colour and are attractive when fruiting. Japanese maples (*Acer japonicum* and *A. palmatum*) also need shelter from strong drying winds. They offer differing textures in their foliage and colours from spring through summer to spectacular autumn displays. The range of cultivars is vast, and there is a plant for every situation. Several books extol their virtues, and one cannot go wrong in consulting these for ideas of what to plant.

Stewartia pseudocamellia Koreana Group and *Stewartia sinensis* again enjoy similar conditions. These are superb small trees, with beautiful white single flowers with a central boss of yellow stamens opening in early to midsummer. In the autumn their foliage takes on yellow, orange, and scarlet colours, and in winter the wonderfully marbled flaking bark can be seen to best advantage. *Stewartia* is in the same family as camellias (*Theaceae*), but until the flowers are seen one could be forgiven for not realizing the relationship.

Styrax japonicus is another superb large bush to small tree which flowers in midsummer. The white bell-shaped flowers are produced in profusion. The following cultivars are worth seeking out: *Styrax japonicus* 'Emerald Pagoda' with larger leaves and flowers, *S. japonicus* 'Fargesii' with lovely rusty red calyx contrasting with the white flowers, *S. japonicus* 'Pink Chimes' with pale pink flowers, and *S. japonicus* 'Purple Dress' whose young foliage is heavily flushed purple.

Evergreen shrubs are important companion plants, and rhododendrons, camellias, and *Pieris* are vital components of the woodland garden. With rhododendrons, the broad-leaved species and the best hardy hybrids are sensible choices, giving a good background for witch hazels in winter, followed by colourful flowers in the spring. Camellias and *Pieris* can be sited to give contrast to the shapes and flowering of witch hazels.

The second situation into which *Hamamelis* fit perfectly is the winter garden, such as can be found at the RHS Garden Wisley, and particularly the Sir Harold Hillier Gardens in Hampshire. Other winter-flowering subjects can be used here. *Mahonia* ×*media* cultivars, such as 'Charity', 'Lionel Fortescue', and 'Winter Sun', together with the scented *Mahonia japonica*, give excellent contrasting foliage as well as bold racemes of pale to bright yellow flowers. *Viburnum tinus* cultivars, especially 'Eve Price' and 'Gwenllian', provide evergreen structure and background and an extraordinary long flowering period, spanning the whole winter and spring. Low-growing evergreens such as *Skimmia japonica* also work well in a winter garden. The male cultivars, such as *S. japonica* 'Fragrans' (syn. 'Fragrant Cloud'), 'Emerald King', and 'Stoneham Red', produce attractive flowers, both in bud as well as when open in spring, with the added bonus of a delicious fragrance. The female cultivars, notably *S. japonica* 'Red Dragon' and 'Tansley Gem', produce clusters of bright red fruits to decorate the winter and spring months, untroubled by birds. *Sarcococca* species, Christmas box, provide good evergreen ground cover and are nicely scented, especially *Sarcococca confusa*. Other species which are garden worthy are *Sarcococca orientalis*, which flowers early and has bold leaves for a Christmas box, and the various forms of *Sarcococca hookeriana*.

Daphne bholua, growing up to 3 m in height, with sweetly scented flowers in mid through late winter, is a must. Look out for the cultivars 'Alba', with near white flowers, 'Jacqueline Postill', very floriferous with purplish pink flowers, and 'Peter Smithers', which has the darkest flowers of all. The winter heath, *Erica carnea*, is a must for the front of borders, where plants can receive full exposure to the sun. Some excellent selections are 'Snow White', 'Pink Spangles' with pale pink flowers, 'March Seedling' with pink flowers, 'Loughrigg' with purple-pink flowers, 'Challenger' with red flowers, and 'Golden Starlet' with yellow foliage.

Deciduous shrubs other than *Hamamelis* can be used in the winter garden. The flowers of *Viburnum farreri* 'Farrer's Pink' are deep pink in bud, opening pale pink, and *V. farreri* 'Candidissimum' produces clear white flowers. Both of these cultivars flower profusely during mild spells. *Viburnum* ×*bodnantense* is a hybrid between the species *V. farreri* and *V. grandiflorum*; it flowers over the winter but is subject to frost. The two best *V.* ×*bodnantense* clones in my opinion are 'Charles Lamont', whose flowers are purer pink and in habit not as gaunt as 'Dawn', and 'Deben', whose flowers are pink in bud, opening white. The fragrance of these shrubs is enjoyed by some but not others.

Two deciduous species of rhododendron, which bear flowers early in the year, are more often than not out in time alongside witch hazels, particularly the late-flowering hybrids. *Rhododendron dauricum* 'Midwinter' produces phlox purple flowers, and *Rhododendron mucronulatum* 'Winter Brightness' has flowers which are a rich rose pink. These make an excellent combination with the yellow-flowered witch hazels such as *Hamamelis* ×*intermedia* 'Arnold Promise' and *H.* ×*intermedia* 'Sunburst'.

The shrubby winter-flowering honeysuckles are also very valuable plants for the winter, with several excellent choices available. *Lonicera* ×*purpusii* 'Winter Beauty' flowers very freely beginning in early winter. *Lonicera setifera* has bristly stems, clothed with sweetly scented, white, flushed pink flowers that resemble those of daphne. *Lonicera standishii* var. *lancifolia* is a more slender leaved form, with white fragrant flowers, tinged pink, and conspicuous yellow stamens.

The winter sweet, *Chimonanthus praecox*, is good if grown in a sunny position or against a wall to ripen growth and promote flower bud formation. Winter sweet succeeds in any well-drained soil. The best form, which needs to be grafted, is *C. praecox* 'Concolor'; the flowers are a clear waxy yellow (lacking the purplish tinting of the species), sweetly scented, and usually borne in late winter.

Stachyurus is a small genus of attractive winter-flowering plants. They are susceptible to late spring frosts when young, but once established they recover quite quickly. The drooping racemes of flowers are a soft creamy yellow, waxy, and freely produced. Two clones are worth seeking out:

Stachyurus chinensis 'Celina' has longer racemes than any other selection, with fifty to sixty flowers; *Stachyurus praecox* 'Rubriflorus' flowers earlier than 'Celina' and the waxy, creamy yellow flowers are tinged red.

The shrubby dogwoods are ideal for coppicing in the winter garden; if hard pruned down to the ground each spring, they will produce vigorous shoots with excellent stem colour. The older the shoot becomes, the less intense the colour, so it is imperative to prune hard down to the ground each spring for the best colour. The following are excellent dogwood selections. *Cornus alba* 'Aurea' is a yellow-leaved form which does not burn in the sun; the stems are a rich red. With its soft yellow foliage, 'Aurea' is a useful plant to bring some interest to winter gardens out of season. *Cornus alba* 'Kesselringii' has purple-black stems; when underplanted with snowdrops (*Galanthus nivalis*), this plant looks superb. *Cornus alba* 'Sibirica' is undoubtedly the best red-stemmed dogwood and can be underplanted with snowdrops or winter aconites (*Eranthis hyemalis*) for a lively effect. *Cornus sanguinea* 'Anny's Winter Orange' has superb shiny red stems. If the plant is not pruned annually, the shoots are more orange, hence the name. *Cornus sanguinea* 'Magic Flame' is another good form with orange yellow stems in the lower half and glossy bright red above. The young shoots of *Cornus sericea* 'Flaviramea' are yellow to olive green. This cultivar looks superb when contrasted with *C. alba* 'Sibirica' and *C. alba* 'Kesselringii'. *Cornus sericea* 'Cardinal' is a vigorous form with coral red stems.

Some of the willows can give superb winter stem colour as well. Growing more vigorously than dogwoods, willows can be planted to the back of a border. One of the best selections with yellow stems is *Salix alba* 'Golden Ness'. *Salix irrorata* has purple shoots covered with an intense white bloom. It will also produce yellow catkins with red stamens on shoots which are only one year old. *Salix purpurea* 'Nancy Saunders' has slender glossy red shoots, with lovely glaucous foliage in the summer. For a different effect in the garden, *Salix* 'Erythroflexuosa' has contorted orange yellow shoots. *Salix* 'Yelverton' is similar to the commonly grown *S. alba* subsp. *vitellina* 'Britzensis' but is a much brighter orange scarlet.

Because they tend to be quite invasive, brambles are hardly ever given a second thought. For the garden with sufficient space, however, they are excellent. The genus *Rubus* is very large and contains many nondescript species. There are a few, however, which produce an attractive bloom on the young shoots, and these are ideal for the winter garden. *Rubus biflorus* is vigorous but not invasive; the stems are covered with a vivid white waxy bloom. *Rubus cockburnianus* has attractive purple, arching stems overlaid with a white bloom. *Rubus cockburnianus* 'Goldenvale' a less vigorous form, has equally good shoots in the winter but with the added bonus of yellow foliage in summer. When underplanted with *Ophiopogon planiscapus* 'Nigrescens', with its black leaves, 'Goldenvale' looks superb. *Rubus thibetanus* has purplish brown stems, overlaid with white bloom, with small reddish spines.

Hardy perennials for use in the winter garden are few and far between, as they need to be evergreen to be effective. *Bergenia* are members of the saxifrage family (*Saxifragaceae*); being evergreen during the winter, they make ideal ground cover subjects. During the winter some forms take on superb mahogany red to beetroot colours in their foliage. They can be grown in any soil and, for best winter colour, need full exposure. *Bergenia purpurascens* is an excellent choice, as long as you purchase a good clone, however, as inferior seed-raised plants are commonplace. *Bergenia* 'Bartok' has superb winter colour, and it is most likely a *B. purpurascens* hybrid. *Bergenia purpurascens* 'Irish Crimson' has beautiful reddish mahogany leaves and is perhaps the best for winter colour. *Bergenia* 'Winterglut' (Winterglow) is a very good seed-raised selection that consistently performs well with winter colour, and I think it has superseded the quality of *B.* 'Rotblum'.

Members of the genus *Epimedium* that remain evergreen are most useful for the winter garden and can be grown in more shady positions than *Bergenia*. *Epimedium perralderianum*, with its glossy green leaves, takes on pretty bronzy tints in the winter and has bright yellow flowers. *Epimedium* ×*perralchium* is a hybrid of *E. perralderianum* with *E. pinnatum* subsp. *colchicum* and has good evergreen foliage with large yellow flowers. *Epimedium pubigerum* has excellent smooth green foliage but unfortunately is not very ornamental in flower.

Most of the spurges look their best in the spring, but there are some which are useful plants in the winter garden. *Euphorbia amygdaloides* var. *robbiae* makes good ground cover, with its dark green foliage. Purple winter foliage makes *Euphorbia characias* subsp. *wulfenii* 'Purpurea' an excellent choice. *Euphorbia characias* subsp. *wulfenii* 'Lambrook Gold' and 'John Tomlinson' are excellent forms; the shoots which will flower the following spring bend over at the tips to form a crook, which looks attractive over the winter months. *Euphorbia* ×*martini* is a hybrid of *E. amygdaloides* and *E. characias*; it has superb flowers, often coming out in winter and lasting right through to early summer.

The genus *Helleborus* has achieved cult status, and a few devotees have painstakingly undertaken breeding work, improving these plants tremendously in recent years. The best group to associate with witch hazels is the *Helleborus* ×*hybridus* group, commonly called Lenten roses, flowering from late winter to early spring. With the *H.* ×*hybridus* group, it pays to cut off the leaves in early winter, whether dead or not. This will enable you to enjoy the flowers more in late winter without the clutter of dead or tatty foliage. The colour range and form of flower in the genus is vast: green or white through to purple-black, variously spotted, and a range of doubles. *Helleborus* should be purchased while in flower to obtain the colours desired and to check the vigour of the plants. *Helleborus argutifolius* has sea green evergreen foliage and domed flower spikes. *Helleborus foetidus* is a superb foliage plant and flowers from midwinter to early spring. *Helleborus foetidus* Wester Flisk Group is a good choice as well.

Ornamental grasses can make a bold statement in the winter months. It is necessary, however, to select those in which the foliage, stems, and flower spikes can stand the gales of winter. These can look particularly attractive in winter garden scenes, especially when coated with a hoar frost or with the low winter sun lighting up the seed heads. *Calamagrostis* ×*acutiflora* 'Karl Foerster' is a selection of the feather reed grass, clump forming and upright, an excellent plant which remains attractive for most of the winter. *Calamagrostis* ×*acutiflora* 'Overdam' is a variegated, less robust form, not reliable in areas that experience hot and humid summers. *Calamagrostis brachytricha* is upright arching in habit and has silver grey winter flower heads which last well, except in very exposed situations. The tufted hair grass and its varieties *Deschampsia cespitosa* 'Bronzeschlier' and *D. cespitosa* 'Goldschlier', with their respective bronzy and yellow inflorescences, also last the winter well. The Japanese silver grass, *Miscanthus sinensis*, is a grass par excellence for winter effect, lasting the winter extremely well. Cultivars abound and the choice is a personal one; favourites of mine are *Miscanthus sinensis* 'China', 'Ferner Osten', 'Flamingo', 'Kaskade', and 'Morning Light'. *Molinia caerulea* subsp. *caerulea* 'Moorhexe', a form of the purple moor grass, is green leaved and of narrow upright habit. *Molinia caerulea* subsp. *arundinacea* 'Transparent' grows much taller but with an arching habit which allows one to see through the flower spikes, hence the cultivar name. The switch grass *Panicum virgatum*, native to the prairies of North America, has some excellent selections such as 'Heavy Metal' with glaucous foliage, 'Shenandoah' with burgundy autumn colour, and the tall 'Warrior'.

Last but not least is that superb grass *Stipa gigantea*, the giant feather grass; the flower spikelets are golden and dramatic, lasting well into the winter.

Bulbs, of course, can and should be used extensively in the winter garden. Winter aconites, *Eranthis hyemalis*, provide welcoming splashes of yellow to contrast with the darker oranges and reds of some witch hazel cultivars. Snowdrops, *Galanthus nivalis*, are perhaps the most important bulbs for the winter; they are hardy and act as harbingers of spring, with the early- to midseason-flowering sorts being most useful to use with witch hazels. Early-flowering *Narcissus* are suitable subjects for planting with witch hazels. *Narcissus* 'Dawn Chorus' is a yellow trumpet sort flowering from midwinter. Another early yellow trumpet cultivar, flowering from midwinter and worth its place in any garden, is *Narcissus* 'Rijnveld's Early Sensation'. Lastly, I suggest that most wonderful plant in all its forms, *Cyclamen coum*, whose flowers are as hardy as those of the witch hazels.

Many keen gardeners have only small to average-sized gardens, and there may only be room for one or two witch hazels. Because the choice of cultivars is important, I direct the reader to Appendix 1, Gardeners' Selection, for the best witch hazel cultivars. By using the recommended pruning techniques described in chapter 10, witch hazels can be enjoyed by everyone who has a garden, however small.

Appendix 1

Gardeners' Selection

Cultivar	Growth habit	Flower colour	Fragrance	Autumn foliage
H. ×*intermedia* 'Angelly'	upright	citron yellow	strong, sweet	yellow
H. ×*intermedia* 'Aphrodite'	spreading	burnt orange	faint	little or none
H. ×*intermedia* 'Arnold Promise'	vase	lemon yellow	strong, sweet	yellow, orange, and red
H. ×*intermedia* 'Aurora'	upright	yellow and red	strong, sweet	yellow, orange, and red
H. ×*intermedia* 'Barmstedt Gold'	upright	golden yellow	medium, sweet	yellow
H. ×*intermedia* 'Diane'	spreading	red	slight scent	orange and red
H. ×*intermedia* 'Frederic'	upright	orange	no scent	yellow, orange, and red
H. ×*intermedia* 'Gingerbread'	spreading	burnt orange	slight	yellow
H. ×*intermedia* 'Glowing Embers'	spreading	copper orange	slight	little or none
H. ×*intermedia* 'Harry'	upright	pale orange	faint	none
H. ×*intermedia* 'Jelena'	vase	copper orange	no scent	yellow, orange, and red

Cultivar	Growth habit	Flower colour	Fragrance	Autumn foliage
H. ×*intermedia* 'Livia'	spreading	carmine red	medium, sweet	tinge of orange-red
H. ×*intermedia* 'Orange Peel'	upright	orange	medium, sweet	yellow, orange, and red
H. ×*intermedia* 'Pallida'	spreading	sulphur yellow	strong, sweet	yellow
H. ×*intermedia* 'Ripe Corn'	rounded	yellow	faint	deep yellow
H. ×*intermedia* 'Robert'	vase	copper orange	medium, sweet	yellow, orange, and red
H. ×*intermedia* 'Rubin'	rounded	clear red	faint	yellow and orange
H. ×*intermedia* 'Sunburst'	vase	sulphur yellow	no scent	some yellow
H. ×*intermedia* 'Vesna'	upright	light orange	strong, sweet	yellow, orange, and red
H. mollis 'Imperialis'	upright	pale yellow	strong, sweet	yellow
H. mollis 'Jermyns Gold'	upright	golden yellow	strong, sweet	yellow
H. mollis 'Wisley Supreme'	upright	light yellow	strong, sweet	yellow

Appendix 2

Places to See Witch Hazels

North America

The Arnold Arboretum
125 Arborway
Jamaica Plain, Massachusetts 02130
Tel. +617-524-1718
www.arboretum.harvard.edu

Bernheim Arboretum and Research Forest
State Highway 245
Clermont, Kentucky 40110
Tel. +502-955-8512
www.bernheim.org

Brookside Gardens
1800 Glenallan Avenue
Wheaton, Maryland 20902
Tel. +301-962-1400
www.mc-mncppc.org/parks/brookside

Chicago Botanic Garden
1000 Lake Cook Road
Glencoe, Illinois 60022
Tel. +847-835-5440
www.chicago-botanic.org

The Dawes Arboretum
7770 Jacksontown Road, SE
Newark, Ohio 43093
Tel. +800-443-1937
www.dawesarb.org

Green Springs Garden Park
4603 Green Spring Road
Alexandria, Virginia 22312
Tel. +703-642-5173
www.co.fairfax.va.us/parks/gsgp

The Holden Arboretum
9500 Sperry Road
Kirtland, Ohio 44094
Tel. +440-946-4400
www.holdenarb.org

Hoyt Arboretum
4000 SW Fairview Boulevard
Portland, Oregon 97221
Tel. +503-228-8733
www.hoytarboretum.org

Morris Arboretum of the University of Pennsylvania
100 Northwestern Avenue
Philadelphia, Pennsylvania 19118
Tel. +215-247-5777
www.upenn.edu/arboretum

The Morton Arboretum
4100 Illinois Route 53
Lisle, Illinois 60532
Tel. +630-968-0074
www.mortonarb.org

J. C. Raulston Arboretum at North Carolina State University
4301 Beryl Road
Raleigh, North Carolina 27695
Tel. +919-515-3132
www.ncsu.edu/jcraulstonarboretum

The Strybing Arboretum and Botanical Gardens
9th Avenue at Lincoln Way
San Francisco, California 94122
Tel. +415-661-1316
www.strybing.org

University of British Columbia Botanical Garden
6804 SW Marine Drive
Vancouver, British Columbia V6T 1Z4, Canada
Tel. +604-822-9666
www.ubcbotanicalgarden.org

U.S. National Arboretum
3501 New York Avenue, NE
Washington, D.C. 20002
Tel. +202-245-2726
www.usna.usda.gov

Washington Park Arboretum at the University of Washington
Graham Visitors' Center
2300 Arboretum Drive
Seattle, Washington 98195
Tel. +206-543-8800
www.depts.washington.edu/wpa

Wegerzyn Gardens Metro Park
1301 E Siebenthaler Avenue
Dayton, Ohio 45414
Tel. +937-277-6545

Europe

Kalmthout Arboretum
Heuvel 2
2920 Kalmthout
Antwerp, Belgium
Tel. +(0)36-666741
Fax +(0)36-663396
www.arboretumkalmthout.be

Batsford Arboretum
Batsford Park
Moreton-in-Marsh
Gloucestershire GL56 9QB, England
Tel. +(0)1386-701441
Fax +(0)1386-701829
www.batsarb.co.uk

RHS Garden Harlow Carr
Crag Lane, Harrogate
Yorkshire HG3 1QB, England
Tel. +(0)1423-565418
Fax +(0)1423-530663
www.rhs.org.uk

RHS Garden Rosemoor
Great Torrington
North Devon EX38 8PH, England
Tel. +(0)1805-624067
Fax +(0)1805-624717
www.rhs.org.uk

RHS Garden Wisley
Woking
Surrey GU23 6QB, England
Tel. +(0)1483-224234
Fax +(0)1483-211750
www.rhs.org.uk

National Collections

Mrs. P. Edwards
Swallow Hayes
Rectory Road
Albrighton
West Midlands WV7 3EP, England
Tel. +(0)1902-372624
Fax +(0)1902-373151

The Sir Harold Hillier Gardens and Arboretum
Jermyns Lane
Ampfield
Romsey
Hampshire SO51 0QA, England
Tel. +(0)1794-368787
www.hilliergardens.org.uk/collect/plants.html

Chris Lane
Witch Hazel Nurseries
The Granary
Callaways Lane
Newington
Sittingbourne
Kent ME9 7LU, England
Tel. +(0)1795-843098
Fax +(0)1795-843098
www.witchhazelnurseries.co.uk

Wim van der Werf
Lansing 23
Boskoop 2771 BK, The Netherlands
Tel. +(0)172-213095
Fax +(0)172-216173

Appendix 3

Where to Buy Witch Hazels

North America

Arbor Village

15606 County Road CC
PO Box 227
Holt, Missouri 64048
Tel. +816-264-3911
Fax +816-264-3760

Collectors' Nursery

16804 NE 102nd Avenue
Battle Ground, Washington 98604
Tel. +360-574-3832
Fax +360-571-8540

Elk Mountain Nursery

PO Box 599
Asheville, North Carolina 28802
Tel. +828-683-9330
www.elk-mountain.com

Fairweather Gardens

PO Box 330
Greenwich, New Jersey 08323
Tel. +856-451-6261
Fax +856-451-0303
www.fairweathergardens.com

Forestfarm

900 Tetherow Road
Williams, Oregon 97544-9599
Tel. +541-846-7269
Fax +541-846-6993
www.forestfarm.com

Gossler Farms Nursery

1200 Weaver Road
Springfield, Oregon 97478-9691
Tel. +541-746-3922
Fax +541-744-7924
www.gosslerfarms.com

Greer Gardens

1280 Goodpasture Island Road
Eugene, Oregon 97401-1794
Tel. +541686-8266
Fax +541-686-0910
www.greergardens.com

Heronswood Nursery

7530 NE 288th Street
Kingston, Washington 98346-9502
Tel. +360-297-4172
Fax +360-297-8321
www.heronswood.com

Rare Find Nursery, Inc.
957 Patterson Road
Jackson, New Jersey 08527
Tel. +732-833-0613
Fax +732-833-1965
www.rarefindnursery.com

Roslyn Nursery
211 Burrs Lane
Dix Hills, New York 11746
Tel. +631-643-9347
Fax +631-427-0894
www.roslynnursery.com

Wayside Gardens
1 Garden Lane
Hodges, South Carolina 29695-0001
Tel. +800-845-1124
Fax +800-817-1124
www.waysidegardens.com

Whitney Gardens and Nursery
PO Box 170
Brinnon, Washington 98320
Tel. +360-796-4411
Fax +360-796-3556
www.whitneygardens.com

Europe

Ashwood Nurseries Ltd.
Greenforge
Kingswinford
West Midlands DY6 0AE, England
Tel. +(0)1384-401996
Fax +(0)1384-401108
www.ashwood-nurseries.co.uk

Barracott Plants
Old Orchard
Calstock Road
Gunnislake
Cornwall PL18 9AA, England
Tel. +(0)1822-832234

Bluebell Nursery and Arboretum
Anwell Lane, Smisby
Nr. Ashby de la Zouch
Derbyshire LE65 2TA, England
Tel. +(0)1530-413700
Fax +(0)1530-417600
www.bluebellnursery.com

Boomkwekerijen Fa C. Esveld
Rijneveld 72
Boskoop 2771 XS, The Netherlands
Tel. +(0)172-213289
Fax +(0)172-215714
www.esveld.nl

Boomkwekerijen Pieter Zwijnenburg Jr.
Botanische kwekerij
Halve Raak 18
Boskoop2771 AD, The Netherlands
Tel. +(0)172-216232
Fax +(0)172-218474

Bridgemere Nurseries
Bridgemere
Nr. Nantwich
Cheshire CW5 6UP, England
Tel. +(0)1270-520381
Fax +(0)1270-520215
www.bridgemere.co.uk

Coblands Broadwater Plants Ltd.
Fairview Lane, Broadwater Forest
Tunbridge Wells
Kent TN3 9LU, England
Tel. +(0)1892-534760
Fax +(0)1892-534760
www.broadwaterplants.co.uk

Goscote Nurseries Ltd.
Syston Road, Cossington
Leicestershire LE7 4UZ, England
Tel. +(0)1509-812121
Fax +(0)1509-814231
www.goscote.co.uk

Larch Cottage Nurseries
Melkinthorpe
Penrith
Cumbria CA10 2DR, England
Tel. +(0)1931-712404
Fax +(0)1931-712727
www.larchcottagenurseries.co.uk

Penwood Nursery
The Drove, Penwood
Newbury
Berks RG15 9EW, England
Tel. +(0)1635-254366

The Place for Plants
East Bergholt Place
East Bergholt
Suffolk CO7 6UP, England
Tel. +(0)1206-299224
Fax +(0)1206-299224

Rein en Mark Bulk
Kwekerij van bijzondere planten
Rijnveld 115
Boskoop 2771 XV, The Netherlands
Tel. +(0)172-212005
Fax +(0)172-213402

Spinners Garden
School Lane, Boldre
Lymington
Hampshire SO41 5QE, England
Tel. +(0)1590-673347
Fax +(0)1590-679506
www.spinnersgarden.com

Starborough Nursery
Starborough Road
Marsh Green
Edenbridge
Kent TN8 5RB, England
Tel. +(0)1732-865614
Fax +(0)1732-862166

Wisley Plant Centre
RHS Garden Wisley
Woking
Surrey GU23 6QB, England
Tel. +(0)1483-211113
Fax +(0)1483-212372

Appendix 4

Metric Conversions

Metric unit	Conversion factor	Imperial unit
millimetres (mm)	divide by 25	inches
centimetres (cm)	divide by 2.5	inches
metres (m)	divide by 0.3	feet
kilometres (km)	divide by 1.6	miles
square metres (m^2)	divide by 0.09	square feet
hectares (ha)	divide by 0.4	acres
grams (g) per cubic metre	multiply by 0.027	ounces per cubic yard
litres (L)	divide by 3.8	gallons

Glossary

abaxial the side of an organ away from the axis, dorsal

acuminate narrowing gradually to a point

adaxial the side of an organ towards the axis, ventral

aestivation the arrangement of the calyx or corolla in a flower bud

alternate placed singly along the stem or axis, not opposite or whorled

androecium the male sex organs (stamens) collectively

anther the part of the stamen that produces pollen

anthesis flowering time

asymmetrical with one side of the leaf larger than the other; having flowers not divisible into equal halves, as the flowers of the genus *Canna*

axil the angle formed by the upper side of a leaf and the stem

axillary in the axil

bifarious twofold, double

bisexual having both stamens and carpels in the same flower

bract a much reduced leaf; especially the small or scale-like leaves associated with a flower or flower cluster

caducous falling off early

calyx the outer perianth, composed of free or united sepals

campanulate bell-shaped

capitulum a head of sessile or almost sessile flowers surrounded by an involucre; the inflorescence especially characteristic of the *Compositae* and *Dipsacaceae*

capsule a dry, dehiscent fruit, formed from a syncarpous ovary

carpel one of the units forming the gynoecium, usually consisting of ovary, style, and stigma

chlorosis an unhealthy condition due to a deficiency of chlorophyll that causes the green parts of the plant to become yellowish

chromosome one of the pairs of strands in a cell's nucleus that bears genes in a linear order; the number of chromosomes in a cell will vary according to the species, cultivar, hybrid, etcetera concerned

ciliate fringed with long hairs

clone a group of plants that have arisen by vegetative reproduction from a single parent and which are therefore genetically identical

connective the part of the stamen, a continuation of the filament, that joins together the two pairs of anther cells

cordate heart-shaped

corolla the inner perianth, composed of free or united petals

cotyledon one of the first leaves of the embryo of a seed plant; typically one in monocotyledons, two in dicotyledons, and two or more in gymnosperms

crenate with rounded teeth

cruciform forming the shape of a cross

cuneate wedge-shaped

cuspidate ending rather abruptly in a sharp point

dehisce open spontaneously when ripe

dentate toothed

dioecious having male and female flowers on different plants of the same species

emasculate to remove the anthers from an unopened flower

embryo a young plant developed sexually or asexually from the ovum; in spermatophytes it is contained within the seed

endemic restricted to a particular country or region

endocarp the innermost layer of the pericarp

endosperm the albumen of a seed, particularly that deposited within the embryo sac

ephemeral lasting for a relatively short period

epicotyl the part of a seedling above the cotyledon(s) that gives rise to the stem and leaves

epigynous with the sepals, petals, and stamens inserted near the top of the ovary

epithet the second word of the name of a species which serves to distinguish it from others in the genus, for example, *virginiana*, in the case of *Hamamelis virginiana*

exocarp the outermost layer of the pericarp

f. (forma) taxonomic unit subordinate to variety, often differing only in a single character (for example, red flowers in a normally yellow-flowered species), which may arise anywhere in a population

fascicles a close cluster or bundle

filament a fine, elongated, thread-like structure, especially the stalk of an anther

filiform thread-like

funicle the stalk connecting an ovule to its placenta

fusiform spindle-shaped

genotype genetic makeup of an individual

genus a botanical rank, comprising one or more similar species; the names of genera are written with a capital initial letter

girt girth, as in measuring a tree

glabrous without hairs

glaucous with a waxy, greyish blue bloom

globose spherical or globe-shaped, as the flower of *Trollius europaeus* (globe flower)

graft a portion of a plant inserted into and uniting with a larger part of another plant, as a scion into a stock

graft union the point where the rootstock and scion join together

gynoecieum the female sex organs (carpels) collectively; in some species, such as *Vicia faba* (broad bean), the gynoecium consists only of a single carpel, whereas in others it is composed of several carpels

hilum the scar left on a seed where it was previously attached to the funicle

hirsute covered in rough, coarse hairs

hybrid a plant resulting form a cross between two or more plants, genetically unlike and belonging to different taxa, for example, *Geum* ×*intermedium*, a cross between two species in the same genus (*G. rivale* and *G. urbanum*) or ×*Pyronia veitchii*, a cross between two species in different genera (*Cydonia oblonga* and *Pyrus communis*)

hypocotyl the part of a seedling below the cotyledons which gives rise to the root

hypogynous with the sepals, petals, and stamens attached to the receptacle or axis below the ovary

inflorescence the arrangement of flowers on the floral axis; a flower cluster

infraspecific below the rank of species

introgression the introduction of characters of one species into the genotype of another, where these species meet in their natural range of distribution

introrse with the anthers facing and opening inwards, towards the centre of the flower

involucrate with an involucre

involucre a ring of bracts surrounding the head of flowers

involute rolled inwards at the margin, that is, towards the adaxial surface

lamina the expanded part of a leaf or frond

lanceolate lance-shaped

lenticel a pore in the stem that allows gases to pass between the outside atmosphere and the interior of a plant

linear long and narrow with parallel sides

lobe any division of an organ, especially if the part is rounded

lobulate having small lobes

locule a compartment of an ovary or an anther

loculicidal splitting at maturity into the locule, more or less midway between the partitions of the capsule

monoecious with male and female flowers on the same plant

morphological relating to the form of a plant

nectariferous bearing nectar-secreting glands

nominate belonging to the first designated name

oblique unequal, as a leaf with one side extending below the other; ascending, as tree branches that slope upwards

obconic top-shaped, inversely conical

obovate inversely ovate, broadest towards the apex and tapering to the stalk

obtuse blunt

orbicular circular

ovary the lower part of a carpel (or carpels) which contains the ovules

ovate with the outline egg-shaped

ovule a structure which, after fertilization, develops into a seed

palmate divided to the base into separate leaflets, all the leaflets arising from the end of the leaf stalk having the veins radiating from the end of the leaf stalk to the tips of the lobes

pedicillate of a flower, stalked

peduncle the stalk of an inflorescence

perianth a collective term for the outer, non-reproductive parts of a flower, often differentiated into calyx and corolla

pericarp the fruit wall that has developed from the ovary wall

perigynous with the sepals, petals, and stamens inserted around the ovary on the hypanthium, a concave structure developed from the receptacle

petiole a leaf stalk

pilose with soft hairs

placenta the part of the ovary to which the ovules are attached

polygamo-monoecious polygamous, but in the main monoecious

polygamous bearing both unisexual and bisexual flowers on the same plant

polynomial pre-Linnaean classification indicated by more than two terms, for instance, *Pistachia nigra Coryli folio*

precocious a flower that opens early in the season, before the leaves appear

puberulous slightly hairy

pubescent covered in soft hairs

punctate marked with dots, depressions, or translucent glands

raceme an indeterminate inflorescence with pedicillate flowers

revolute rolled downwards at the margin, that is, towards the abaxial surface

rootstock a frequently subterranean stem or rhizome

sac a small pouch or bag-shaped structure

scaberulous slightly rough

scabrous with the surface rough to the touch, due to minute projections

scarious thin, dry, and membranous

scion a young shoot which is inserted into a rooted stock in grafting

sepal a single segment of the calyx

septicidal splitting at maturity along or into the partitions (septa) of the capsule

serrated with a saw-toothed margin

sessile not stalked

sinuate having the blade of the leaf flat but with the margin winding strongly inward and outwards

sinus the recess between two teeth or lobes, for example, on a leaf margin

spatulate spatula-shaped

species a group of closely related, mutually fertile individuals, showing constant differences from allied groups, the basic unit of classification; the names of species are written with a small initial letter

stamen one of the male sex organs, usually consisting of anther, connective, and filament

staminodium a sterile stamen

stellate star-shaped

stigma the apex of the style, usually enlarged, on which the pollen grains alight and germinate

stipule a leafy outgrowth, often one of a pair arising at the base of the petiole

stolon a lateral stem growing horizontally at ground level, rooting at the nodes, and producing new plants from its buds, as in the genus *Fragaria* (strawberry)

stratification the manner in which something is stratified, such as seed in layers of sand

style the often elongated apical part of a carpel or gynoecium that bears the stigma at its tip

subcordate more or less heart-shaped

subsessile almost devoid of a stalk

syncarpous having united carpels

synonym another name for the same taxon, either an alternative name that is valid under a different classification, or a name now invalid according to the International Code for Botanical Nomenclature that has been superseded by a later name

taxon (pl. taxa) a unit of classification of any rank, such as *Bellis perennis* (species), *Bellis* (genus), *Compositae* (family)

tomentose densely covered in soft hairs

torus the end of the stem which bears the flower parts

tubercle a small tuber; a small, rounded projection

unisexual having only male or female organs in the flower; the male and female flowers may be on separate plants (dioecism) or on the same individual (monoecism)

valve one of the pieces into which an anther splits at maturity to release the pollen; one of the pieces into which a fruit splits at maturity to release the seeds

vascular relating to the vessels that convey water and nutrients within the plant, that is, the xylem and phloem

villous covered with long, shaggy hairs

Bibliography

Anderson, A. W. 1951. Dr. F. P. Siebold. *Gardeners' Chronicle* 129(3345): 52.

Anderson, A. W. 1956. Are they wych or witch hazels? *Gardeners' Chronicle: Gardening Illustrated* December 140(25): 649.

Anderson, E. 1933. Variation in flower color in *Hamamelis vernalis. Journal of the Arnold Arboretum* 14: 253–257.

Anderson, E. 1934. *Hamamelis vernalis* Sarg. *Arnold Arboretum Bulletin of Pop. Inf. IV.* 2: 1–4, 2 pl.

Anderson, E. 1936. Early blooming shrubs at the arboretum. *Arnold Arboretum Bulletin of Pop. Inf.* 4: 23–24, 1 pl.

Anderson, E., and K. Sax. 1935. Chromosome numbers in the *Hamamelidaceae* and their phylogenetic significance. *Journal of the Arnold Arboretum* 16: 210–215.

Anon. 1888. *Hamamelis zuccariniana. Gardeners' Chronicle* (3rd ser.) 3: 278.

Anon. 1891. The witch hazels. *The Garden* 39: 546–547.

Anon. 1903. *Hamamelis mollis. Gardeners' Chronicle* (3rd ser.) 33: 185.

Anon. 1951. *Hamamelis.* In *RHS Dictionary of Gardening,* Vol. 2. Oxford: Clarendon Press, 950–951.

Anon. 1953. Notes from Wisley. *Journal of the Royal Horticultural Society* 78: 2–4.

Anon. 1961. Plants to which awards have been made. *Journal of the Royal Horticultural Society* 84: 324–325.

Anon. 1969. *Hamamelis.* In *RHS Dictionary of Gardening,* supplement. Oxford: Clarendon Press, 335.

Anon. 1971. *Illustrated Important Forest Trees of Japan.* Vol. 3. Japan Forest Technical Association. Tokyo, Japan: Chikyusha Co. Ltd., 40.

Anon. 1972. *Hilliers' Manual of Trees and Shrubs.* Winchester, England: Hillier & Sons, 135–137.

Anon. 1991. *The Hillier Manual of Trees and Shrubs.* 6th ed. Newton Abbott, England: David & Charles, 196–198.

Anon. 1993. *The Hillier Colour Dictionary of Trees and Shrubs.* 2nd ed. Newton Abbot, England: David & Charles, 106.

Anon. 1999. *Hamamelis.* In *The New RHS Dictionary of Gardening,* Vol. 2. London: Macmillan Reference Ltd., 487–488.

Anon. 2002. *The Hillier Manual of Trees and Shrubs.* Newton Abbott, England: David & Charles, 135–137.

Bean, W. J. 1898. A new witch hazel. *Gardeners' Chronicle* (3rd ser.) 24: 363–364.

Bean, W. J. 1976. *Trees and Shrubs Hardy in the British Isles.* 8th rev. ed., Vol. 2. Ed. G. Taylor. London: John Murray, 315–321.

Bean, W. J. 1988. *Trees and Shrubs Hardy in the British Isles.* 8th rev. ed., Supplement. Ed. D. L. Clarke. London: John Murray, 259–260.

Berry, E. W. 1923. *Tree Ancestors: A Glimpse into the Past.* Baltimore, Williams & Wilkins Co., 188–190.

Bradford, J. L., and D. L. Marsh. 1977. Comparative studies of the witch hazels *Hamamelis virginiana* and *Hamamelis vernalis. Proceedings of the Arkansas Academy of Sciences* 31: 29–31.

Bretschneider, E. 1898. *History of European Botanical Discoveries in China*. Vol. 2. London: Sampson Low, Marston & Co., 741–744.

Brown, G. E. 1974. Growing witch hazels. *Journal of the Royal Horticultural Society* 99: 15–19.

Carder, V. A. 1974. Some notes on witch hazels at Kew. *Journal of the Royal Horticultural Society* 99: 11–15.

Chaney, R. W., and D. I. Axelrod. 1959. *Miocene Floras of the Columbia Plateau*. Carnegie Institute Publ. no. 476, 1–72.

Chang, H., and S. Yan. 1979. *Hamamelidaceae: Hamamelis*. In *Flora Republicae Popularis Sinicae*, Vol. 35, no. 2. Beijing: Academia Sinica, 73–74.

Christiansen, J., and M. Fonnesbech. 1975. Prevention by polyvinylpyrrolidone of growth inhibition of *Hamamelis* shoot tips grown in vitro and of browning of the agar medium. *Acta Horticulturae* 54: 101–104.

Coker, W. C., and H. R. Totten. 1937. *Trees of the Southeastern States*. Chapel Hill, N.C.: University of North Carolina Press, 194–195.

Connor, S. 1995. Mystical, medicinal witch hazel. *Arnoldia* 55(2): 20–21.

Coombes, A. J. 1996. Winter magic. *The Garden* 121(1): 28–33.

Cresson, C. O. 1986. The de Belder witch hazels. *The Green Scene* 14(4): 14–15.

Cubberley, B. 1989. *Hamamelis* ×*intermedia* 'Arnold Promise'. *Field Notes, American Nurseryman* 170: 178.

Darlington, C. D., and A. P. Wylie. 1955. *Chromosome Atlas of Flowering Plants*. London: George Allen & Unwin Ltd., 177.

de Belder, J., and B. Wouters. 2001. *Winterbloeiers*. Tielt, Belgium: Uitgeverij Lannoo nv., 30–41.

de Belder, J., A. Verhaeghe, and B. Wouters. 1988. *Het Arboretum van Kalmthout*. Tielt, Belgium: Uitgeverij Lannoo nv., 21–39.

de Belder, R. 1969. The Arboretum at Kalmthout. *Journal of the Royal Horticultural Society* 94: 81–94.

Del Tredici, P., P. Meyer, R. Hao, C. Mao, K. Conrad, and R. W. Thomas. 1995. Plant collecting on Wudang Shan. *Arnoldia* 55(1): 12–20.

de Ridder, M., and D. O. Wijnands. 1980. De systematiek van *Hamamelis*. *Dendroflora* 17: 6–8.

de Steven, D. 1982. Seed production and seed mortality in a temperate forest shrub (witch-hazel, *Hamamelis virginiana*) [in Michigan]. *Journal of Ecology* 70(2): 437–443.

de Vogel, P. 1968. Keuringen. *Dendroflora* 5: 69.

Dillwyn, L. W. 1843. *Hortus Collinsonianus*. Swansea, England: Murray and D. Rees.

Dirr, M. A. 1975. *Manual of Woody Landscape Plants*. Champaign, Ill.: Stipes, 216–219.

Dirr, M. A. 1983. Witch hazels deserve a spot in the landscape. *American Nurseryman* 158: 60–63.

Dirr, M. A. 1998. *Manual of Woody Landscape Plants: Their Identification, Ornamental Characteristics, Culture, Propagation and Uses*. 5th ed. Champaign, Ill.: Stipes, 416–424.

Dirr, R. J. 1994. *Hamamelis: und andere zaubernussgewachse*. Stuttgart: Eugen Ulmer GmbH & Co., 10–53.

Dummer, P. 1969. A new stock for grafting *Hamamelis. Plant Propagator* 15: 18–19.

Edwards, P. 1997. Showtime for *Hamamelis* beauty. *Plants News* 3(3): 92–94.

Edwards, P. 2000. "Strain no. 2" becomes *Hamamelis* 'Swallow Hayes'. *Plants News* 6(3): 36.

Ernst, W. R. 1963. The genera of *Hamamelidaceae* and *Platanaceae* in the south-eastern United States. *Journal of the Arnold Arboretum* 44: 193–201.

Ewan, J., ed. 1968. *William Bartram: Botanical and Zoological Drawing, 1756–1788.* Lunenburg, Vt.: Stinehour Press.

Ewan, J., and N. Ewan. 1970. *John Banister and His Natural History of Virginia, 1678–1692.* Urbana: University of Illinois Press.

Fenicchia, R. A. 1967. Unusual plants and their propagation. *Proceedings of the International Plant Propagators' Society* 17: 158–164.

Forbes, F. B., and W. B. Hemsley. 1886–1905. *Index Florae Sinensis.* Vols. 1–7. London: The Linnean Society.

Fordham, A. J. 1960. Germination of double dormant seeds. *Proceedings of the International Plant Propagators' Society* 10: 207.

Fordham, A. J. 1968. Question box. *Proceedings of the International Plant Propagators' Society* 18: 327–329.

Fordham, A. J. 1976. Propagation of some *Hamamelidaceae* (witch hazel family). *Proceedings of the International Plant Propagators' Society* 26: 296–298.

Fulling, E. H. 1953. American witch hazel: History, nomenclature and modern utilisation. *Economic Botany* 7: 359–381.

Gaggini, J. B. 1974. New techniques improve propagation prospects for high value *Hamamelis. Nurseryman & Garden Centre* 158(12): 466–469.

Gaut, P. C., and J. N. Roberts. 1984. *Hamamelis* seed germination. *Proceedings of the International Plant Propagators' Society* 34: 334–342.

Gleason, H. A. 1922. The witch hazels. *Journal of the New York Botanical Garden* 23: 17–19.

Gleason, H. A. 1923. *Hamamelis vernalis. Addisonia* 8: 9–10, pl. 261.

Goldblatt, P., and P. K. Endress. 1977. Cytology and evolution in *Hamamelidaceae. Journal of the Arnold Arboretum* 58(1): 67–71.

Graenicher, S. 1906. Some notes on the pollination of flowers, *Hamamelis virginiana. Bulletin of the Wisconsin Natural History Society* 2(4): 16–18.

Grant, M. 2003. Nomenclatural notes. *The New Plantsman* 2(2): 117–119.

Grootendoorst, H. J. 1965. *Hamamelis.* Keuringsrapport. *Dendroflora* 2: 11–17, 45.

Grootendoorst, H. J. 1980. *Hamamelis.* Keuringsrapport. *Dendroflora* 17: 9–17.

Gronovius, J. F. 1743. *Flora Virginica.* Vol. 2. Lugdani Batavorum, Cornelium Haak, 139.

Gumbleton, W. E. 1888. *Hamamelis zuccariniana. Gardeners' Chronicle* (3rd ser.) 3: 278.

Handel-Mazzettii, H. 1929–1936. *Symbolae Sinicae.* Vol. 7. Vienna: von Julius Springer, 241.

Heywood, V. H., ed. 1978. *Flowering Plants of the World.* Oxford: Oxford University Press, 55–57.

Hickey, M., and C. King. 2000. *The Cambridge Illustrated Glossary of Botanical Terms.* Cambridge: Cambridge University Press.

Hightshoe, G. L. 1988. *Native Trees, Shrubs and Vines for Urban and Rural America.* New York: Van Nostrand Reinhold, 220–221, 576–577.

Hohn, T. C. 1991–1992. Witch hazel winters. *Washington Park Arboretum Bulletin* 54(4): 15–20.

Hohn, T. C. 1993. Bewitched! *American Nurseryman* 77(2): 64–73.

Hooker, J. D. 1882. *Hamamelis japonica. Curtis's Botanical Magazine* 108: pl. 6659.

Hooker, J. D. 1883. *Hamamelis virginiana. Curtis's Botanical Magazine* 109: pl. 6684.

Hooker, J. D. 1903. *Hamamelis mollis. Curtis's Botanical Magazine* 129: pl. 7884.

Houtman, R. T. 1996. Tentoonstelling Winter glorie. *Dendroflora* 30: 95–103.

Houtman, R. T., and W. J. van der Werf. 2002. *Hamamelis* sortimentsonderzoek en keuringsrapport. *Dendroflora* 39: 30–61.

Humphrey, B., chairman. 1979. Discussion group report: Propagation of *Hamamelis* and related plants. *Proceedings of the International Plant Propagators' Society* 29: 256–260.

Huttleston, D. G. 1989. International registrations of cultivar names for unassigned woody genera. *HortScience* 24(3): 430–432.

Jenne, G. E. 1966. *A Study of Variation in North American Hamamelis L. (Hamamelidaceae).* Unpubl. M.Sc. thesis, Vanderbilt University, Nashville, TN.

Kitamura, S., and G. Murata. 1979. *Coloured Illustrations of Woody Plants of Japan.* Vol. 2. Osaka, Japan: Hoikusha Ltd., 128–134.

Koch, H. 1974. Kalidüngüng begünstigt erwünschüted laübfall (Potassium fertilisation promotes a desired leaf fall). *Mitteilüngen der Deütchen Dendrologischen Gesellschaft* 67: 88.

Kort, A. 1902a. *Hamamelis japonica* var. *zuccariniana. Revue de l'Horticulture Belge et Etrangere* 28: 62.

Kort, A. 1902b. Les *Hamamelis. Revue de l'Horticulture Belge et Etrangere* 28: 61–63.

Kort, A. 1907. L'*Hamamelis virginica* en therapeutique. *Revue de l'Horticulture Belge et Etrangere* 33: 188.

Krussman, G. 1986. *Manual of Cultivated Broad Leaved Trees and Shrubs.* Vol. 2. Trans. M. E. Epp. London: B.T. Batsford Ltd., 124–127.

Lamb, J. G. D. 1976. The propagation of understocks for *Hamamelis. Proceedings of the International Plant Propagators' Society* 26: 127–129.

Lamb, J. G. D., and F. Nutty. 1984. The propagation of *Hamamelis. Plantsman* 6(1): 45–48.

Lancaster, R. 1967. Plantsman's notebook: *Hamamelis vernalis. Gardeners' Chronicle* 161(1): 15.

Lancaster, R. 1970. Complete guide to *Hamamelis*: The witch hazels. *Gardeners' Chronicle* 167(21): 32–35; (22): 34; (23): 26–29; (24): 24–27; (25): 25.

Lancaster, R. 1976. Notes from fellows: *Hamamelis vernalis* 'Sandra' for autumn colour. *The Garden* 101: 102–103.

Lancaster, R. 1983. The Wudang Mountains of northwest Hubei. *International Dendrological Society Yearbook* 1983: 50–54.

Lane, C. G. 1995. Propagation and production of *Hamamelis* cultivars in the field by chip budding. *Proceedings of the International Plant Propagators' Society* 45: 149–150.

Lane, C. G. 1998. *Hamamelis* in small spaces. *The Garden* 123(1): 38–41.

Lane, C. G. 1999. The wonder of witch hazels. In *The National Plant Collections Directory.* Wisley, England: National Council for the Conservation of Plants and Gardens, 74–80.

Lane, C. G. 2000. The development of *Hamamelis* ×*intermedia. Proceedings of the International Plant Propagators' Society* 50: 341–345.

Lange, J. 1953. *Hamamelis japollis* hybr. n. *Dansk Dendrologisk Arsskrift* 2: 139–145.

Leiss, J. 1969. *Hamamelis* propagation. *Proceedings of the International Plant Propagators' Society* 19: 349–352.

Little, E. L., Jr. 1953. *Check List of Native and Naturalized Trees of the United States.* Washington, D.C.: U.S. Department of Agriculture, Forest Service, 203.

Malmo, B. G. 1958. *Hamamelidaceae. University of Washington Arboretum Bulletin* 21: 3–6, 30–31.

Maries, C. 1882. Rambles of a plant collector. *The Garden* 22: 359–361.

Marks, T. R., and S. E. Simpson. 1990. Reduced phenolic oxidation at culture initiation in vitro following the exposure of field-grown stockplants to darkness or low levels of irradiance. *Journal of Horticultural Science* 65(2): 103–111.

Marquard, R. D. 1996. Breeding witch hazel at the Holden Arboretum. *Proceedings of the International Plant Propagators' Society* 46: 524–527.

Marquard, R. D., E. P. Davis, and E. L. Stowe. 1997. Genetic diversity among witch hazel cultivars based on randomly amplified polymorphic DNA markers. *Journal of the American Society of Horticultural Science* 122(4): 529–535.

M[asters], M. T. 1874. *Hamamelis arborea. Gardeners' Chronicle* (new ser.) 1(6): 187.

McMillan Browse, P. D. A. 1979. *Hardy Woody Plants from Seed.* London: Grower Books.

Merrill, E. D. 1917. *Flora of South China.* Berkeley: University of California Press.

Meyer, F. G. 1979. *Hamamelis vernalis* Sargent 'January Pride' (Meyer) new cultivar. *AABGA Bulletin* 88–90.

Meyer, F. G. 1997. *Hamamelidaceae*: *Hamamelis.* In *Flora of North America*, Vol. 3. Oxford: Oxford University Press, 362–365.

Mulligan, B. O. 1978. Growth of a collector's garden. Part II. *University of Washington Arboretum Bulletin* 41(4): 33.

Nash, G. V. 1918. *Hamamelis japonica. Addisonia* 3: 35–36, pl. 98.

Nash, G. V. 1919. *Hamamelis virginiana. Addisonia* 4: 43–44, pl. 142.

Nutty, F. J. 1986. *Propagation of Hamamelis mollis. Proceedings of the International Plant Propagators' Society* 36: 282–284.

Ogisu, M. 1980. Mansaku no nakama: Genus *Hamamelis* and its species and varieties. *Garden Life* 19(2): 23–29.

Ohwi, J. 1965. *Flora of Japan.* English ed. Washington, D.C.: Smithsonian Institution, 516–517.

Ohwi, J. (M. Kitagawa). 1983. *New Flora of Japan.* Tokyo: Shibundo Co. Ltd., 820–822.

Okuyama, S. 1982. *Wild Plants of Japan: Spring to Early Summer.* New and enlarged ed. Tokyo: Seibundo-Shinkosa.

Oliver, D. 1888. *Hamamelis mollis. Hooker's Icones Plantarum* (3rd ser.) 18: pl. 1742.

Palmer, E. J. 1932. Leaves from a Collectors Notebook. *Journal of the Arnold Arboretum* 13: 436.

Peattie, D. C. 1950. *A Natural History of Trees.* Boston: Houghton Mifflin, 300–303.

Prain, D. 1914. *Hamamelis vernalis. Curtis's Botanical Magazine* 140: pl. 8573 (*H. vernalis* description; *H. virginiana* illustration).

Preston, F. G. 1954. The genus *Hamamelis. Gardeners' Chronicle* (3rd ser.) 136(3527): 69–70.

Purcell, G. V. 1973. The budding of *Hamamelis. Proceedings of the International Plant Propagators' Society* 23: 129–132.

Pursh, F. 1814. *Flora Americae Septentrionalis, Or a Systematic Arrangement and Description of the Plants of North America.* Vol. 1. London: White, Cochrane & Co., 116.

Rao, P. R. M. 1974. Seed anatomy in some *Hamamelidaceae. Phylogeny, Phytomorphology* 24(1/2): 113–139.

Ray, J. 1686–1704. *Historia Plantarum.* Vol. 3. London: Henricum Faithorne, 1928.

Rehder, A. 1920. New species, varieties and combinations. *Journal of the Arnold Arboretum* 1: 256.

Rehder, A. 1922. New species, varieties and combinations. *Journal of the Arnold Arboretum* 3: 210.

Rehder, A. 1925. *Hamamelis japonica* var. *flavo-purpurascens. Journal of the Arnold Arboretum* 6: 208.

Rehder, A. 1928. New species, varieties and combinations. *Journal of the Arnold Arboretum* 9: 30.

Rehder, A. 1940. *Manual of Cultivated Trees and Shrubs Hardy in North America.* 2nd ed. Reprint. 1986. Portland, Or.: Dioscorides Press, 318–319.

Rehder, A. 1945. Notes on some cultivated trees and shrubs. *Journal of the Arnold Arboretum* 26: 69–70.

Royle, D. 1979. Witch hazel: A crop with eye appeal. *Grower* 92(2): 13–14.

Sanders, C. R. 1982. Letters to the editor: Comments on *Hamamelidaceae. The Plantsman* 4(2): 126–127.

Sanders, C. R. 1990. Witch hazels of note. *Proceedings of the International Plant Propagators' Society* 40: 308–313.

Sargent, C. S. 1893. *Hamamelis virginiana.* In *The Silva of North America,* Vol. 2. New York: Houghton, Mifflin & Co., 3–5.

Sargent, C. S. 1911. *Trees and Shrubs.* Vol. 2. New York: Houghton, Mifflin & Co., 137–138.

Sargent, C. S. 1913. *Plantae Wilsonianae.* Vol. 1, no. 3. Cambridge, Mass.: Harvard University Press, 431–432.

Sargent, C. S. 1920. Notes on North American trees. Part VI. *Journal of the Arnold Arboretum* 1: 246–247.

Sargent, C. S. 1922. *Manual of the Trees of North America.* Vol. 1. Cambridge, Mass.: H. O. Houghton & Co., 368–371.

Satake, Y., H. Hara, S. Watari, and T. Tominari, eds. 1989. *Wild Flowers of Japan: Woody Plants.* Tokyo: Heibonsha Ltd., 153–155, pl. 170, 171.

Schloemer-Jager, A. 1958. Altertiare Pflanzen aus Flazen der Brogger-Halbinsel Spitsbergens. *Palaeontographica* 104B: 39–103.

Schopmeyer, C. S., ed. 1974. *Seed of Woody Plants in the United States.* Handbook no. 450. Washington, D.C.: U.S. Department of Agriculture, 443–444.

Sharp, Xolocotzi, Crum, and Fox. 1950. *Boletin-Sociedad Botanica de Mexico* II: 1–4.

Siebold, P. F. 1843. *Florae Japonicae.* Lugdani Batavorum: Auctorem.

Simpson, J. B. 1953. In J. Walton, ed. *An Introduction to the Study of Fossil Plants.* London: Adam & Charles Black, 181.

Standley, P. C. 1937. Studies of American plants. Part VII. *Botanical Series, Field Museum of Natural History* 17(2): 192–193.

Steyermark, J. A. 1934. *Hamamelis virginiana* in Missouri. *Rhodora* 36: 97–100.

Steyermark, J. A. 1956. Eastern witch hazel. *Missouri Botanical Garden Bulletin* 44: 99–101.

Stimson, M. 1980. Plantsman's notebook: For winter colour. *Garden Centre & Horticultural Trade Journal* 11 April: 28–30; 25 April: 17.

Strand, C. 1988. Asian witch hazels and their hybrids: A history of *Hamamelis* in cultivation. *The New Plantsman* 5(4): 231–245.

Synge, P. M., ed. 1958. Plants to which awards have been made in 1958. *Journal of the Royal Horticultural Society* 83: 183.

Thomas, G. S. 1967. *Colour in the Winter Garden.* London: Charles T. Branford Co., 17–20.

Thomas, G. S. 1992. *Ornamental Shrubs, Climbers and Bamboos.* London: John Murray, 194–197.

Torrey, J., and A. Gray. 1840. *Flora of North America.* Vol. 1. New York: Wiley & Putnam, 597.

Trehane, P., ed. 1995. *International Code of Nomenclature for Cultivated Plants.* Wimborne, U.K.: Quarterjack.

Turrill, W. B. 1963. *Hamamelis japonica* var. *zuccariniana. Curtis's Botanical Magazine* (new ser.) 174: table 420.

Upward, E. M. 1963. Witch hazels of quality. *Gardeners' Chronicle: Gardening Illustrated* 153(6): 103.

van de Laar, H. J. 1977. Keuringen. *Dendroflora* 13/14: 75.

van de Laar, H. J. 1988. Tentoonstelling Flora Nova '87. *Dendroflora* 24: 47–64.

van de Laar, H. J. 1994. Keuringen 1993. *Dendroflora* 30: 77–83.

van Gelderen, D. M. 1996. *100 jaar keuringswerk 1895–1995.* Boskoop: Koninklijke Vereniging voor Boskoopse Culturen.

van Gemert, J. 1938. Journal of a tour of arboreta, botanical gardens and nurseries of northern Europe. Part 2. *Morton Arboretum Bulletin of Popular Information* 13(4): 16.

van Groeningen, I. 1995. Kalmthout Arboretum. *The Garden* 120(4): 186–188.

Veitch, J. H. 1906. *Hortus Veitchii.* London: James Veitch & Sons Ltd.

Vines, R. A. 1960. *Trees, Shrubs, and Woody Vines of the Southwest.* Austin: University of Texas Press, 323–325.

von Dohlen, C. D. 1989. Geographic variation and evolution in the life cycle of the witch-hazel leaf gall aphid, *Hormaphis hamamelidis. Oceologia* 78(2): 165–175.

Weaver, R. E. 1976. The witch hazel family (*Hamamelidaceae*). *Arnoldia* 36(3): 69–109.

Weaver, R. E. 1981. *Hamamelis* 'Arnold Promise'. *Arnoldia* 41(1): 30–33.

Wilson, E. H. 1929. *China: Mother of Gardens.* Boston: Stratford.

Wright, D. 1982–1983. *Hamamelidaceae*: A survey of the genera. *The Plantsman* 4(1): 29–53.

Wyman, D. 1963. New plants registered. *Arnoldia* 23(9): 111–114.

Wyman, D. 1969. *Shrubs and Vines for American Gardens.* New York: Macmillan, 171–173.

Plant Index

Acer capillipes 'Honey Dew', 192
Acer ×*conspicuum* 'Phoenix', 192
Acer ×*conspicuum* 'Silver Vein', 192
Acer davidii, 79
Acer davidii 'Serpentine', 192
Acer japonicum, 192
Acer palmatum, 192
Acer 'White Tigress', 192
American witch hazel, see *Hamamelis virginiana*

Bergenia 'Bartok', 196
Bergenia purpurascens, 196
Bergenia purpurascens 'Irish Crimson', 196
Bergenia 'Rotblum', 196
Bergenia 'Winterglut', 196
Betula albosinensis 'China Ruby', 191
Betula ermanii 'Grayswood Hill', 191
Betula nigra, 187
Betula nigra 'Duraheat', 191
Betula nigra 'Heritage', 191
Betula pendula 'Tristis', 191
Betula platyphylla 'Whitespire', 192
Betula utilis 'Grayswood Ghost', 191
birch, see *Betula*
blue moor grass, see *Molinia caerulea*
bramble, see *Rubus*

Calamagrostis ×*acutiflora* 'Karl Foerster', 197
Calamagrostis ×*acutiflora* 'Overdam', 197
Calamagrostis brachytricha, 197
Castanea seguinii, 79
Chimonanthus praecox, 194
Chimonanthus praecox 'Concolor', 194
Chinese witch hazel, see *Hamamelis mollis*
Christmas box, see *Sarcococca*
Cornus alba 'Aurea', 195
Cornus alba 'Kesselringii', 195
Cornus alba 'Sibirica', 195
Cornus japonica var. *chinensis*, 79
Cornus sanguinea 'Anny's Winter Orange', 195
Cornus sanguinea 'Magic Flame', 195
Cornus sericea 'Cardinal', 195
Cornus sericea 'Flaviramea', 195
Corylopsis sinensis, 79
Corylopsis willmottiae, 79
Corylus avellana, 19
Cyclamen coum, 198

daffodil, see *Narcissus*
Daphne bholua 'Alba', 193
Daphne bholua 'Jacqueline Postill', 193
Daphne bholua 'Peter Smithers', 193
Deschampsia cespitosa 'Bronzeschlier', 197
Deschampsia cespitosa 'Goldschlier', 197
Disanthus cercidifolius, 21
Distylium racemosum, 175
dogwood, see *Cornus*

Epimedium ×*perralchium*, 196
Epimedium perralderianum, 196
Epimedium pinnatum subsp. *colchicum*, 196
Epimedium pubigerum, 196
Eranthis hyemalis, 195, 198
Erica carnea 'Challenger', 194
Erica carnea 'Golden Starlet', 194

Erica carnea 'Loughrigg', 194
Erica carnea 'March Seedling', 194
Erica carnea 'Pink Spangles', 194
Erica carnea 'Snow White', 194
Euphorbia amygdaloides, 196
Euphorbia amygdaloides var. *robbiae*, 196
Euphorbia characias, 196
Euphorbia characias subsp. *wulfenii*, 196
Euphorbia characias subsp. *wulfenii* 'Purpurea', 196
Euphorbia ×*martini*, 196

feather reed grass, see *Calamagrostis* ×*acutiflora*

Galanthus nivalis, 195, 198
giant feather grass, see *Stipa gigantea*

Hamamelis 'Amethyst', 149
Hamamelis androgyna, see *H. virginiana*
Hamamelis arborea, see *H. japonica* 'Arborea'
Hamamelis bitchiuensis, see *H. japonica* var. *bitchiuensis*
Hamamelis 'Brevipetala', 150
Hamamelis carnea, see *H. vernalis* f. *carnea*
Hamamelis caroliniana, see *H. virginiana*
Hamamelis communis, see *H. virginiana*
Hamamelis corylifolia, see *H. virginiana*
Hamamelis 'Dany', see *H.* 'Danny'
Hamamelis 'Danny', 151
Hamamelis dentata, see *H. virginiana*
Hamamelis dioica, see *H. virginiana*
Hamamelis 'Dishi', 152
Hamamelis 'Doerak', 152
Hamamelis estivalis, see *H. virginiana*
Hamamelis 'Fire Blaze', 153
Hamamelis flavopurpurascens, see *H. japonica* var. *japonica* f. *flavopurpurascens*
Hamamelis 'Girard Orange', 154
Hamamelis hyemalis, see *H. virginiana*
Hamamelis incarnata, see *H. japonica* var. *obtusa* f. *incarnata*
Hamamelis ×*intermedia*, 95, 159
Hamamelis ×*intermedia* 'Adieu', 96
Hamamelis ×*intermedia* 'Adonis', see *H.* ×*intermedia* 'Ruby Glow'
Hamamelis ×*intermedia* 'Advent', 97
Hamamelis ×*intermedia* 'Agnes', 97
Hamamelis ×*intermedia* 'Alexander', 98
Hamamelis ×*intermedia* 'Allgold', 99
Hamamelis ×*intermedia* 'Amanon', 99
Hamamelis ×*intermedia* 'Andrea', 100
Hamamelis ×*intermedia* 'Angelly', 101
Hamamelis ×*intermedia* 'Antoine Kort', 102
Hamamelis ×*intermedia* 'Aphrodite', 102
Hamamelis ×*intermedia* 'Arnold Promise', 103
Hamamelis ×*intermedia* 'Arnold's Promise', see *H.* ×*intermedia* 'Arnold Promise'
Hamamelis ×*intermedia* 'August Lamken', see *H.* ×*intermedia* 'Orange Beauty'
Hamamelis ×*intermedia* 'Aureolin', see *H.* ×*intermedia* 'Ripe Corn'
Hamamelis ×*intermedia* 'Aurora', 104
Hamamelis ×*intermedia* 'Barmstedt Gold', 105
Hamamelis ×*intermedia* 'Barmstedt's Gold', see *H.* ×*intermedia* 'Barmstedt Gold'
Hamamelis ×*intermedia* 'Bernstein', 106
Hamamelis ×*intermedia* 'Birgit', 106
Hamamelis ×*intermedia* 'Böhlje's Feuerzauber', 107
Hamamelis ×*intermedia* 'Brandes', see *H.* ×*intermedia* 'Brandis'

Hamamelis ×*intermedia* 'Brandis', 108
Hamamelis ×*intermedia* 'Carmine Red', 108
Hamamelis ×*intermedia* 'Citronella', 109
Hamamelis ×*intermedia* 'Copper Beauty', see *H.* ×*intermedia* 'Jelena'
Hamamelis ×*intermedia* 'Copper Cascade', 110
Hamamelis ×*intermedia* 'Cyrille', 110
Hamamelis ×*intermedia* 'Danny', see *H.* 'Danny'
Hamamelis ×*intermedia* 'Dany', see *H.* 'Danny'
Hamamelis ×*intermedia* 'Diane', 111
Hamamelis ×*intermedia* 'Dishi', see *H.* 'Dishi'
Hamamelis ×*intermedia* 'Double Gold', 112
Hamamelis ×*intermedia* 'Early Bird', 113
Hamamelis ×*intermedia* 'Feuerzauber', 113
Hamamelis ×*intermedia* 'Fiery Orange', see *H.* ×*intermedia* 'Gingerbread'
Hamamelis ×*intermedia* 'Fire Blaze', see *H.* 'Fire Blaze'
Hamamelis ×*intermedia* 'Fire Charm', see *H.* ×*intermedia* 'Feuerzauber'
Hamamelis ×*intermedia* 'Firecracker', see *H.* ×*intermedia* 'Feuerzauber'
Hamamelis ×*intermedia* 'Frederic', 114
Hamamelis ×*intermedia* 'Frederique', see *H.* ×*intermedia* 'Frederic'
Hamamelis ×*intermedia* 'Friesia', 115
Hamamelis ×*intermedia* 'Georges', 115
Hamamelis ×*intermedia* 'Gimborn's Perfume', 116
Hamamelis ×*intermedia* 'Ginger Bread', see *H.* ×*intermedia* 'Gingerbread'
Hamamelis ×*intermedia* 'Gingerbread', 117
Hamamelis ×*intermedia* 'Girard's Orange', see *H.* 'Girard Orange'
Hamamelis ×*intermedia* 'Girard's Purple', see *H. vernalis* 'Girard Purple'
Hamamelis ×*intermedia* 'Glowing Embers', 118, 164
Hamamelis ×*intermedia* 'Golden', 118
Hamamelis ×*intermedia* 'Harlow Carr', 119
Hamamelis ×*intermedia* 'Harry', 120
Hamamelis ×*intermedia* 'Heinrich Bruns', 121
Hamamelis ×*intermedia* 'Hiltingbury', 121
Hamamelis ×*intermedia* 'Improved Winter Beauty', see *H.* ×*intermedia* 'Glowing Embers'
Hamamelis ×*intermedia* 'Iwado', see *H.* ×*intermedia* 'Glowing Embers'
Hamamelis ×*intermedia* 'Jelena', 122
Hamamelis ×*intermedia* 'Jelena's Sister', see *H.* ×*intermedia* 'Sister Jelena'
Hamamelis ×*intermedia* 'John', 123
Hamamelis ×*intermedia* 'Kort's Select', see *H. mollis* 'Kort's Yellow'
Hamamelis ×*intermedia* 'Limelight', 124
Hamamelis ×*intermedia* 'Livia', 125
Hamamelis ×*intermedia* 'Luna', 125
Hamamelis ×*intermedia* 'Magic Fire', see *H.* ×*intermedia* 'Feuerzauber'
Hamamelis ×*intermedia* 'Moonlight', 126
Hamamelis ×*intermedia* 'New Red', see *H.* ×*intermedia* 'Diane'
Hamamelis ×*intermedia* 'Newington', see *H.* ×*intermedia* 'Harlow Carr'
Hamamelis ×*intermedia* 'Nina', 127
Hamamelis ×*intermedia* 'Ninotchka', 128
Hamamelis ×*intermedia* 'Old Copper', 128
Hamamelis ×*intermedia* 'Orange', see *H.* ×*intermedia* 'Orange Beauty'
Hamamelis ×*intermedia* 'Orange Beauty', 129

Hamamelis ×intermedia 'Orange Encore', 130
Hamamelis ×intermedia 'Orange Glow', see *H. ×intermedia* 'Heinrich Bruns'
Hamamelis ×intermedia 'Orange Peel', 131
Hamamelis ×intermedia 'Ostergold', 131
Hamamelis ×intermedia 'Pallida', 132
Hamamelis ×intermedia 'Parasol', 134
Hamamelis ×intermedia 'Perfume', see *H. ×intermedia* 'Gimborn's Perfume'
Hamamelis ×intermedia 'Primavera', 134
Hamamelis ×intermedia 'Ripe Corn', 135
Hamamelis ×intermedia 'Robert', 136
Hamamelis ×intermedia 'Robin', see *H. ×intermedia* 'Old Copper'
Hamamelis ×intermedia 'Rubin', 136
Hamamelis ×intermedia 'Rubinstar', 137
Hamamelis ×intermedia 'Ruby Glow', 138
Hamamelis ×intermedia 'Sara', see *H. ×intermedia* 'Sarah'
Hamamelis ×intermedia 'Sarah', 139
Hamamelis ×intermedia 'Savill Starlight', 139
Hamamelis ×intermedia 'Selection Kort', see *H. mollis* 'Kort's Yellow'
Hamamelis ×intermedia 'Selection Orange', see *H. ×intermedia* 'Bernstein'
Hamamelis ×intermedia 'Sister Jelena', 140
Hamamelis ×intermedia 'Spanish Spider', 141
Hamamelis ×intermedia 'Strawberries and Cream', 142
Hamamelis ×intermedia 'Strawberry and Cream', see *H. ×intermedia* 'Strawberries and Cream'
Hamamelis ×intermedia 'Sunburst', 142
Hamamelis ×intermedia 'Swallow Hayes', 143
Hamamelis ×intermedia 'Treasure Trove', 144
Hamamelis ×intermedia 'Twilight', 144
Hamamelis ×intermedia 'Vesna', 145
Hamamelis ×intermedia 'Vezna', see *H. ×intermedia* 'Vesna'
Hamamelis ×intermedia 'Westerstede', 146
Hamamelis ×intermedia 'Wiero', 147
Hamamelis ×intermedia 'Winter Beauty', 147
Hamamelis ×intermedia 'Zitronenjette', 148
Hamamelis ×japollis, see *H. ×intermedia*
Hamamelis ×japollis 'Nina', see *H. ×intermedia* 'Nina'
Hamamelis japonica, 61–65
Hamamelis japonica 'Arborea', 71
Hamamelis japonica 'Brentry', 71
Hamamelis japonica 'Canary Yellow', 72
Hamamelis japonica 'Flavopurpurascens Superba', see *H. ×intermedia* 'Ruby Glow'
Hamamelis japonica 'Paleface', 73
Hamamelis japonica 'Pendula', 73
Hamamelis japonica 'Rubin', see *H. ×intermedia* 'Rubin'
Hamamelis japonica 'Rubra', 74
Hamamelis japonica 'Rubra Superba', see *H. ×intermedia* 'Ruby Glow'
Hamamelis japonica 'Sulphurea', 75
Hamamelis japonica 'Superba',
Hamamelis japonica 'Zuccariniana', 76
Hamamelis japonica f. *discolor*, see *H. japonica* var. *obtusata* f. *discolor*
Hamamelis japonica f. *obtusata*, see *H. japonica* var. *obtusata*
Hamamelis japonica subsp. *megalophylla*, see *H. japonica* var. *megalophylla*

Hamamelis japonica var. *arborea*, see *H. japonica* 'Arborea'
Hamamelis japonica var. *bitchiuensis*, 65
Hamamelis japonica var. *flavopurpurascens*, see *H. japonica* var. *japonica* f. *flavopurpurascens*
Hamamelis japonica var. *japonica*, 66
Hamamelis japonica var. *japonica* f. *flavopurpurascens*, 67
Hamamelis japonica var. *megalophylla*, 68
Hamamelis japonica var. *obtusata*, 68
Hamamelis japonica var. *obtusata* f. *discolor*, 69
Hamamelis japonica var. *obtusata* f. *flavopurpurascens*, 70
Hamamelis japonica var. *obtusata* f. *incarnata*, 70
Hamamelis 'Kim', 155
Hamamelis 'Lansing', 155
Hamamelis macrophylla, see *H. virginiana*
Hamamelis megalophylla, see *H. japonica* var. *megalophylla*
Hamamelis mexicana, see *H. virginiana* var. *mexicana*
Hamamelis mollis, 77–81
Hamamelis mollis 'Aurantiaca', see *H.* 'Brevipetala'
Hamamelis mollis 'Bonny Brook', 81
Hamamelis mollis 'Boskoop', 81
Hamamelis mollis 'Brevipetala', see *H.* 'Brevipetala'
Hamamelis mollis 'Coombe Wood', 83
Hamamelis mollis 'Doerak', see *H.* 'Doerak'
Hamamelis mollis 'Early Bright', 83
Hamamelis mollis 'Emily', 84
Hamamelis mollis 'Fred Chittenden', 85
Hamamelis mollis 'Goldcrest', 86
Hamamelis mollis 'Gold Edge', 86
Hamamelis mollis 'Imperialis', 87
Hamamelis mollis 'Iwado', 87
Hamamelis mollis 'James Wells', 88
Hamamelis mollis 'Jermyns Gold', 90
Hamamelis mollis 'Kort's Select', see *H. mollis* 'Kort's Yellow'
Hamamelis mollis 'Kort's Yellow', 90
Hamamelis mollis 'Pallida', see *H. ×intermedia* 'Pallida'
Hamamelis mollis 'Perfume', see *H. ×intermedia* 'Gimborn's Perfume'
Hamamelis mollis 'Princeton Gold', 91
Hamamelis mollis 'Rochester Superba', see *H.* 'Rochester'
Hamamelis mollis 'Select', see *H. mollis* 'Princeton Gold'
Hamamelis mollis 'Sunburst', see *H. ×intermedia* 'Sunburst'
Hamamelis mollis 'Superba', see *H.* 'Rochester'
Hamamelis mollis 'Wells Form', see *H. mollis* 'James Wells'
Hamamelis mollis 'Wisley Supreme', 92
Hamamelis mollis superbum, see *H.* 'Rochester'
Hamamelis mollis var. *oblongifolia*, see *H. mollis*
Hamamelis mollis var. *pallida*, see *H. mollis* 'Fred Chittenden'
Hamamelis monoica, see *H. virginiana*
Hamamelis nigra, see *H. virginiana*
Hamamelis obtusata, see *H. japonica* var. *obtusata*
Hamamelis obtusata var. *discolor*, see *H. japonica* var. *obtusata* f. *discolor*
Hamamelis obtusata var. *flavopurpurascens*, see *H. japonica* var. *obtusata* f. *flavopurpurascens*
Hamamelis parvifolia, see *H. virginiana*
Hamamelis purpurea, see *H. vernalis* 'Washington Park'

Hamamelis riparia, see *H. virginiana*
Hamamelis 'Rochester', 156
Hamamelis rotundifolia, see *H. virginiana*
Hamamelis vernalis, 45–47
Hamamelis ×*vernalis*, see *H. vernalis*
Hamamelis vernalis 'Amethyst', see *H.* 'Amethyst'
Hamamelis vernalis 'Autumn Embers', 48
Hamamelis vernalis 'Blue Moon', 48
Hamamelis vernalis 'Boesger', see *H. vernalis* 'Kohankie Red'
Hamamelis vernalis 'Brotzman Purple', see *H.* 'Amethyst'
Hamamelis vernalis 'Carnea', see *H. vernalis* 'Kohankie Red'
Hamamelis vernalis 'Carney', see *H. vernalis* 'Kohankie Red'
Hamamelis vernalis 'Christmas Cheer', 49
Hamamelis vernalis 'Girard Purple', 50
Hamamelis vernalis 'Holden', 50
Hamamelis vernalis 'January Pride', 51
Hamamelis vernalis 'Kohankie Red', 52
Hamamelis vernalis 'Lansing', see *H.* 'Lansing'
Hamamelis vernalis 'Lombarts Weeping', 53
Hamamelis vernalis 'New Year Gold', 54
Hamamelis vernalis 'New Year's Gold', see *H. vernalis* 'New Year Gold'
Hamamelis vernalis 'Orange Glow', 54
Hamamelis vernalis 'Orange Spangles', 55
Hamamelis vernalis 'Pendula', see *H. vernalis* 'Lombarts Weeping'
Hamamelis vernalis 'Purple Seedling', see *H.* 'Amethyst'
Hamamelis vernalis 'Purpurea', see *H. vernalis* 'Washington Park'
Hamamelis vernalis 'Quasimodo', 56
Hamamelis vernalis 'Red Imp', 56
Hamamelis vernalis 'Sandra', 57
Hamamelis vernalis 'Sashay', see *H. vernalis* 'Sashet'
Hamamelis vernalis 'Sashet', 58
Hamamelis vernalis 'Spring Magic', 58
Hamamelis vernalis 'Squib', 59
Hamamelis vernalis 'Washington Park', 60
Hamamelis vernalis f. *carnea*, 47
Hamamelis vernalis f. *tomentella*, 47
Hamamelis virginiana, 29–33
Hamamelis virginiana 'Champlin's Red', 40
Hamamelis virginiana 'Green Thumb', 41
Hamamelis virginiana 'Harvest Moon', 41
Hamamelis virginiana 'Little Suzie', 42
Hamamelis virginiana 'Mohonk Red', 43
Hamamelis virginiana 'Pendula', 43
Hamamelis virginiana 'Tennessee Beauty', 44
Hamamelis virginiana f. *parvifolia*, see *H. virginiana*
Hamamelis virginiana f. *rubescens*, 39, 40
Hamamelis virginiana var. *angustifolia*, see *H. virginiana*
Hamamelis virginiana var. *henryi*, 35, 39
Hamamelis virginiana var. *mexicana*, 37, 38
Hamamelis virginiana var. *orbiculata*, see *H. virginiana*
Hamamelis virginiana var. *virginiana*, 33, 35, 36, 39
Hamamelis virginica, see *H. virginiana*
Hamamelis virginica var. *parvifolia*, see *H. virginiana*
Hamamelis zuccariniana, see *H. japonica* 'Zuccariniana'

Hamamelis zuccariniana rubra, see *H. japonica* 'Rubra'
hazel, see *Corylus avellana*
Helleborus argutifolius, 197
Helleborus foetidus, 197
Helleborus foetidus 'Wester Flisk Group', 197
Helleborus ×*hybridus*, 197
Himalayan birch, see *Betula utilis*
Hosta ventricosa, 79

Japanese silver grass, see *Miscanthus sinensis*
Japanese witch hazel, see *Hamamelis japonica*

Korean feather reed grass, see *Calamagrostis brachytricha*

laurel, see *Prunus laurocerasus*
laurustinus, see *Viburnum tinus*
Lenten lily, see *Helleborus* ×*hybridus*
Liquidambar styraciflua, 21
Lonicera ×*purpusii* 'Winter Beauty', 194
Lonicera setifera, 194
Lonicera standishii var. *lancifolia*, 194

Mahonia japonica, 193
Mahonia ×*media* 'Charity', 193
Mahonia ×*media* 'Lionel Fortescue', 193
Mahonia ×*media* 'Winter Sun', 193
megesea, see *Bergenia*
Miscanthus sinensis, 197
Miscanthus sinensis 'China', 197
Miscanthus sinensis 'Ferner Osten', 197
Miscanthus sinensis 'Flamingo', 197
Miscanthus sinensis 'Kaskade', 197
Miscanthus sinensis 'Morning Light', 197
Molinia caerulea subsp. *arundinacea* 'Transparent', 197
Molinia caerulea subsp. *caerulea* 'Moorhexe', 197

Narcissus 'Dawn Chorus', 198
Narcissus 'Rijnveld's Early Sensation', 198
Narcissus 'W. P. Milner', 198

oak, see *Quercus*
Ophiopogon planiscapus 'Nigrescens', 196
Ozark witch hazel, see *Hamamelis vernalis*

Panicum virgatum, 197
Panicum virgatum 'Heavy Metal', 197
Panicum virgatum 'Shenandoah', 197
Panicum virgatum 'Warrior', 197
pine, see *Pinus sylvestris*
Pinus sylvestris, 191
Pistachia nigra coryfolius, see *H. virginiana*
Pistachia nigra corylifolio, see *H. virginiana*
Pistachia virginica nigra corylifoliis, see *H. virginiana*
Prunus laurocerasus, 182

Quercus robur, 191
Quercus serrata, 79

Rhododendron dauricum 'Midwinter', 194
Rhododendron mucronulatum 'Winter Brightness', 194
Rhododendron simsii, 79
river birch, see *Betula nigra*
Rubus biflorus, 195
Rubus cockburnianus, 196
Rubus cockburnianus 'Goldenvale', 196
Rubus thibetanus, 196

Salix alba 'Golden Ness', 195
Salix alba 'Yelverton', 195
Salix alba subsp. *vitellina* 'Britzensis' 195
Salix 'Erythroflexuosa', 195
Salix irrorata, 195
Salix purpurea 'Nancy Saunders', 195
Sarcococca confusa, 193
Sarcococca hookeriana, 193
Sarcococca orientalis, 193
silver birch, see *Betula pendula*
Skimmia japonica 'Emerald King', 193
Skimmia japonica 'Fragrant Cloud', 193
Skimmia japonica 'Red Dragon', 193
Skimmia japonica 'Stoneham Red', 193
Skimmia japonica 'Tansley Gem', 193
snowdrop, see *Galanthus nivalis*
Sorbus commixta 'Embley', 192
Sorbus hupehensis, 192
Sorbus hupehensis 'Pink Pagoda', 192
Sorbus 'Joseph Rock', 192
Sorbus 'Rose Queen', 192
Sorbus sargentiana, 192
spurge, see *Euphorbia*
Stachyurus chinensis 'Celina', 195
Stachyurus praecox 'Rubriflorus', 195
Stewartia pseudocamellia Koreana Group, 192
Stewartia sinensis, 192
Stipa gigantea, 198
Styrax japonicus 'Emerald Pagoda', 193
Styrax japonicus 'Fargesii', 193
Styrax japonicus 'Pink Chimes', 193
Styrax japonicus 'Purple Dress', 193
sweet gum, see *Liquidambar styraciflua*
switch grass, see *Panicum virgatum*

Taxus baccata, 19
Trilopus dentata, see *Hamamelis virginiana*
Trilopus estivalis, see *Hamamelis virginiana*
Trilopus nigra, see *Hamamelis virginiana*
Trilopus nigra var. *catesbiana*, see *Hamamelis virginiana*
Trilopus parvifolia, see *Hamamelis virginiana*
Trilopus riparia, see *Hamamelis virginiana*
Trilopus rotundifolia, see *Hamamelis virginiana*
Trilopus virginica, see *Hamamelis virginiana*
tufted hair grass, see *Deschampsia cespitosa*

Ulmus glabra, 19

Viburnum ×*bodnantense* 'Charles Lamont', 194
Viburnum ×*bodnantense* 'Dawn', 194
Viburnum ×*bodnantense* 'Deben', 194
Viburnum farreri 'Candidissimum', 194
Viburnum farreri 'Farrer's Pink', 194
Viburnum tinus 'Eve Price', 193
Viburnum tinus 'Gwenllian', 193

Weigela japonica var. *sinica*, 79
willow, see *Salix*
winter aconite, see *Eranthis hyemalis*
winter honeysuckle, see *Lonicera*
winter sweet, see *Chimonanthus*
witch hazel, see *Hamamelis*
wych elm, see *Ulmus glabra*

yew, see *Taxus*